DQ645748

THE ELIZABETH CADY STANTON–
SUSAN B. ANTHONY READER
Correspondence, Writings, Speeches

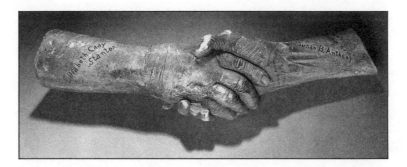

Bronze cast of the clasped hands of Elizabeth Cady Stanton and Susan B. Anthony, a replica of the original plaster cast created as a gift from Stanton for Anthony's seventieth birthday celebration. The cast is on display at the Elizabeth Cady Stanton House. Courtesy of the Women's Rights National Historical Park and the Elizabeth Cady Stanton Foundation.

THE ELIZABETH CADY STANTON–SUSAN B. ANTHONY READER

Correspondence, Writings, Speeches

REVISED EDITION

Edited and with a Critical Commentary by ELLEN CAROL DuBOIS

Foreword by GERDA LERNER

Northeastern University Press
BOSTON

Northeastern University Press

Parts One through Three copyright 1981 by Schocken Books Inc. Published by arrangement with Schocken Books Inc. Introduction and Part Four copyright 1992 by Ellen Carol DuBois.

All rights reserved. Except for the quotation of short passages for the purposes of criticism and review, no part of this book may be reproduced in any form or by any means, electronic or mechanical, including photocopying, recording, or any information storage and retrieval system now known or to be invented, without written permission of the publisher.

Library of Congress Cataloging-in-Publication Data

Stanton, Elizabeth Cady, 1815–1902.
   The Elizabeth Cady Stanton–Susan B. Anthony reader :
   correspondence, writings, speeches / edited and with a critical
   commentary by Ellen Carol DuBois ; Foreword by Gerda Lerner.—Rev. ed.
      p.   cm.
   Rev. ed. of: Elizabeth Cady Stanton, Susan B. Anthony.
   correspondence, writings, speeches. 1981.
   Includes index.
      ISBN 1-55553-149-0 (alk. paper)—ISBN 1-55553-143-1 (pbk. : alk. paper)
      1. Stanton, Elizabeth Cady, 1815–1902. 2. Anthony, Susan B.
   (Susan Brownell), 1820–1906. 3. Feminists—United States—
   Correspondence. 4. Feminism—United States—History—19th century.
   I. Anthony, Susan B. (Susan Brownell), 1820–1906. II. DuBois, Ellen
   Carol, 1947–   . III. Elizabeth Cady Stanton, Susan B. Anthony,
   correspondence, writings, speeches. IV. Title.
   HQ1412.S72   1992
   305.4'092'2—dc20   92-28160

Designed by Nancy Dale Muldoon

Printed and bound by Edwards Brothers, Inc., Ann Arbor, Michigan. The paper is Glatfelter Offset, an acid-free sheet.

MANUFACTURED IN THE UNITED STATES OF AMERICA
97 96 95 94 93 92   5 4 3 2 1

OUR right is always rising higher and sinking deeper.—The very truths you are now contending for, will, in fifty years, be so completely imbedded in public opinion that no one need say one word in their defence; whilst at the same time new forms of truth will arise to test the faithfulness of the pioneer minds of that age, and so on eternally; for truth will forever elaborate new forms by its creative energy, and thus furnish food for all growing minds.

Angelina Grimké Weld to Elizabeth Cady Stanton, 1851

CONTENTS

PART THREE: 1874–1906

PART FOUR: SUPPLEMENTARY DOCUMENTS

FOREWORD

Elizabeth Cady Stanton and Susan B. Anthony are the two women most widely known and acclaimed for their lifelong leadership of the nineteenth-century women's rights movement. Yet their writings and speeches have been difficult of access to the general public, except for a few Stanton speeches reprinted in anthologies. Professor DuBois's volume provides a welcome selection of important documents, speeches, and letters by Stanton and Anthony, which highlight their intellectual and personal development, and it offers an important reinterpretation in the introductory essays.

Stanton and Anthony projected a public image of unity, teamwork, and a collaboration so close they seemed to merge their identities into one. Readers of this volume will, by comparing the writings of both women during the same time periods, discover two separate identities, not infrequently in conflict, and often stressing different aspects of a problem. Stanton's forceful leadership during the early phases of the formation of the women's rights movement is well known. Her controversial insistence on including the demand for woman suffrage in the Declaration of Sentiments of the 1848 Seneca Falls women's rights convention has frequently been treated by historians as a utopian stance and a tactical error. Professor DuBois makes us understand that Stanton, in demanding political equality for women, was firmly rooted in the American tradition and that, more importantly, she had the vision to see that the demand for suffrage was the key which transformed personal grievances into political consciousness. In DuBois's words, "By demanding political power, women could struggle collectively against their degradation, rather than each against her own father and husband." The "utopian demand" would in the long run prove more practical as a unifying force than the more limited reforms of education and property rights.

The documents trace in detail the agonizing conflict of the two women during the crisis over the adoption of the Fourteenth and Fifteenth Amendments to the Constitution, when they saw their former allies among abolitionists and radical Republicans ignore the demand for woman suffrage in favor of securing Black suffrage. Their embattled position of making themselves independent of the leadership of abolitionist men and radical Republican politicians is seen by Professor DuBois as a major turning point in the development of feminism. Although in the short range the resulting split in the ranks of the women's movement weakened it, in the long range it was Stanton and Anthony's insistence on building a movement based primarily on the leadership of women which laid the foundation for future victories.

In the decades after the Civil War the two women focused each on different aspects of woman's oppression, as they developed their feminist argument. Anthony concentrated her attention on the economic needs of women and, in 1868, helped to form a short-lived but pioneering organization of working women. At a time when most middle-class women were unsympathetic to the emergent labor movement, Anthony tried to integrate feminist and trade union goals. Stanton, following in the tradition of Frances Wright and other utopian feminists, concentrated her attacks on the sexual oppression of women. She championed the concept of "woman's control over her own body," which she termed "self-sovereignty," and by which she and her contemporaries understood the right of women to control their own bodies in the marriage relationship. Stanton advocated easier divorce laws, an end to prostitution, women's control over the frequency of sexual intercourse in marriage, and redress for wives against the excesses of violent or drunken husbands. These were practical demands, which appealed to Victorian women more readily than did the demand for suffrage. As DuBois shows, Stanton and Anthony together extended the assertion of women's "natural rights" into programmatic attacks on women's major economic and sexual grievances. Thus, the demand for woman's suffrage became expanded into a "radical and multifaceted feminism." DuBois's reinterpretation of Victoria Woodhull and her impact on Stanton and Anthony adds a new dimension to the picture.

In the eighties and nineties Stanton and Anthony developed in different directions and disagreed, at various times, over tactics and long-range goals. Anthony, growing more assertive and confident as her organizational leadership was recognized and rewarded by small gains in the struggle for a woman suffrage amendment, became increasingly pragmatic. Now it was Anthony who believed that the suffrage movement should stay aloof from other reforms, while Stanton advocated that the suffrage campaign be rooted firmly in a broad-ranging radical political program. In old age, she became more and more uncompromising in her writing and lecturing. In 1890, as Anthony's major effort went into unifying all women around the demand for the vote, Stanton insisted on opening up for debate, rather than burying, the profound disagreement among suffragists over what constituted the rights of women. Her advocacy of freethought, her attack on the Christian church and on the literal truth of the Bible, isolated her not only from conservatives in politics and society, but from the mainstream of the women's rights movement. Yet it was Stanton who, in spiritual isolation, kept alive the radical critique of American society and of traditionalist sexual mores. It was she, rather than Anthony, who prepared the ground for the radical re-definition of twentieth-century feminism, which, while demanding equal access and political participation of women in a society defined and controlled by men, would insist on the need for a transformation in the sexual division of labor and in the social relation of the sexes.

The documents in this volume revive the powerful voices of two great Americans, who have been alternately disregarded or mythologized. Stanton and Anthony, as they emerge from this volume, were distinct individuals, searching and visionary in their thought, forceful in their actions, indomitable in their dedication to women's emancipation. Seen in the round, with their weaknesses as well as their strengths, they were truly movers and shakers of their time.

Ellen DuBois, whose work on this volume is based on years of research in primary sources, brings to it her special insights as the chief interpreter of post–Civil War feminism in her widely acclaimed *Feminism and Suffrage: The Emergence of an Independent Women's Movement in America, 1848–1869.* She has made Anthony and Stanton accessible to present-day readers, letting them speak for themselves and helping us to see them more clearly in a new light. This volume should be as useful and appealing to the general reader as it will be to students of history, women's history, and American biography.

GERDA LERNER
Robinson-Edwards Professor of History
University of Wisconsin, Madison

INTRODUCTION TO THE
REVISED EDITION

In the years since I compiled this collection, the historical reputations of Elizabeth Cady Stanton and Susan B. Anthony have risen from virtual obscurity; they are on their way to richly deserved positions as significant figures in American history. Elizabeth Stanton's home in Seneca Falls has been carefully restored to its original condition and, along with the site of the Wesleyan Chapel in which the 1848 women's rights convention was held, has been designated a National Women's Rights Historical Park. Susan B. Anthony was commemorated with a new one-dollar piece, and although the coin was ultimately withdrawn, she was the first woman ever so honored. Both Stanton and Anthony have been the subjects of modern biographies.[1] Perhaps most important, copies of all their letters, speeches, pamphlets, and assorted writings have been collected from far-flung repositories and obscure nineteenth-century newspapers and assembled on microfilm for scholars to use.[2] We know a good deal more about them than we did in 1981, and at the same time our knowledge of the history of women's rights and of feminism is far broader, so that their particular lives and choices no longer have to stand for an entire movement.

Even though our knowledge of women's history is much richer than it was a decade ago, the essential themes of this collection still seem to me good ones. Stanton and Anthony, I argue here, were part of the women's rights tradition, which was a distinctive perspective on women's condition and provided an open challenge to the doctrine of "separate spheres" (or "true womanhood") that dominated mid-nineteenth-century American thought and culture. In particular, secularism, individualism, and an emphasis on the similarities of the sexes characterized women's rights ideas; this distinguished them from more conventional gender ideologies, which started from religious premises, located women in the family, and concentrated on elaborating and elevating women's differences from men. I believe that the ability of Stanton and Anthony to see so far beyond the conventions of their day regarding woman's sphere came—perhaps ironically—from their application to women of liberal definitions of freedom that had always been intended only for men, principles such as economic independence, natural rights, and personal liberty.

Although both Stanton and Anthony believed deeply in other social reforms, the bond between them was built around the supreme value they both placed on winning women's equal right to suffrage, the foremost badge of freedom and the major marker between women's world of private responsibilities and men's world of public concerns. For Stanton and Anthony, the promise of the vote lay not only in the elevation of the individual woman but in the collective empowerment of the whole sex. When they began their work, women were not supposed to be interested or involved in the sordid world of politics; by the end of their careers they had led the way to a much more positive understanding among their sex of the possibilities of politics.[3]

In 1981 I relied on the term "feminism" with a kind of convenient imprecision. On the one hand, I used the term, usually with a modifier such as "egalitarian" or "domestic," to mean the variety of intellectual and cultural traditions that aspired to "elevate" women's condition, whatever that might mean. On the other hand, I also tried to reserve "feminism" for the variant on which this book focuses—the women's rights movement of Elizabeth Stanton and Susan B. Anthony. Since I originally edited this collection, historians have begun a debate about how best to use the term.[4] Women did not speak of themselves as feminists in the United States until the 1910s, and when they did they were responding to very different social conditions and political alternatives from those Stanton and Anthony faced.[5] But to limit "feminism" to the twentieth-century politics that first used the word will deny us a term we need to help reconstruct longer traditions of thought about women's condition: in this case, the individualistic ideas of the nineteenth-century women's rights movement, which constituted an important resource for the feminism of the 1910s. Whatever way this problem is resolved—and my own inclination is to develop a historical taxonomy of multiple feminisms—we need to understand the important differences between various approaches to women's elevation, so that we can compare and debate them and work for changes in our own time with greater precision and authority.

In 1981 I used "feminism" in one other way, modified by the adjective "radical," to capture not so much the content as the spirit and intensity of the challenge that Stanton and Anthony mounted against women's subordination. This radical feminist spirit is, after all, one of the reasons that their legacy remains meaningful and inspiring almost a century after their deaths. Stanton's deep reservoir of rage at male power and privilege and Anthony's absolute faith in women's capacity to act together and to transform themselves in the process speak to us across the years and remain, now as in their lifetimes, sources of their political power and historical significance.

But I also insisted on the different paths that Stanton and Anthony followed toward the end of their careers, because I believe that these disagreements suggest a recurring tension at the heart of the radical feminist spirit. For Anthony, women's rights preserved its radicalism by keeping itself separate from other political movements and parties, whose male leaders she believed would inevitably relegate women's interests to a helpmeet position. Stanton, while appreciative of the need for a strong and independent women's movement, feared that without sufficient connection to the larger traditions of liberal thought and democratic politics, without attachments to other progressive movements, women's politics could become narrow and conservative. Rare is the historian of women's rights who does not have her special sympathies, and in this debate I am a partisan of Stanton's position. But even more, I believe and hope that it is possible to reconcile feminist autonomy and a broad vision of social justice. Within a decade after the deaths of Stanton and Anthony, such a combination resurfaced, as a strong and confident women's movement provided much of the leadership for the vigorous reform movements of the Progressive era.[6]

There is one issue with respect to which my evaluation of the historic role that Stanton and Anthony played has changed, and this is the question of the racial character of the woman suffrage movement that they helped to build. How one understands the nature and implications of their feminist militance is inseparable from how one evaluates their response in the late 1860s to the ratification of the fourteenth and fifteenth amendments. In 1981 I stressed how Stanton and Anthony broke out of their long alliance with male abolitionists and Republicans and committed themselves to the creation of an independent, women-based movement. Other scholars insisted that the opposition that Stanton and Anthony created (or at least encouraged) between Black and women's rights fundamentally compromised the future inclusiveness of the movement they were setting in motion. Given the centrality of the crisis of the late 1860s not only to the historical reputations of Stanton and Anthony but to the subsequent history of the woman suffrage movement, we should continue to evaluate and reevaluate the historical significance of that moment.[7]

My own sense of the importance of the Reconstruction crisis has moved closer to that of my critics. To my appreciation for what was gained at that moment I have added a profound sense of what was lost.[8] In leaving behind their political connection to male abolitionists and Republicans, Stanton and Anthony sacrificed their historic connection to Black women. As part of the antislavery movement, they had learned to rethink the condition of their sex by replacing the "true woman" with the "slave mother" as the emblem of the female condition.[9] With the collapse in the late 1860s of the universal suffrage strategy for uniting woman suffrage with Black suffrage, they no longer approached women's rights by linking the claims of race and sex but by counterposing (and in the case of Elizabeth Stanton even antagonizing) them. At that moment the case for woman suffrage became simultaneously more gender-based and more elitist and racist.[10] Historians have begun to explore the subtle ways in which "whiteness" was embedded in the nineteenth-century labor movement, and are challenging us in the late twentieth century to rethink and untangle the historic intersections of workers' insurgency and white supremacy.[11] Painful as it may be, such an exploration and untangling desperately needs to be undertaken for the history of women's rights.[12]

In an odd sort of way, I think such a prospect graces the memory of Stanton and Anthony, even if it means a somewhat harsher evaluation of their particular historic contribution. History has not yet resolved many of the basic political questions posed by their lives and careers, but we can learn from their mistakes as well as their best aspirations. The reconstitution of a genuinely nonhierarchical womanhood, which repudiates the inequalities not only of gender but of race and class, is one such challenge. Another unmet goal that we have inherited from them—if possible an even more profound one—is to make political life genuinely democratic and popularly meaningful. Our modern political disempowerment is no less debilitating to us as women for being *de facto* rather than *de jure*. Any restrospective appreciation for the historic role of the woman suffrage movement and of Elizabeth Cady Stanton and Susan B. Anthony at its head should have a forward-looking component as well. This is necessary to direct our attention to what women can do to enhance our political power and how we can act to reinvigorate democratic citizenship in general.[13]

Los Angeles　　　　　　　　　ELLEN CAROL DuBOIS
April 1992

NOTES

1. Lois Banner, *Elizabeth Cady Stanton: A Radical for Woman's Rights* (Boston: Little, Brown, 1980); Elisabeth Griffith, *In Her Own Right: The Life of Elizabeth Cady Stanton* (New York: Oxford University Press, 1984); Kathleen Barry, *Susan B. Anthony: A Biography of a Singular Feminist* (New York: New York University Press, 1988).

2. *Papers of Elizabeth Cady Stanton and Susan B. Anthony*, ed. Patricia G.

Holland and Ann D. Gordon (Wilmington, Del., Scholarly Resources Inc., 1991).

3. Despite the widespread notion that women regarded politics with total aversion, nineteenth-century women showed their political and partisan side in a variety of ways. See for instance Mary Ryan, *Women in Public: Between Banners and Ballots, 1825–1880* (Baltimore: Johns Hopkins University Press, 1990); also Lori Ginsburg, *Women and the Work of Benevolence* (New Haven: Yale University Press, 1990).

4. Karen Offen, "Defining Feminism: A Comparative Historical Approach," *Signs*, Vol. 14 (Autumn 1988), pp. 119–57; responses from Ellen DuBois, Nancy Cott, and Karen Offen, *Signs*, Vol. 15 (Autumn 1989), pp. 195–209; Elsa Barkley Brown, "Womanist Consciousness: Maggie Lena Walker and the Independent Order of Saint Luke," *Signs*, Vol. 14 (Spring 1989), pp. 610–33.

5. Nancy F. Cott, *The Grounding of Modern Feminism* (New Haven: Yale University Press, 1987).

6. See the essays in Noralee Frankel and Nancy S. Dye, eds., *Gender, Class, Race & Reform in the Progressive Era* (Lexington: University Press of Kentucky, 1991).

7. My initial interpretation is developed fully in *Feminism and Suffrage: The Emergence of an Independent Women's Movement in America, 1848–1869* (Ithaca: Cornell University Press, 1978). For the counterinterpretation, see especially Angela Davis, *Women, Race and Class* (New York: Random House, 1981), and Bettina Apthetker, *Women's Legacy: Essays on Race, Sex and Class in American History* (Amherst: University of Massachusetts Press, 1982). An important recent contribution to this literature is Dorothy Sterling's biography of Abby Kelly Foster, *Ahead of Her Time: Abby Kelly and the Politics of Slavery* (New York: W. W. Norton, 1991). Kelly was a leader of the wing of the women's rights movement that embraced rather than challenged the postwar amendments.

8. Ellen C. DuBois, "Outgrowing the Compact of the Fathers: Equal Rights, Woman Suffrage and the United States Constitution, 1820–1878," *Journal of American History*, Vol. 74, no. 3 (December 1987), pp. 836–62.

9. Jean Yellin, *Women and Sisters: The Anti-Slavery Feminists in American Culture* (New Haven: Yale University Press, 1989). As Chana Lee has pointed out to me, it is possible to interpret the symbolic importance of slave women to early women's rights in a different and much less positive way: as an objectification of Black women's victimization.

10. For a re-reading of the history of American feminism from the viewpoint of African-American women, see Paula Giddings, *When and Where I Enter: The Impact of Black Women on Race and Sex in America* (New York: William Morrow, 1984).

11. Alexander Saxton, *The Indispensable Enemy: Labor and the Anti-Chinese Movement in California* (Berkeley: University of California Press,

1971), and *The Rise and Fall of the White Republic* (London and New York: Verso, 1990); David Roedigger, *The Wages of Whiteness* (New York: Routledge, 1991).

12. Gwendolyn Mink has made an excellent start in "The Lady and the Tramp: Gender, Race and the Origins of the American Welfare State," in *Women, the State, and Welfare*, ed. Linda Gordon (Madison: University of Wisconsin Press, 1990), pp. 92–122.

13. See Anne Phillips, *Engendering Democracy* (State College: Pennsylvania State University Press, 1990).

From the INTRODUCTION to the 1981 Edition

ALTHOUGH we know Stanton and Anthony better than we know most women in American history, we do not understand them as well as we should. It is for this reason that the following documents and commentary, which chronicle the political careers of Elizabeth Cady Stanton and Susan B. Anthony, are offered as part of a current reappraisal of the woman suffrage movement and the history of political feminism.[1] The documents are divided into three sections, corresponding to different periods in the history of American reform politics and therefore of the woman suffrage movement. The first section covers the pre–Civil War period and the development of women's rights ideas within the context of a multifaceted and radical reform movement. This section traces Stanton and Anthony as they developed their basic perspective for women's emancipation: political power and equality with men. The second section covers the Reconstruction period and reformers' struggles to inject their concerns into the Republican party's political program. The documents in this section focus on the efforts of Stanton and Anthony to develop a comprehensive political program for women's emancipation, especially with respect to economic and sexual equality. The final section covers the post-Reconstruction period, and the reorganization of reform interests in an increasingly class-stratified soci-

---

1. New work on suffragism includes: essays in *A Not Unreasonable Claim: Women and Reform in Canada, 1880s–1920s*, ed. Linda Kealey (Toronto: The Women's Press, 1979); Jill Liddington and Jill Norris, *One Hand Tied Behind Us: The Rise of the Woman's Suffrage Movement* (London: Virago Press, 1979); *The Concise History of Woman Suffrage*, ed. Mari Jo Buhle and Paul Buhle (Urbana: University of Illinois Press, 1978); and my own *Feminism and Suffrage: The Emergence of an Independent Women's Movement in America, 1848–1869* (Ithaca: Cornell University Press, 1978).

ety. The documents in this section emphasize the growing conflict between Stanton and Anthony over the direction that the
woman suffrage movement should take. Selections document
Stanton's minority radicalism in the 1880s and 1890s, and Anthony's role in the reconciliation between suffragism and what
historians have come to call the "domestic feminist" approach to
the elevation of women's position.

In making selections for this collection, I chose documents that
conveyed the particular kind of leadership that Stanton and
Anthony each gave to the feminist movement. I included many
of Stanton's speeches, to emphasize her power as a political
orator, and the passionate and militant character of her thought.
I also selected documents that stressed Anthony's contributions
as an organizer, and her ability to draw out women's anger and
commitment to "the Cause." In addition, I selected documents
that would augment and/or modify the published and easily
available material on Stanton and Anthony; accordingly, more
than a third of the documents are taken from unpublished
sources—manuscript speeches, letters, diaries—and others come
from nineteenth-century newspapers and published materials
long out of print. Finally, I selected documents that would give a
full sense of the historical context in which Stanton and Anthony
were situated—the many political movements with which they
were associated, the variety of issues they addressed, and the
changing historical circumstances in which they operated. In
editing, I altered punctuation where doing so would make the
material, especially the speeches, easier to read. I also eliminated
unnecessary and tedious repetition. In general, however, I sought
to preserve the original character, full breadth, and historical
specificity of each document. Accordingly, the selections are for
the most part fairly lengthy.

Several archivists and librarians were especially helpful in
locating manuscript material: Mary Huth of the University of
Rochester; Frances Goudy of Vassar College; Archie Motley of
the Chicago Historical Society; Eva Moseley and Barbara Haber
of the Schlesinger Library; and Harriet McLoone of the Huntington Library. For permission to reprint manuscript materials in
their collections, I wish to thank the Chicago Historical Society,

the Vassar College Library, and the Schlesinger Library of Radcliffe College. Rhoda Jenkins of Greenwich, Connecticut, graciously granted me permission to reprint unpublished writings of her great-grandmother, Elizabeth Cady Stanton. Earlier drafts of my historical commentary were read by Mari Jo Buhle, Eric Foner, Linda Gordon, and Anne Firor Scott, and I profited a great deal from their suggestions. Finally, two people, Gerda Lerner and Eli Zaretsky, gave me special support for this work, and I want to thank them for all their help, advice, and faith in this project.

PART ONE
1815–1861

Feminism before Seneca Falls

The 1848 women's rights convention at Seneca Falls was part of a tradition of political thought about women reaching back at least half a century. In general, this tradition involved the extension of natural rights egalitarianism from men to women— especially the principles of individualism, the universal capacity for reason, and political democracy. In the multifaceted debate over the proper position of women in bourgeois society, this tradition, which was called "women's rights," tended to supply more advanced arguments—reaching deeper into the structures of women's subordination, claiming more territory as women's province, going farther in envisioning a totally different sexual order—than other ways of approaching the problem of woman's place.

Mary Wollstonecraft, the Englishwoman who wrote *Vindication of the Rights of Women* (1791), is generally recognized as the first major figure in this tradition. Wollstonecraft wrote in response to the Enlightenment antifeminist Rousseau, who argued that since female nature was different from male, women's rights must be different from men's. Wollstonecraft insisted that women's nature was basically the same as men's—free, rational, and independent—and that, like men, women's "first duty is to themselves as rational creatures," their primary objective being "to obtain a character as a human being regardless of the distinction of sex." Although Wollstonecraft acknowledged that women had "different duties to fulfill" and urged them to become "affectionate wives and rational mothers," her frame of reference for women was not the domestic sphere, but the public world from which they were so largely excluded. "In order to render [women's] private virtue a public benefit," she insisted "they must have a civil existence in the state, married or single." Wollstonecraft believed that education would improve women's position and character, but what distinguished her from more conservative advocates of this reform was her commitment to the kind of education that would narrow the moral and intellectual distance between men and women, and counter the selfish, antidemocratic tendencies of home life. Thus, she specifically advocated coeducation, and a system of public, or "national," schools for all classes "for only by jostlings of equality can we form a just opinion of ourselves."[1]

In the United States, where an energetic debate on women's education was taking place in the 1790s, Wollstonecraft's writings were widely circulated. The publication of the *Vindication* and the clarity and conviction of Wollstonecraft's arguments helped to build sentiment in favor of improving education for women. Yet the larger framework of her thought—her egalitarianism and her belief in the importance of a public role for women—were not well received. Two factors limited Wollstonecraft's influence: her association with the secular radicalism of the French Revolution, which was increasingly in disfavor as a popular ideology after 1800; and—closely related—the revelation that Wollstonecraft had been a free lover and borne a child out of wedlock. The publication of the *Vindication* permitted many American women to speak out more confidently in favor of the intellectual and moral capacities of their sex and at the same time dissociate themselves from Wollstonecraft's larger radicalism. "I confess I admire many of her sentiments," the young Eliza Southgate wrote in 1801, "notwithstanding, I believe should any one adopt her principles, they would conduct [themselves] in the same manner, and upon the whole her life is the best comment on her writings."[2]

Instead, most American proponents of women's education in the early nineteenth century tended to base their arguments on women's special domestic responsibilities and unique moral position rather than on the common human nature and identical social responsibilities of the sexes. Hannah Mather Crocker, writing in 1818, argued that women were the mental and moral equals of men, but her defense of women's education was laced with warnings against "the impropriety of females ever trespassing on masculine ground," or intruding too far into public life. Crocker rested her best hopes for women's education, not

on the extension of public life and egalitarian principles to
women, but on the perfection of "family government" and "a
religious course of life." Similarly, Emma Willard, pioneer of
women's education in the United States and founder of the
Troy Female Seminary (which the young Elizabeth Cady attended) was a staunch advocate of the intellectual equality of
the sexes and, at the same time, believed that women's education must be "adapted to that difference of character and duties,
to which the softer sex should be formed."[3]

In the 1820s, egalitarian feminism found a brilliant new advocate, Frances Wright. Wright, a follower of the utopian socialist Robert Owen, settled in the United States as the most
likely place to realize her goal of true equality. There were links
between Wright and Wollstonecraft, most notably the forma-
tive impact of William Godwin, lover and comrade of Wollstonecraft, on Robert Owen. Like Wollstonecraft, Wright believed that girls and boys should be educated in the same way
and at the same schools. She was a particularly trenchant critic
of the domestic institutions that were emerging to structure
nineteenth-century women's lives. She advocated "free and voluntary affection" as an alternative to lifelong, monogamous
marriage, and a childrearing system based on state-run coedu-
cational boarding schools instead of the private family.[4] The attacks on Wright in the American press as a free lover, infidel,
and monstrously public woman were very similar to the attacks
on Wollstonecraft twenty years earlier. Although the attacks
were severe, and Wright's anticlericalism and socialism made
her anathema to many, she had an important impact on the
American debate on woman's sphere. Other freethinking radicals took up her ideas that egalitarianism, secularism, and sexual
freedom were the basis on which women's true position should
be established. Wright's coworker, Robert Dale Owen (Robert
Owen's son), and the Polish feminist and freethinker, Ernestine
Rose, were particularly important to later advocates of women's
rights.

Egalitarian radicals seem to have played an important part in
the early efforts to reform the property laws affecting married
women. In New York, a married women's property act was

submitted in 1836 by Judge Thomas Hertell, a radical and freethinking member of the state legislature; Ernestine Rose spoke and circulated a petition on behalf of Hertell's bill. In the same year, Robert Dale Owen submitted married women's property legislation in Indiana, where he was a member of the legislature. Owen also worked for reform in the divorce law, in particular to allow women to divorce men who were drunkards, and divorce reform was pursued in conjunction with married women's property legislation in Massachusetts as well.[5] Although not all supporters of the new property laws for women were egalitarian feminists, the opposition was entirely based on conservative ideas about woman's place and the sacred character of the marriage contract. The property law for women was not changed in New York until 1848, which seems to have been an important year for this reform elsewhere: in Pennsylvania, the law was changed in 1848; and in Massachusetts and Vermont, agitation also began in that year.

Despite the efforts of Wright and her followers to win equality for women in civil society, the dominant approach to the improvement of women's position remained the idea of elevating woman's role in the domestic sphere. Catherine Beecher, a major exponent of what one historian has called "the program of woman's sphere," began to rise to prominence in the early 1830s.[6] Whereas Wright was a critic of monogamous marriage and the private household, Beecher was their staunch defender and placed domesticity at the very center of her strategy for American women. She believed that woman's influence must be different from man's and should rest on her ability to inculcate the "spirit of benevolence" into the American character through the children that she raised. Beecher's major innovation was to argue that teaching was a function similar to mothering, and was therefore an appropriate activity for women. Through such womanly efforts, Beecher believed, women could simultaneously secure increased social power for themselves and provide the crucial antidote to the individual ambition and self-striving which seemed to be threatening the very core of American society, especially after the financial panic of 1837. There were many important points of conflict between Wright and Beecher: the former was a militant secularist while the latter advised women to put religious matters before worldly affairs; Wright was a critic of the unequal distribution of property while Beecher defended it as the indispensable "stimulus to industry"; and while Wright criticized the utilitarian dedication to the specialization and professionalization of learning, Beecher urged that it be extended to include housewifery. There were similarities in the thought of the two women—both favored better education and a more active social role for women, and both were committed to elevating woman's status and winning her new respect—but there were enormous differences of strategy and vision. Beecher explicitly offered her ideas as an alternative to those, like Wright, "who are bewailing themselves over the fancied wrongs and injuries of women in this Nation."[7]

Ideas like Beecher's were well received, especially among middle- and upper-class white women. By the 1830s, such women provided the audience for a burgeoning female literature, sentimental novels, maternal and domestic advice books, and magazines which gave voice to their discontent and their aspirations for a wider sphere. *Godey's Lady's Book*, for instance, reached the extraordinary circulation of 150,000 in the late 1830s. Its editor, Sarah Josepha Hale, shared many of Beecher's opinions, was openly hostile to "women's rights," and favored women's education and their entry into professions, particularly medicine, which she thought compatible with true womanliness.[8] Growing numbers of women attended female seminaries and academies, where they were both educated in the arts and sciences and indoctrinated in the virtues and duties of their sex.

Throughout the 1830s and 1840s, women especially took to heart the notion that their sex gave them the right and capacity to exert a special social influence, and formed networks of local, all-women's organizations to pursue these wider moral obligations. Their concerns ranged from the care of indigents and the education of orphans, to the elimination of prostitution and the reform of sexual morality. In the context of these all-women's organizations, women were sometimes able to express their profound resentment of the social and economic power that men had over their lives. In moral reform societies in particular, they attacked the double standard and the sexual and economic exploitation of women with great militance. Women's barely submerged anger, combined with their conviction of the importance of bringing their special, moral influence to bear on society, led them to the very edges of "woman's sphere." The moral reform societies pursued male licentiousness all the way to the New York legislature, where they petitioned for a law making the sexual seduction of "any unmarried female of previous chaste character" a crime. Petitioning, although a political activity, was an extraordinary one which women could undertake occasionally without risking their womanliness. Once the moral reform women succeeded in "influencing" the legislature to pass the antiseduction law, they returned to the more acceptable tasks of caring for friendless women and children. Believing in the special needs and capacities of women, they nevertheless continued to defer to the authority of men, at least to their institutionalized political and religious power.[9]

When female antislavery activity began in the early 1830s, it was on similar terms. Women abolitionists believed that they had a particular obligation with respect to religious and moral concerns and, on the grounds that slavery was a threat to the moral character of American society, they argued that it was appropriate for women to work for its abolition. Initially they observed the proprieties by meeting separately from men and making their particular concern the women and children who were victims of slavery.[10] Like female moral reformers, they sought to achieve their goals by trying to influence men, both in their private relations and by public petition campaigns.

However, antislavery activity, far more than moral reform or temperance, brought women into conflict with established centers of power, and this in turn helped to lead them beyond the "woman's sphere" way of conceiving their social role. As Elizabeth Stanton explained, slavery was a "question of religion, philanthropy, political economy, commerce, education, and social life, on which depends the very existence of this so called republic."[11] In 1837, two women abolitionists, Sarah and Ange-

lina Grimké, were attacked by the Congregational clergy of
Massachusetts for becoming "public reformers" and speaking to
mixed groups of men and women. They responded by embrac-
ing the odious tradition of women's rights to defend their abolitionism. Significantly, they were also rebuked by Catherine
Beecher, who reminded them that "woman is to win everything
by peace and love . . . but this is all to be accomplished in the
domestic circle . . . [by] woman's retaining her place as dependent and defenceless and making no claims and maintaining no
rights."[12] Angelina Grimké responded that the antislavery
movement had taught her that "human beings have *rights* because they are *moral* beings; . . . as all men have the same moral
nature, they have essentially the same rights." Applying this
"fundamental principle" to women, she realized that sex was a
"mere circumstance," falsely "enthroned upon the summit, ad-
ministering upon rights and responsibilities." Sarah Grimké answered the clerical criticisms of her public activity in a similar
fashion. She repudiated "the distinction now so strenuously insisted upon between masculine and feminine virtues" and insisted on the great benefits, to men and women both, of "equality of the sexes."[13]

The Grimkés' defense of women's rights catalyzed a great
deal of feminist sentiment among abolitionists. Many other
women and a few men supported and encouraged them, and finally, in 1839, antifeminists, finding themselves in the minority,
withdrew from the American Anti-Slavery Society (AASS).
Abolitionist women subsequently dissolved their separate
auxiliaries, took office in the organization, became traveling
public lecturers, and generally obliterated all distinctions between men's and women's activity in the AASS. In this atmosphere, feminism and feminists flourished. Elizabeth Cady
Stanton, Susan B. Anthony, Lucy Stone, Jane Elizabeth Jones,
and other leaders of the women's rights movement in the 1850s
were active in the AASS of the 1840s. Thirty years later, when
Stanton and Anthony surveyed the influences leading up to the
Seneca Falls convention of 1848, they identified three precipi-
tating factors: the radical ideas of Wright and Rose on religion
and democracy; the initial reforms in women's property law in

the 1830s and 1840s; and "above all other causes," women's experiences in the antislavery movement.[14]

Elizabeth Cady Stanton and Seneca Falls

Elizabeth Cady Stanton was an extraordinary woman. She bore seven children and lived eighty-seven years in nearly perfect health, mental as well as physical. She was brilliant and learned, and she was also sensuous, defending her own weight (175 pounds in 1860, over 240 when she was an old woman), her propensity to take frequent naps, and the sexuality of all women when none of these things was considered respectable.[15] She had a powerful wit which she used to demolish her enemies and keep her friends at a respectful distance. Above all, she was committed to unearthing and understanding the long history of women's oppression, and to leading women to revolt against it. Her strength of character, intelligence, and vitality were so great, her anger at the oppression of women so profound, that coming to know her now, more than seventy-five years after her death, is still as inspiring an experience as it must have been when she was in her prime.

She was born in 1815 to one of New York's "blue-blooded first families."[16] Her mother was a Livingston, and this aristocratic background provided her with a tendency to elitism and a special measure of self-confidence that came from generations of landed wealth. She attended Emma Willard's Troy Seminary, where she received the best woman's education available at the time. There, she was caught up in a powerful religious revival, and, as with many other women of her generation, the effort to experience spiritual conversion and convince herself of her total depravity and dependence on God nearly led to an emotional breakdown. Removed from the pressures of the revival "epidemic," and exposed to secular philosophy, "my religious superstition gave place to rational ideas based on scientific facts, and in proportion as I looked at everything from a new standpoint, I grew more happy day by day."[17] After graduation, she read law in the office of her father, the noted jurist Daniel Cady, and became a student of legal and constitutional history.[18] Her knowledge of the law and respect for its significance, as well as her hostility to religious enthusiasm and the organized clergy, distinguished her from many other women who believed that religion was woman's sphere and government and politics were alien, masculine activities.

In this same period, she was introduced into the abolitionist movement by her cousin, Gerrit Smith. Smith was a major figure in the transformation of abolitionism from an evangelical enterprise, which relied on moral suasion and individual conversion to defeat slavery, into a political movement, which focused on the law and the power of the state. In 1839 and 1840, Smith was meeting with other abolitionists convinced of the necessity of political organization, prominent among whom was Henry B. Stanton. Stanton, who had begun his career as a theological student and brilliant abolitionist organizer, had been one of the first abolitionists to recognize the limitations of the moral suasion strategy. In a famous incident in 1839, he had challenged William Lloyd Garrison, the leading abolitionist exponent of moral suasion, to admit that he opposed political action. "Do you believe that voting is a sin?" Stanton insisted, to which Garrison would only answer, "A sin for me."[19]

Elizabeth Cady and Henry Stanton met at Gerrit Smith's home. They shared many things, including a belief in the importance of political organization for the achievement of reform. In defense of Henry Stanton's role in the formation of the new, antislavery Liberty party, Elizabeth Cady wrote: "I am in favor of political action. . . . So long as we are to be governed by human laws, I shall be unwilling to have the making and administration of these laws left entirely to the selfish and unprincipled part of the community, which would be the case should all honest men refuse to mingle in political affairs." Political organization, she argued, in this case "a party formed and candidates nominated," "give a reality to antislavery principles."[20] Their courtship was brief and tempestuous, due in part to Judge Cady's opposition and in part to political upheaval within the abolitionist movement. Their marriage took place on May 9, 1840, sandwiched in between the founding convention of the

Liberty party and the meeting at which the American Anti-Slavery Society split over the question of women's rights.

Marriage to Henry Stanton brought Elizabeth into personal contact with the pioneering feminists of the antislavery movement. The first stop on their wedding trip was the home of Angelina Grimké Weld, Theodore Weld, and Sarah Grimké. "We were very much pleased with Elizabeth Stanton who spent several days with us," Angelina wrote to a friend, "and I could not help wishing that Henry was better calculated to help mould such a mind."[21] From there, the Stantons went to London to attend the World's Anti-Slavery Convention, where the recent split in the American abolitionist movement led to a bitter controversy over women's rights. The American women delegates, one of whom was Lucretia Mott, were refused admission to the convention. Mott and Elizabeth Stanton spent a great deal of time together in London and, when they returned to the United States, began to correspond.

Meeting Lucretia Mott greatly accelerated Elizabeth Stanton's development as a feminist. "Before meeting Mrs. Mott, I had heard a few men of liberal opinions discuss various political, religious and social theories," Stanton wrote some years later, "but with my first doubt of my father's absolute wisdom, came a distrust of all men's opinions on the character and sphere of women." Mott was the first woman she had met who was as liberal-minded as the men she had known and "who had sufficient confidence in herself to frame and hold an opinion in the face of opposition," especially male.[22] Despite her Quakerism and her piety, Mott was familiar with and sympathetic to the traditions of secular radicalism. Stanton credited her with "banishing religious doubts and fears from my mind."[23] Mott had read Wollstonecraft and Paine, knew Robert Owen the elder, and, perhaps most important for Stanton's development, was acquainted with and sympathetic to the feminist ideas of Frances Wright. Mott cultivated Stanton's intellect and encouraged her feminism. She urged her to read Wollstonecraft, Wright, and the Grimkés' writings, which Stanton herself circulated in the early 1840s.[24] "The more I think on the present condition of woman," Stanton wrote to Mott in 1842, "the more am I oppressed with the reality of their degradation."[25] Finally, in 1848, Stanton's feminist apprenticeship was completed. With the help of Mott, her sister, Martha Wright, and another Quaker woman, Mary McClintock, Stanton conceived and organized the first women's rights convention.

There has been considerable historical speculation about the timing of the Seneca Falls convention. Why did it not occur until 1848, especially inasmuch as the two key figures had met and discussed women's rights eight years before? First of all, Stanton's domestic situation had changed, considerably intensifying her personal discontent. By 1848, she was a thirty-three-year-old housewife and mother of three, living in central New York, away from the centers of intellectual and political excitement. Her husband earned only a modest income, was often away from home on political business, and she cared for her children and did most of her housework herself or with the help of one servant.

Larger political influences were also at work. In April, the New York legislature finally passed the law, for which Stanton and others had lobbied, giving married women control over their inherited property. At the same time, revolutionary movements were flaring up all over Europe, demanding the overthrow of despotism, the extension of democratic political rights, and the achievement of full equality. Finally, it became increasingly apparent that both major parties and the national government were committed to the defense and expansion of slavery, and this accelerated political developments among abolitionists. Less than a month after the women's rights convention at Seneca Falls, Henry Stanton played a major role in the organization of an openly antislavery faction within the Democratic party, and by November he had been elected to the New York legislature as a Free Soil Democrat.

Elizabeth Stanton was the dominant force behind the convention at Seneca Falls (see document 1).[26] It was her idea to call it, she suggested that the Declaration of Independence be adapted for use as a women's rights manifesto, and she assembled the list of grievances designed to prove that "the history of mankind is the history of repeated injuries and usurpations on the part of man toward woman." The Seneca Falls Declaration of Sentiments bore many hallmarks of her influence. It was shaped by a powerful, eloquent conviction of men's "absolute tyranny" over women, which Stanton infused into everything she said and wrote about women. She also gave the Declaration a sense of great historical significance, almost as if this convention were the first time that women had ever repudiated the false and unequal position into which men had placed them, and demanded the full equality and true freedom that was their right. Finally, she was responsible for the focus on political equality, and especially the demand for the vote, which distinguished Seneca Falls from the women's rights activity that had preceded it.

In the half century since Mary Wollstonecraft, the debate over sexual egalitarianism had shifted ground. The primary question for feminists was no longer education, but the more distant realms of public activity reserved for men, especially politics. Frances Wright had recognized the importance of political organization, and had spoken and written on "the science of government," but at a time when the principle of political equality had not yet even been won with respect to white men, she did not demand that women be enfranchised. Nor was political equality the focus for feminists in the abolitionist movement, most of whom were suspicious of politics and committed to the strategy of moral suasion.[27] It fell to Elizabeth Stanton, a militant feminist who understood the importance of political organization for reformers, to recognize that feminism, like abolition, had to become a political movement to "give reality" to its principles. This was the basis on which she demanded woman suffrage.

In the Seneca Falls Declaration of Sentiments, Stanton argued that political equality was the key to women's overthrow of male despotism and the achievement of the "equal status to which they are entitled." The first in her list of grievances against men was that women were denied their "inalienable right to the elective franchise." From this flowed men's ability to pass laws that deprived women of control over property and wages, subjected them to the authority of their husbands in marriage, deprived them of their children in the case of divorce, and left them "oppressed on all sides." By focusing on the demand for political equality, Stanton gave feminism a clear strategy and set it on firm ground for becoming an organized social movement. She understood that law played a major role in setting men over women. By demanding political power, women could struggle collectively against their degradation, rather than each against her own father or husband. The demand for the vote touched the nerve of woman's subordination by contending that women could have a role in society other than that of wife and mother. "Depend upon it, this is the point to attack," Stanton wrote prophetically, "the stronghold of the fortress— *the one* woman will find the most difficult to take, *the one* man will most reluctantly give up."[28]

Although the Seneca Falls convention was intended to stimulate widespread agitation for women's civil and political equality, it was almost two years before a women's rights convention was held outside New York. Finally in April, 1850, feminists in the abolitionist stronghold of Salem, Ohio, organized a women's rights meeting to exert pressure on the state constitutional convention. Later that year, feminists from seven states met in Worcester, Massachusetts; the leading figure was Paulina Wright Davis, a former moral reformer who had become active in the antislavery movement. Davis tried to set a non-militant, harmonious tone at Worcester, and in her call to the convention stressed "the absolute unity of interest" between the sexes, the impossibility of "antagonism" or "hostile attitudes . . . either in the apprehension or amendment of the wrongs which exist."[29] The convention set up a rudimentary form of organization: a coordinating committee, a plan for woman suffrage petition campaigns in eight states, and committees to report on women's educational, industrial, legal, and social status.[30] In 1851 Indiana women organized a convention, and the next year Pennsylvania women did the same, even though they remained wary of women becoming involved in "the violence and intrigue which are frequently practised by party politicians."[31]

Stanton was unable to attend most of these early women's

rights conventions because of the continuing demands of household and children, but nothing kept her from writing. She sent letters of encouragement to those she did not attend and began to plan a book on women's history.[32] Horace Greeley invited her to write occasional articles for *The New York Tribune*, but when another Seneca Falls resident, Amelia Bloomer, began to publish a monthly women's temperance newspaper, Stanton saw the opportunity for a regular outlet for her women's rights ideas. Under her influence, Bloomer's newspaper, *The Lily*, became "the only [medium] in the whole country—for spreading among women accurate news of the women's rights movement."[33]

Feminists of all sorts began to turn to Stanton. "Every article you write hits the nail on the head," wrote Mary Gove Nichols, a health reformer and early proponent of free love. "I like you vastly."[34] The pioneering woman physician, Harriott Hunt, wanted to come to Seneca Falls to meet her. "Our deep interest in the Woman's cause which is opening so wonderfully draws me very near to you my dear Mrs. Stanton and I do not feel as addressing a stranger."[35] There was widespread impatience among feminists to see Stanton released from her domestic responsibilities. "Oh Liz, if you were not tied hand and foot by domestic duties," Sarah Grimké wrote, "what a glorious work you would do for woman. As it is you do much, very much."[36] "When your children are a little more grown, you will surely be heard," Lucy Stone wrote, soon after they met, "for it cannot be possible to repress what is in you."[37]

Susan B. Anthony and Women's Temperance Activity

Stanton's involvement with *The Lily* brought her into contact with a young temperance worker, Susan B. Anthony. Anthony was born in 1820 into an antislavery and liberal Quaker family. Her father had struggled against religious orthodoxy, but Susan did not have to do so, and she tended to be both more casual and more practical about the power of the established churches than Stanton. In 1837, her father lost his cotton mill during the panic, and when the family reached its

lowest point economically, Susan and her sisters went out to
teach. Within a few years, she had become passionately attached to the idea of self-support and personal independence for
women. She was the only women's rights leader of the first
generation to remain unmarried. By 1850, she was looking for a
wider field for her labors than teaching, and turned to temperance. She subscribed enthusiastically to the ideas and moral reform perspective of the movement, and became active in the
Daughters of Temperance, its female wing, where her dedicated
work and strong personality soon brought her into prominence
in western New York.[38]

The temperance movement was undergoing a revival in the
early 1850s and had begun to take a turn toward politics.[39] After
years of treating intemperance as a sin and moral failing, reformers were beginning to recognize the role that the state
played in organizing and facilitating the liquor industry. In
Maine, temperance advocates succeeded in getting the legislature to pass a law prohibiting the production or sale of liquor,
and agitation grew for a "Maine law" in other states, including
New York. Like most women in the temperance movement,
Anthony believed that the only influence women could bring to
bear against alcohol was private, in their homes, and indirect,
"through husband, son, father, or brother."[40] Yet she was very
much in favor of bringing the issue into politics, and frustrated
because there was no role for women in this work (see document 2).

Amelia Bloomer introduced Anthony to Stanton sometime in
1851. Perhaps Anthony had expressed a desire to meet the
woman who was preaching political equality for women; perhaps Bloomer recognized the affinity between Stanton's ideas
about women and the equality of the sexes, and Anthony's
drive and capacity. Anthony was immediately drawn to Stanton by the power of her ideas. She was attracted by Stanton's
political and secular viewpoint, and her disdain for what Anthony was soon calling the "pharasaical priests" who had considerable control over the temperance movement. Stanton lib-
erated the feminism in Anthony, particularly her anger at the
sentimental and trivializing treatment of women by male tem-

perance leaders. When Anthony was prohibited from speaking at a temperance convention because to do so would violate woman's sphere, she decided to organize a new, independent women's temperance society which would place no such limitations on her. She persuaded Elizabeth Stanton to work with her, and, in April 1852, the New York State Women's Temperance Society held its founding meeting. Five hundred women were present, Elizabeth Stanton was made president, and Anthony became the traveling organizer.[41]

Stanton proposed a women's rights program for the new society, the two most radical elements of which were woman suffrage, "so that woman may vote on this great political and social evil," and a liberalized divorce law, to permit women to divorce drunken husbands (see document 2). Like Frances Willard, who would lead the Women's Christian Temperance Union twenty-five years later, Stanton recognized that women's enthusiasm for temperance often embodied a protest against their vulnerability to and dependence on irresponsible and abusive men, and believed that this spirit could be turned in a feminist direction. Unlike Willard, however, many of her ideas were too radical for temperance women to accept. This was particularly true of her advocacy of divorce reform. More important, there was no independently established women's rights movement, as there would be in the 1870s, to pull women's temperance activity in a feminist direction. At the first anniversary of the Women's State Temperance Society, Stanton and Anthony were successfully challenged by an alliance of temperance men and conservative women. Once the prohibition against men voting in the Society was overturned, Stanton was deposed from the presidency and the women's rights program of divorce and woman suffrage was repudiated. Although Anthony was re-elected to office, she withdrew in solidarity with Stanton.[42]

The temperance episode solidified the comradeship that Stanton and Anthony had begun to develop. The effect on Stanton was enormous. "In turning the intense earnestness and religious enthusiasm of this great-souled woman into this channel," Stanton wrote, "I soon felt the power of my convert goading me forward to more untiring work."[43] Starting with the temperance movement of the 1850s, Anthony drew Stanton into active reform work among women and kept her there. Anthony was familiar with the network of female benevolent organizations and much more than Stanton appreciated the loyalty to sex that women were beginning to cultivate there. She believed that this sisterhood could be extended into a feminist movement. She was more consistently optimistic about women's development than Stanton, readier to see the signs of developing feminism in them. Although she played a crucial role in this period by relieving Stanton of some of her domestic burdens and acting as her proxy at reform conventions, she may have had an even more important effect in helping her to resist the psychological lure of "narrow family selfishness."[44] Anthony's entire existence was the world of female reform and she provided Stanton with a strong and vital link to that world. "I do believe that I have developed into much more of a woman under her jurisdiction," Stanton wrote thirty-five years later, "than if left to myself reading novels in an easy chair."[45]

Women's Rights and Antislavery in the 1850s

Anthony's conversion from moral reform to political feminism was a total one, and she immediately put her prodigious energies directly in the service of women's rights in New York State. Using the skills and contacts she had acquired while traveling for temperance reform, she organized an ambitious petition campaign for women's rights during the winter of 1853–1854. Sixty women circulated petitions under her direction, and, within a few months, secured more than ten thousand signatures to send to the New York legislature.[46] Women's rights activists had for some time wanted a more systematic approach, but most of them were too attached to the individualistic style of agitational reform to undertake it. The call to the 1852 national convention had urged "a well digested plan of operation whereby [our] social rights may be secured," but many women's rights leaders found organizations objectionable because they "fettered" and "distorted" the individual spirit.[47] Anthony, fresh from the network of women's benevolent societies, had no such objections to the constraint of organization, and no difficulty disciplining her energies to it. Her willingness to undertake the slow, backbreaking work necessary to teach women the importance of political equality and to force legislatures to grant it proved to be her greatest contribution to feminism. Her total dedication, year after year, eventually won her enormous loyalty from American women and a solid historical reputation as "mother" of the women's movement.

The petition campaign culminated in a grand women's rights convention in Albany in February, 1854, the central event of which was Elizabeth Stanton's "Address to the Legislature" (see document 3). Stanton was unusually nervous about this speech, spent over two months writing it, and consulted several men to make sure that there were no errors in her legal scholarship. The basic premise of her arguments was, as it had been at Seneca Falls, that women's position before the law denied the fundamental truth that "men and women are alike," thus "we ask for no better laws than those you have made for yourself." In three of the four categories in which she surveyed women's legal oppression, the remedies she proposed followed this rule of the identity of men and women before the law: women as citizens must have equal civil status with men, especially the right to vote and sit on juries; women as widows must have equal inheritance rights when their spouses died intestate; and women as wives must have a revised marriage code which subjected marriage "to the same laws which controlled all other contracts" and made it dissolvable at the will of either party. It was only when Stanton considered the unjust laws under which women suffered as mothers that she shifted her philosophical ground, arguing, Beecher-like, that women had a unique role in "moulding the character of the son" and thus special responsibility for developing "a higher and purer morality." "Thy address to the Legislature we circulate unsparingly," wrote Lucretia Mott. "It gives great satisfaction."[48] "The hearing has confirmed my previous suspicion that you are the head and font of this offence against the oppressors of womanhood," another admirer wrote.[49] "May I tell you, dear, of one little defect in your address?" Sarah Grimké wrote. "It was too caustic."[50]

Both Stanton and Anthony went through personal transformations as they developed the skills and sense of self necessary to work for women's rights (see document 4). After her 1854 speech, Stanton arrived at a "fierce decision" to work for women's rights in earnest, and to "speak when I can do myself credit," but she encountered painful opposition from her father, friends, and husband. "I wish you to consider this letter strictly confidential," she wrote to Anthony in 1855. "Sometimes, Susan, I struggle in deep waters." Anthony faced a different challenge as she began to build the kind of life that would sustain her as an unmarried woman and full-time political reformer. She experienced deep loneliness and, when Lucy Stone and Antoinette Brown, to whom she had looked for companionship and intimacy, each married, she was profoundly angered. "I have *very weak* moments," she wrote to Stanton in despair, "and long to lay my weary head somewhere and nestle my full soul close to that of another in full sympathy. I sometimes fear that I too shall faint by the wayside, and drop out [of] the ranks of the faithful few."

It took more than six years of grueling, sustained work before the New York legislature met any of the women's rights demands. In her 1854 speech Stanton had boldly proclaimed that "the mass speak through us"—"women who support themselves and their children . . . the drunkards' wives . . . the woman who has worked hard all her days to help her husband to accumulate a large property . . . the laboring women . . . those women who teach in our seminaries . . . the unfortunate ones in our workhouses." But the truth was that it took a long time for women's rights to win any popular support, even among women. The dominant ideology of womanhood continued to be that of separate spheres and female domesticity, and women's rights feminists faced the enormous task of challenging these beliefs. In Washington, D.C., Anthony heard a prominent clergyman preach that "it is . . . in the home that . . . all women's chiefest duties lie," and she was enraged (see document 5); when a male reformer, not unfriendly to women's rights, claimed that "women's inherent nature is Love & Man's Wisdom," her "heart sank."[51] Among women, ideas like those of

Catherine Beecher continued to be more acceptable than those of women's rights, but slowly, in response to conventions, lectures, articles, and petition campaigns, support began to grow. "In my circle, I hear the movement talked of and earnest hopes for its spread expressed," Mrs. Charles G. Finney, wife of the powerful evangelist minister, told Anthony. "But these women dare not speak out their sympathy."[52] In 1860, after six years of county canvasses, petition campaigns, and memorials to the legislature, New York feminists secured the first comprehensive reform in women's legal status, including full property, parental, and widow's rights, but not enfranchisement.

The major factor affecting the women's rights movement in the late 1850s was the growing intensity of the conflict over slavery. In 1850, Congress passed the Fugitive Slave Law providing federal protection for slaveowners' rights. A series of dramatic conflicts between abolitionists and slave-catchers followed as did heightened antislavery sentiment in the North. Four years later, the Kansas-Nebraska Act inaugurated bloody civil war between proslavery and antislavery settlers in the Kansas Territory. In 1857, the Supreme Court, in its Dred Scott decision, ruled that slavery was fully constitutional. As the power of the federal government was mobilized in favor of slaveholders, antislavery sentiment increasingly moved into national politics, and, in 1855, free-soilers established the Republican party.

Although Stanton and Anthony had been identified with abolitionism for many years, they did not become active in the antislavery movement until the late 1850s. In 1857, Anthony was asked to replace Lucy Stone as a paid organizer for the American Anti-Slavery Society, which worked outside the electoral system to agitate against slavery.[53] For the next four years she traveled tirelessly for abolition, while she was directing the women's rights campaigns in New York. At first Stanton saw some hope in the Republican party, in which her husband was active, but the pace of events soon outran the possibility of electoral solutions and she became convinced "that we shall be in the midst of violence, blood, and civil war before we look at it."[54] By 1857 she had identified herself with the American

Anti-Slavery Society because it alone seemed to recognize the
enormity of "the monster slavery."[55] In 1860, she was invited as
the foremost representative of American feminism to address
the annual meeting of the AASS (see document 6). Her subject
was the link between abolitionism and women's rights, between
the Black slave and the white woman. Although her speech was
criticized by some for giving too much attention to women's
rights, Stanton was herself increasingly caught up in the struggle over slavery.[56] In late 1859, John Brown raided the U.S. Ar-
senal at Harpers Ferry, Virginia, in an effort to instigate a slave
revolt, and was captured and martyred by hanging. Stanton's
cousin Gerrit Smith was a backer of Brown and the episode
temporarily drove him mad. Stanton, who loved her cousin and
revered Brown, was moved to protest her "dwarfed womanhood," feeling that, "in times like these, every one should do the
work of a full grown man."[57] In early 1861, she undertook the
first short traveling canvass of her life and joined Anthony in a
series of antislavery meetings around western New York. In
city after city, they were harassed and physically attacked for
demanding that the newly elected Republican president, Abra-
ham Lincoln, commit himself to the abolition of slavery. In
April of that year, the federal forces at Fort Sumter were attacked by the secessionist government of South Carolina, and
war was declared. From that point on the political life of the
North was totally dominated by the war, and the issues of
women's rights awaited its end and the ultimate resolution of
the slavery issue.

NOTES

1. Mary Wollstonecraft, *Vindication of the Rights of Woman*
(New York: W. W. Norton, 1967), pp. 145, 9–10, 7, 148–49, 168–73.
2. Clarence Cook, ed., *A Girl's Life Eighty Years Ago: Letters of
Eliza Southgate Bowne* (New York: G. Scribner's Sons, 1887) cited
by Nancy F. Cott, ed., *Root of Bitterness* (New York: E. P. Dutton &
Co., 1972), pp. 107–08. Also see Nicholas McGuinn, "George Eliot
and Mary Wollstonecraft," *The Nineteenth Century Woman*, eds.
Sara Delamont and Lorna Duffin (London: Croom Helm, 1978).
3. Hannah Mather Crocker, *Observations of the Real Rights of
Women, and their Appropriate Duties, Agreeable to Scripture, Rea-*

son and Common Sense (Boston: By the Author, 1818); Emma Hart Willard, *Address to the Public: Particularly to the Members of the Legislature of New York, Proposing a Plan for Improving Female Education* (Albany: I. W. Clark, 1819); both excerpted in *Up From the Pedestal: Selected Writings in the History of American Feminism*, ed. Aileen S. Kraditor (Chicago: Quadrangle Books, 1968), pp. 40, 43–44, 82.

4. Alice S. Rossi, "Woman of Action: Frances Wright," in *The Feminist Papers from Adams to de Beauvoir* (New York: Columbia University Press, 1973); the quotation is cited on p. 93. Also see Frances Wright, *Course of Popular Lectures* (New York: Office of The Free Enquirer, 1830).

5. On Rose and Hertell, see Yuri Suhl, *Ernestine Rose and the Battle for Human Rights* (New York: Reynal and Company, 1959), pp. 53–55. On Robert Dale Owen, see *History of Woman Suffrage*, Vol. 1, eds. Elizabeth Cady Stanton, Susan B. Anthony, and Matilda J. Gage (Rochester: Susan B. Anthony, 1881), p. 293 (hereafter referred to as *HWS*). In Massachusetts, Mary Upton Ferrin agitated both for married women's property legislation and divorce reform; see *HWS*, Vol. 1, p. 208.

6. The phrase is Nancy Cott's, from *The Bonds of Womanhood: "Woman's Sphere" in New England, 1780–1835* (New Haven: Yale University Press, 1977), p. 202.

7. Catherine E. Beecher, *A Treatise on Domestic Economy* (New York: Schocken Books, 1977), especially chap. 15 and pp. 9 and 183.

8. The circulation figure for *Godey's Lady's Book* is from Eleanor Flexner, *Century of Struggle: The Women's Rights Movement in the United States* (New York: Atheneum, 1968), p. 65. For Hale's opinions on women's rights, see Keith Melder, *Beginnings of Sisterhood: The American Women's Rights Movement 1800–1850* (New York: Schocken Books, 1977), p. 132.

9. Barbara Berg, *The Remembered Gate: Origins of American Feminism* (New York: Oxford University Press, 1978), especially p. 210; also Carroll Smith Rosenberg, "Beauty, the Beast and the Militant Woman: A Case Study in Sex Roles and Social Stress in Jacksonian America," *American Quarterly*, Vol. 23 (1971), pp. 562–84.

10. Louis Filler, *The Crusade Against Slavery, 1830–1860* (New York: Harper and Brothers, 1960), p. 129.

11. Elizabeth Cady Stanton, "Speech to the 1860 Anniversary of the American Anti-Slavery Society," *The Liberator*, May 18, 1860, p. 78 (see document 6).

12. Catherine E. Beecher, *An Essay on Slavery and Abolitionism with Reference to the Duty of American Females* (Philadelphia: Henry Perkins, 1837), pp. 100–02.

13. Angelina Grimké, *Letters to Catherine E. Beecher in Reply to an Essay on Slavery and Abolitionism* (Boston: Isaac Knapp, 1838),

pp. 115–16; Sarah Grimké, *Letters on the Equality of the Sexes and the Condition of Women Addressed to Mary S. Parker* (Boston: Isaac Knapp, 1838), pp. 16 and 54.

14. *HWS*, Vol. 1, pp. 51–52.

15. As a young woman, Stanton mentioned her weight in a letter to Elizabeth Smith Miller, her cousin, June 24, 1860, Autograph Collection, Vassar College Library. For the 240-lb. figure, see Stanton to Miller, September 11, 1888, Theodore Stanton Papers, Douglass College Library, as cited by Elisabeth Griffith, "Elizabeth Cady Stanton: Grand Old Woman" (unpublished manuscript, 1978). For her attitude toward female sexuality, see her comments about Walt Whitman in her September 6, 1883, diary entry in *Elizabeth Cady Stanton As Revealed in Her Letters, Diary and Reminiscences*, eds. Theodore Stanton and Harriot Stanton Blatch (New York: Harper & Brothers Publishers, 1922), p. 210 (hereafter referred to as *Stanton Letters*).

16. "Interview with Elizabeth Cady Stanton," *Sunday New York Herald*, January 22, 1899.

17. Elizabeth Cady Stanton, *Eighty Years and More: Reminiscences, 1815–1897* (New York: T. Fischer Unwin, 1898), pp. 43–44.

18. Stanton described herself as "reading law" in a questionnaire she filled out for the Troy Seminary many years later. I want to thank Anne Firor Scott for bringing this document to my attention.

19. Filler, *Crusade Against Slavery*, p. 156.

20. Elizabeth Cady Stanton to Elisabeth Pease, as cited by Alma Lutz, *Created Equal: A Biography of Elizabeth Cady Stanton* (New York: The John Day Company, 1940), p. 36

21. Angelina Grimké Weld to Gerrit and Anne Smith, June 18, 1840, *Letters of Theodore Dwight Weld, Angelina Grimké Weld, and Sarah Grimké, 1822–1844*, Vol. 2, eds. Gilbert H. Barnes and Dwight L. Dumond (New York: Appleton-Century Company, 1934), p. 842.

22. *HWS*, Vol. 1, p. 419.

23. As quoted in *James and Lucretia Mott, Life and Letters*, ed. Anna D. Hallowell (Boston: Houghton, Mifflin and Company, 1884), p. 186.

24. Mott to Stanton, March 16, 1855, Elizabeth Cady Stanton Papers, Library of Congress; and Mott to Richard Webb, September 5, 1855, in Hallowell, *James and Lucretia Mott*, p. 357. Melder, *Beginnings of Sisterhood*, p. 145, mentions that Stanton circulated the Grimkés' writings.

25. Stanton's letter is quoted by Mott to Richard and Hannah Webb, February 25, 1842, in Hallowell, *James and Lucretia Mott*, p. 223.

26. Stanton, *Eighty Years*, chap. 9, especially p. 148, and *HWS*, Vol. 1, chap. 4.

27. This included the Grimkés and Mott. In her first major women's rights speech, delivered in 1849, Mott said, "Far be it from

me to encourage women to vote or to take an active part in politics in the present state of our affairs" (cited in Hallowell, *James and Lucretia Mott*, p. 500). The position of the Grimkés, especially Angelina, on politics, was quite ambiguous. In her letters to Catherine Beecher, Angelina wrote that she believed in "woman's right to have a voice in all the laws and regulations by which she is to be *governed,*" but she only defended the right to petition and nowhere directly asserted the right to vote (p. 119).

28. Letter from Elizabeth Cady Stanton to the Salem, Ohio, Convention, April 7, 1850, *HWS*, Vol. 1, pp. 810–12.

29. *HWS*, Vol. 1, p. 221.

30. On the plan for petition campaigns, see Elizabeth Cady Stanton to Amy Post, December 4, 1850, *Stanton Letters*, pp. 24–25.

31. *HWS*, Vol. 1, p. 833.

32. Lucretia Mott to Stanton, October 3, 1848, Elizabeth Cady Stanton Papers, Library of Congress.

33. Alma Lutz, *Created Equal*, p. 46.

34. M. S. Gove Nichols to Stanton, August 21, 1852, *Stanton Letters*, p. 44.

35. Harriott Hunt to Stanton, June 30, 1852, Elizabeth Cady Stanton Papers, Library of Congress.

36. Sarah Grimké to Stanton, March 29, 1854, ibid.

37. Lucy Stone to Stanton, August 14, 1853, ibid.

38. Ida Harper, *The Life and Work of Susan B. Anthony*, Vol. 1 (Indianapolis: the Bowen-Merrill Company, 1899), chap. 6. Anthony supervised this two-volume biography and so it is somewhat autobiographical.

39. For a brief overview of temperance in the 1850s, see Ronald Walters, *American Reformers, 1815–1860* (New York: Hill & Wang, 1978).

40. From an appeal written by Anthony in 1852, as quoted in Harper, *Life of Anthony*, Vol. 1, p. 71.

41. Ibid., chap. 6; see also *HWS*, Vol. 1, chap. 14.

42. *HWS*, Vol. 1, pp. 493–99.

43. Stanton, *Eighty Years*, p. 187.

44. Ibid., p. 165.

45. Harper, *Life of Anthony*, Vol. 2, p. 667.

46. Ibid., Vol. 1, p. 105.

47. *HWS*, Vol. 1, pp. 518 and 541–42.

48. Lucretia Mott to Stanton, n.d., *Stanton Letters*, p. 56.

49. Stanton's correspondent was probably the Reverend Amory D. Mayo, February 15, 1854, Elizabeth Cady Stanton Papers, Library of Congress.

50. Sarah Grimké to Stanton, March 29, 1854, ibid.

51. Anthony to Stanton, September 29, 1857, ibid. (see document 4).

52. Anthony quoted Mrs. Finney in a letter to Stanton, May 26, 1856, Elizabeth Cady Stanton Papers, Vassar College Library (see document 4).

53. Harper, *Life of Anthony*, Vol. 1, chap. 10.

54. Stanton to Anthony, November 4, 1855, *Stanton Letters*, pp. 62–63 (see document 4). Stanton to Elizabeth Smith Miller, November 15, 1856, ibid.

55. Stanton to Anthony, December, 1857, ibid., p. 71.

56. Letter to *The Liberator*, May 18, 1860, as cited in ibid., p. 78.

57. Stanton to Anthony, December 23, 1859, ibid., pp. 74–75 (see document 4).

DOCUMENT 1

STANTON, "ADDRESS DELIVERED AT SENECA FALLS," JULY 19, 1848

Despite her claim of "diffidence," there was nothing timid about this speech, Stanton's first on women's rights. She began by accusing men of the moral crime of assuming that women's nature was different than their own, and criticized not only the ideology of male superiority, but also the idea that the sexes were different but equal. Nor did she hesitate to point out to women the contribution they made to their own degradation, and the "indifference" and "contempt" with which they greeted women's rights. Stanton expected that the remedy she proposed, equality of civil status and political power, would seem "strange to many," and she predicted that it would lead both to domestic upheaval and social reform.

wrong

"This is my first lecture. . . . It contains all I knew at the time," Stanton wrote on the manuscript of this speech in 1866 before she handed it over to Harriot and Margaret Stanton. "I give this manuscript to my precious daughters, in the hope that they will finish the work which I have begun."*

Address Delivered at Seneca Falls and Rochester, New York (New York: Robert J. Johnson Printers, 1870)

* Cited in Laura Curtis Bullard, "Elizabeth Cady Stanton," *Our Famous Women: An Authoritative Record of the Lives and Deeds of Distinguished American Women of Our Times* (Hartford, Conn.: A. D. Worthington, 1886), pp. 617–18.

I SHOULD feel exceedingly diffident to appear before you at this time, having never before spoken in public, were I not nerved by a sense of right and duty, did I not feel the time had fully come for the question of woman's wrongs to be laid before the public, did I not believe that woman herself must do this work; for woman alone can understand the height, the depth, the length, and the breadth of her own degradation. Man cannot speak for her, because he has been educated to believe that she differs from him so materially, that he cannot judge of her thoughts, feelings, and opinions by his own. Moral beings can only judge of others by themselves. The moment they assume a different nature for any of their own kind, they utterly fail. . . .

Among the many important questions which have been brought before the public, there is none that more vitally affects the whole human family than that which is technically called Woman's Rights. Every allusion to the degraded and inferior position occupied by women all over the world has been met by scorn and abuse. From the man of highest mental cultivation to the most degraded wretch who staggers in the streets do we meet ridicule, and coarse jests, freely bestowed upon those who dare assert that woman stands by the side of man, his equal, placed here by her God, to enjoy with him the beautiful earth, which is her home as it is his, having the same sense of right and wrong, and looking to the same Being for guidance and support. So long has man exercised tyranny over her, injurious to himself and benumbing to her faculties, that few can nerve themselves to meet the storm; and so long has the chain been about her that she knows not there is a remedy. . . .

As the nations of the earth emerge from a state of barbarism, the sphere of woman gradually becomes wider, but not even under what is thought to be the full blaze of the sun of civilization, is it what God designed it to be. In every country and clime does man assume the responsibility of marking out the path for her to tread. In every country does he regard her as a being inferior to himself, and one whom he is to guide and control. From the Arabian Kerek, whose wife is obliged to steal from her husband to supply the necessities of life; from the Mahometan who forbids pigs, dogs, women and other impure animals, to enter a Mosque, and does not allow a fool, madman or woman to proclaim the hour of prayer; from the German who complacently smokes his meerschaum, while his wife, yoked with the ox, draws the plough through its furrow; from the delectable carpet-knight, who thinks an inferior style of conversation adapted to woman; to the legislator, who considers her incapable of saying what laws shall govern her, is the same feeling manifested. . . .

Let us consider . . . man's superiority, intellectually, morally, physically.

Man's intellectual superiority cannot be a question until woman has had a fair trial. When we shall have had our freedom to find out our own sphere, when we shall have had our colleges, our professions, our trades, for a century, a comparison then may be justly instituted. When woman, instead of being taxed to endow colleges where she is forbidden to enter—instead of forming sewing societies to educate "poor, but pious," young men, shall first educate herself, when she shall be just to herself before she is generous to others; improving the talents God has given her, and leaving her neighbor to do the same for himself, we shall not hear so much about this boasted superiority. . . .

In consideration of man's claim to moral superiority, glance now at our theological seminaries, our divinity students, the long line of descendants from our Apostolic fathers, the immaculate priesthood, and what do we find there? Perfect moral rectitude in every relation of life, a devoted spirit of self-sacrifice, a perfect union of thought, opinion and feeling among those who profess to worship the one God, and whose laws they feel themselves called upon to declare to a fallen race? Far from it. . . . Is the moral and religious life of this class what we might expect from minds said to be fixed on such mighty themes? By no means. . . . The lamentable want of principle among our lawyers, generally, is too well known to need comment. The everlasting backbiting and bickering of our physicians is proverbial. The disgraceful riots at our polls, where man, in performing the highest duty of citizenship, ought surely to be sober-minded, the perfect rowdyism that now characterizes the debates in our national Congress,—all these are great facts which rise up against man's claim for moral superiority. In my opinion, he is infinitely woman's inferior in every moral quality, not by nature, but made so by a false education. In carrying out his own selfishness, man has greatly improved woman's moral nature, but by an almost total shipwreck of his own. Woman has now the noble virtues of the martyr. She is early schooled to self-denial and suffering. But man is not so wholly buried in selfishness that he does not sometimes get a glimpse of the narrowness of his soul, as compared with woman. Then he says, by way of an excuse for his degradation, "God made woman more self-denying than man. It is her nature. It does not cost her as much to give up her wishes, her will, her life, even, as it does him. He is naturally selfish. God made him so."

No, I think not. . . . God's commands rest upon man as well as woman. It is as much his duty to be kind, self-denying and full of good works, as it is hers. As much his duty to absent himself from scenes of violence as it is hers. A place or position that would require the sacrifice of the delicacy and refinement of woman's nature is unfit for man, for these virtues should be as carefully guarded in him as in her. The false ideas that prevail with regard to the purity necessary to constitute the perfect character in woman, and that requisite for man, has done an infinite deal of mischief in the world. I would not have woman less pure, but I would have man more so. I would have the same code of morals for both. . . .

Let us now consider man's claim to physical superiority. Methinks I hear some say, surely, you will not contend for equality here. Yes, we must not give an inch, lest you take an ell. We cannot accord to man even this much, and he has no right to claim it until the fact has been fully demonstrated. . . . We cannot say what the woman might be physically, if the girl were allowed all the freedom of the boy in romping, climbing, swimming, playing whoop and ball. Among some of the Tartar tribes of the present day, women manage a horse, hurl a javelin, hunt wild animals, and fight an enemy as well as a man. The Indian women endure fatigues and carry burdens that some of our fair-faced, soft-handed, moustached young gentlemen would consider quite impossible for them to sustain. The Croatian and Wallachian women perform all the agricultural operations in addition to their domestic labors, and it is no uncommon sight in our cities, to see the German immigrant with his hands in his pockets, walking complacently by the side of his wife, whilst she bears the weight of some huge package or piece of furniture upon her head. Physically, as well as intellectually, it is use that produces growth and development.

But there is a class of objectors who say they do not claim superiority, they merely assert a difference. But you will find by following them up closely, that they soon run this difference into the old groove of superiority. . . .

We have met here to-day to discuss our rights and wrongs, civil and political, and not, as some have supposed, to go into the detail of social life alone. We do not propose to petition the legislature to make our husbands just, generous and courteous, to seat every man at the head of a cradle, and to clothe every woman in male attire. None of these points, however important they may be considered by leading men, will be touched in this Convention. . . .

We are assembled to protest against a form of government, existing without the consent of the governed—to declare our right to be free as man is free, to be represented in the government which we are taxed to support, to have such disgraceful laws as give man the power to chastise and imprison his wife, to take the wages which she earns, the property which she inherits, and, in case of separation, the children of her love; laws which make her the mere dependent on his bounty. It is to protest against such unjust laws as these that we are assembled to-day, and to have them, if possible, forever erased from our statute-books, deeming them a shame and a disgrace to a Christian republic in the nineteenth century. . . .

And, strange as it may seem to many, we now demand our right to vote according to the declaration of the government under which we live. . . . We have no objection to discuss the question of equality, for we feel that the weight of argument lies wholly with us, but we wish the question of equality kept distinct from the question of rights, for the proof of the one does not determine the truth of the other. All white men in this country have the same rights, however they may differ in mind, body or estate. The right is ours. The question now is, how shall we get possession of what rightfully belongs to us. We should not feel so sorely grieved if no man who had not attained the full stature of a Webster, Clay, Van Buren, or Gerrit Smith could claim the right of the elective franchise. But to have drunkards, idiots, horse-racing, rumselling rowdies, ignorant foreigners, and silly boys fully recognized, while we ourselves are thrust out from all the rights that belong to citizens, it is too grossly insulting to the dignity of woman to be longer quietly submitted to. The right is ours. Have it we must. Use it we will. The pens, the tongues, the fortunes, the indomitable wills of many women are already pledged to secure this right. The great truth, that no just government can be formed without the consent of the governed, we shall echo and re-echo in the ears of the unjust judge, until by continual coming we shall weary him. . . .

But what would woman gain by voting? Men must know the advantages of voting, for they all seem very tenacious about the right. Think you, if woman had a vote in this government, that all those laws affecting her interests would so entirely violate every principle of right and justice? Had woman a vote to give, might not the office-holders and seekers propose some change in her condition? Might not Woman's Rights become as great a question as free soil?

"But you are already represented by your fathers, husbands, brothers and sons?" Let your statute books answer the question. We have had enough of such representation. In nothing is woman's true happiness consulted. Men like to call her an angel—to feed her on what they think sweet food—nourishing her vanity; to make her believe that her organization is so much finer than theirs, that she is not fitted to struggle with the tempests of public life, but needs their care and protection!! Care and protection—such as the wolf gives the lamb—such as the eagle the hare he carries to his eyrie!! Most cunningly he entraps her, and then takes from her all those rights which are dearer to him than life itself—rights which have been baptized in blood—and the maintenance of which is even now rocking to their foundations the kingdoms of the Old World.

The most discouraging, the most lamentable aspect our cause wears is the indifference, indeed, the contempt, with which women themselves regard the movement. Where the subject is introduced, among those even who claim to be intelligent and educated, it is met by the scornful curl of the lip, and by expression of ridicule and disgust. But we shall hope better things of them when they are enlightened in regard to their present position. When women know the laws and constitutions under which they live, they will not publish their degradation by declaring themselves satisfied, nor their ignorance, by declaring they have all the rights they want. . . .

Let woman live as she should. Let her feel her accountability to her Maker. Let her know that her spirit is fitted for as high a sphere as man's, and that her soul requires food as pure and exalted as his. Let her live *first* for God, and she will not make imperfect man an object of reverence and awe. Teach her her responsibility as a being of conscience and reason, that all earthly support is weak and unstable, that her only safe dependence is the arm of omnipotence, and that true happiness springs from duty accomplished. Thus will she learn the lesson of individual responsibility for time and eternity. That neither father, husband, brother, or son, however willing they may be, can discharge her high duties of life, or stand in her stead when called into the presence of the great Searcher of Hearts at the last day. . . .

Let me here notice one of the greatest humbugs of the day, which has long found for itself the most valuable tool in woman—"The Education Society." The idea to me, is simply absurd, for women, in their present degradation and ignorance, to form sewing societies for the education of young men for the ministry. An order of beings above themselves, claiming to be gifted with superior powers, having all the avenues to learning, wealth and distinction thrown freely open to them, who, if they had but the energy to avail themselves of all these advantages, could easily secure an education for themselves, while woman herself, poor, friendless, robbed of all her rights, oppressed on all sides, civilly, religiously and socially, must needs go ignorant herself. Now, is not the idea preposterous, for such a being to educate a great, strong, lazy man, by working day and night with her needle, stitch, stitch, and the poor widow always throws in her mite, being taught to believe that all she gives for the decoration of churches and their black-coated gentry, is given unto the Lord. I think a man, who, under such conditions, has the moral hardihood to take an education at the hands of woman, and at such an expense to her, should, as soon as he graduates, with all his honors thick upon him, take the first ship for Turkey, and there pass his days in earnest efforts to rouse the inmates of the harems to a true sense of their degradation, and not, as is his custom, immediately enter our pulpits to tell us of his superiority to us, "weaker vessels,"—his prerogative to command, ours to obey, his duty to preach, ours to keep silence. . . . The last time when an appeal of this kind was made to me, I told the young girl that I would send her to school a year, if she would go, but I would never again give one red cent to the Education Society. And I do hope that every Christian woman, who has the least regard for her sex, will make the same resolve. We have worked long enough for man, and at a most unjust and unwarrantable sacrifice of self, yet he gives no evidence of gratitude, but has, thus far, treated his benefactors with scorn, ridicule and neglect. . . .

One common objection to this movement is, that if the principles of freedom and equality which we advocate were put into practice, it would destroy all harmony in the domestic circle. Here let me ask, how many truly harmonious households have we now? . . . The only happy households we now see are those in which husband and wife share equally in counsel and government. There can be no true dignity or independence where there is subordination to the absolute will of another, no happiness without freedom. Let us then have no fears that the movement will disturb what is seldom found, a truly united and happy family. . . .

There seems now to be a kind of moral stagnation in our midst. Philanthropists have done their utmost to rouse the nation to a sense of its sins. . . . Our churches are multiplying on all sides, our missionary societies, Sunday schools, and prayer meetings and innumerable charitable and reform organizations are all in operation, but still the tide of vice is swelling, and threatens the destruction of everything, and the battlements of righteousness are weak against the raging elements of sin and death. Verily, the world waits the coming of some new element, some purifying power, some spirit of mercy and love. The voice of woman has been silenced in the state, the church, and the home, but man cannot fulfill his destiny alone, he cannot redeem his race unaided. There are deep and tender chords of sympathy and love in the heart of the down-fallen and oppressed that woman can touch more skillfully than man. The world has never yet seen a truly great and virtuous nation, because in the degradation of woman the very fountains of life are poisoned at their source. It is vain to look for silver and gold from mines of copper and lead. It is the wise mother that has the wise son. So long as your women are slaves you may throw your colleges and churches to the winds. . . . Truly are the sins of the fathers visited upon the children to the third and fourth generation. God, in his wisdom, has so linked the whole human family together that any violence done at one end of the chain is felt throughout its length, and here, too, is the law of restoration, as in woman all have fallen, so in her elevation shall the race be recreated.

. . . We do not expect our path will be strewn with the flowers of popular applause, but over the thorns of bigotry and prejudice will be our way, and on our banners will beat the dark storm-clouds of opposition from those who have entrenched themselves behind the stormy bulwarks of custom and authority, and who have fortified their position by every means, holy and unholy. But we will steadfastly abide the result. Unmoved we will bear it aloft. Undaunted we will unfurl it to the gale, for we know that the storm cannot rend from it a shred, that the electric flash will but more clearly show to us the glorious words inscribed upon it, "Equality of Rights."

DOCUMENT 2A

ANTHONY, LETTER ON TEMPERANCE, AUGUST 26, 1852

DOCUMENT 2B

STANTON, "APPEAL FOR THE MAINE LAW," JANUARY 21, 1853

Although a women's temperance movement, the Daughters of Temperance, had existed in New York for some time, Stanton and Anthony considered it too conservative and limited in scope for their feminist purposes, and formed their own organization, the New York State Women's Temperance Society, in April, 1852. Anthony was one of the society's traveling agents, and in this letter to *The Lily*, she described the women's temperance activity around the state with great sympathy and enthusiasm. Like the women she met, Anthony was a "soul dissatisfied," frustrated by the "senseless, hopeless work that man points out for woman to do."

Stanton, who had just given birth to her fifth child, was unable to travel away from Seneca Falls, but presided over the organization by proxy. Her address to the New York State Assembly was read for her in January, 1853, by Anthony. In it, she elaborated the women's rights program she wanted the women's temperance forces to adopt, the basic elements of which were woman suffrage and liberalized divorce laws.

More generally, she demonstrated an appreciation for
the central role of government in supporting both the
liquor industry and the oppression of women. The
temperance legislation which she advocated for New
York was modeled on a Maine law which prohibited
the production or sale of liquor within state bound-
aries.

Rochester, August 26, 1852

DEAR Mrs. Bloomer:
... I attended the great Temperance demonstration held at
Albion, July 7th, and as I took a view from a different stand
point, from any of those who have heretofore described that
monster gathering, I will say a few words. Messrs. Barnum,
Cary and Chapin, were the speakers for the day. They talked
much of the importance of carrying the Temperance question
into politics, but failed to present a *definite* plan, by which to
combine the temperance votes and secure concert of action
throughout the State and country. . . .

According to long established custom, after serving strong
meats to the "lords of creation," the lecturers dished up a course
of what they doubtless called delicately flavored soup for the
Ladies. Barnum said it was a fact, and might as well be owned
up, that this nation is under *petticoat* government; that every
married man would acknowledge it, and if there were any
young men who would not now, it was only necessary for them
to have one week's experience as a husband, to compel them to
admit that such is indeed the fact;—all of which vulgarity could
but have grated harshly upon the ears of every intelligent,
right-minded woman present.

At the close of the Mass Meeting, the women, mostly Daughters of Temperance—were invited to meet at the Presbyterian
Church, at 3 o'clock P.M., to listen to an address from Susan B.

The Lily, September, 1852, pp. 73–74

Anthony, of Rochester. The Church was filled,—quite a large
number of men, (possessed no doubt of their full share of
Mother Eve's curiosity,) were in attendance. They were reminded, that they ought highly to appreciate the privilege
which woman permitted them to enjoy,—that of remaining in
the house and being silent lookers on.

It was really hopeful to see those hundreds of women, with
thoughtful faces—faces that spoke of disquiet within,—of souls
dissatisfied, unfed, notwithstanding the soft eloquence, which
had been that A.M., so bounteously lavished upon *"angel
woman."* I talked to them in my plain way,—told them that to
merely relieve the suffering wives and children of drunkards,
and vainly labor to reform the drunkard was no longer to be
called *temperance* work, and showed them that woman's temperance sentiments were not truthfully represented by man at
the Ballot Box. On the whole, I am of the opinion that those
women went away no better satisfied with the part that man has
ever assigned to woman in this great reform, than when they
came.

In the evening, S. F. Cary, T. W. Brown, and Mr. Chapin,
addressed a large audience in the Presbyterian Church. Most
excellent addresses, all of them, if they had only omitted the
closing paragraphs to the *Ladies.* Oh! I am sick and tired of the
senseless, hopeless work that man points out for woman to do.
Would that the women of our land would rise, *en masse,* and
proclaim with one united voice, that they repudiate the popular
doctrine that teaches them to follow in the wake of the sin and
misery, degradation and woe, which man for the gratification of
his cupidity, chooses to inflict upon the race, to minister to their
wretched victims words of comfort, and kindly point out to
them how they may again enjoy the blessings of a good conscience. Such work is vain, worse than vain;—if woman may do
nothing toward removing the CAUSE of drunkenness, then is
she indeed powerless—then may she well sit down, and with
folded hands weep over the ills that be.

During the month of July, I spoke at Caryville, Alabama
Centre, Richville, Ackron, Clarence and Williamsville. Found
Unions of D. of T. in the first four villages; the one at Ackron

numbers 40, and is in a very flourishing condition. The Caryville Union donated the sum of three dollars to the Treasury of
the Women's State Temperance Society, and that of Ackron the
liberal sum of five dollars. . . .

At Buffalo, I called on Mrs. H. B. Williams, an active member
of the "Ladies' Temperance Union." That society numbers
fourteen hundred Women, and has done a great deal during the
last twenty years, by way of ameliorating the condition of
the wretched victims of Intemperance and its attendant vices.
Mrs. W. read me a copy of a letter, which the Buffalo "Ladies'
Temperance Union," sent to the Annual Meeting of the State
Temperance Society, held at Syracuse in June last. It called the
Temperance question home to the ballot box. The D. of T. of
that City, also sent a letter to that memorable meeting, but both
of those letters were, with woman's voice, suppressed by those
Pharasaical Priests, who pretended to be the representatives of
the State Temperance Society.

I hope you have told your readers . . . of the first Women's
Temperance Meeting, on the evening of the 6th [in Elmira].
Miss Clark spoke on the 7th and 9th. I again addressed the citizens of that village. The meetings were all fully attended and
much interest was manifested. While stopping at the Depot, the
A.M. of the 10th, a lady addressed me and said: "It is rude to
thus speak to a stranger, but I want to say to you, that you have
done one thing in Elmira." "And what is that?" "You have convinced me that it is proper for women to talk Temperance in
public as well as in private. A gentleman told me that Miss
Anthony was going to lecture on Temperance; said I, she had
better be home washing dishes. He replied, 'perhaps she does
not know how.' Well, said I, let her come to my house, & I will
give her a few lessons. . . ."

The women of Elmira formed a woman's temperance society,
auxiliary to the State society—obtained about one hundred
members, and forthwith appropriated their funds to the purchase of Temperance tracts and newspapers for gratuitous circulation. . . . By the way, Mrs. Bloomer, the temperance newspapers are trying to work themselves and their leaders into the
belief that the position which we, as a temperance society, take,

"that Confirmed Drunkenness is a just ground of Divorce," is all wrong and calculated to produce much evil in society. Now I am a firm believer in the doctrine which man is continually preaching, that woman's influence over him is all powerful; hence I argue that for man to know, that his pure minded and virtuous wife, would, should he become a confirmed Drunkard, assuredly leave him, and take with her the property and the children, it would prove a powerful incentive to a correct, consistent life. As public sentiment and the laws now are, the vilest wretch of a husband knows that his wife will submit to live on in his companionship, rather than forsake him, and by so doing subject herself to the world's cold charity, and be robbed of her home and her children. Men may prate on, but we women are beginning to know that the life and happiness of a *woman* is of equal value with that of a *man;* and that for a woman to sacrifice her health, happiness and perchance her earthly existence in the hope of reclaiming a drunken, sensualized man, avails but little. In nine cases out of ten, if the man *ever* reforms, it is not until after the wife sinks into an untimely grave; or if not in her *grave*, is physically and mentally unnerved, and unfitted for any earthly enjoyment. . . .

During last week I visited Palmyra, Marion, Walworth, Farmington and Victor. . . . Auxiliary Temperance Societies have been formed in very nearly all the towns I have visited and the women are beginning to feel that they have something to do in the Temperance Cause—that woman may speak and act in public as well as in the home circle—and now is the time to inscribe upon our banner, "NO UNION WITH DISTILLERS, RUM-SELLERS, AND RUMDRINKERS."

Yours for Temperance without Compromise,
S. B. ANTHONY.

Appeal for the Maine Law, Written by Mrs. Stanton and Read by Miss Anthony in the Assembly Chamber:

This is, I believe, the first time in the history of our State, that Woman has come before this Honorable Body to state the legal disabilities under which, as women, we have thus far lived and labored. Though our grievances are many, and our causes of complaint, if set forth, would be as numerous as those made by our forefathers against their King; yet, in behalf of the women of this State, I appeal to you at this time, for the redress of those only, growing out of the legalized traffic in ardent spirits. . . . |W|e come to propose to you to do for us one of two things—either so remodel your State constitution, that woman may vote on this great political and social evil, and thus relieve herself of the terrible injustice that now oppresses her, or, be in fact what, as men, you now claim to be, her faithful representatives, her legal protectors, her chivalrous knights.

If you wisely choose the first proposition, and thus relieve yourself of the burthen of all special legislation for one million and a half of disenfranchised subjects, giving us equal rights, as citizens, with all "white male citizens," then we have nothing to ask. Our course, under such circumstances, would be clear and simple. We should not long stand gaping into the heavens as our temperance saints now do, voting rum into high places, and then praying it to walk out. But if you still hug the delusion that you can legislate for us far better than we could for ourself, and still insist on looking after our best interests, and protecting us in our sacred rights, at least permit us from time to time, to tell you of our wants and needs. . . .

1st. Then, as our "faithful representatives," we ask you to give us the Maine Law which has been so glorious in those States where it has been fairly tried. Now that we see a door of escape open, from the long line of calamities that intemperance has brought upon the head of woman, we would fain enter in and be at peace. We have long and impatiently waited for you to take some effective action on this abominable traffic, and now, feeling that the time has fully come, we pray you to act promptly and wisely. . . . But if you are not prepared to give us the Maine Law, and thus suppress this traffic altogether, then, as you love justice, remove from it all protection. Do not legalize it in any way. Let the trade be free and then let all contracts in which rum is involved be null and void. A man cannot come into court with his gambling debts, neither let him with his rum

debts; for what better is rumselling than gambling, or the rum-
seller than the gamester? Then, do away with all license laws,
and take no cognizance of the monster evil; for what a government licenses, it does not condemn. Now this traffic is either
right or wrong. If right, let it be subject to the same laws as all
other articles of commerce; if wrong, let those who carry it on
be treated as criminals by the government, throwing on them
the responsibility of all the pauperism and crime they directly
or indirectly produce. . . .

But above all, we conjure you not to let this session pass,
without giving us a law making drunkenness a just cause of divorce. Such a law would be far greater in its permanent results
than the Maine Law, even. Suppose we have the Maine Law to-
day—you have then disposed of all intoxicating drinks; but you
have still the animal natures,—the morbid appetite for stimu-
lants and excitement entailed on generation after generation
which will work themselves out in some direction. But back up
the Maine Law by the more important one on Divorce and you
make a permanent reform in so regulating your laws on marriage that the pure and noble of our sex may be sustained by the
power of Government in dissolving all union with gross and vicious natures. It would create a strong public sentiment against
drunkenness for you to declare, that, in your opinion, it is a
crime so enormous, as to furnish just cause for the separation of
man and wife. . . .

2d. As our legal protectors, we ask you to release us from taxation. Under the present system, the drunkard's wife is doubly
taxed. As she has no right to what she has helped to earn, the
rumseller can take all she has for her husband's debts, and leave
her to-day, houseless, homeless, and penniless. . . . Verily, "no
just government can be formed but by the consent of the governed." . . . You have in your hands the means of self-protection. Not so with us. The law gives to man the right to all he can
get, and to what we get too. The new property law protects
what we inherit, but not what we jointly earn; hence you see
how hopeless is the condition of the drunkard's wife. . . . Seeing
that you would consider women voters a terrible scourge on the
body politic,—if you would not have us press our claims to the

exercise of our right to the elective franchise, see that we have justice at your hands. The women of this State are not satisfied with such representation and protection, as we have had thus far,—and unless our interests can be better looked after, unless you can give us more equable laws—we demand the right to legislate for ourselves.

3d. As our chivalrous knight, . . . we only ask, that in your leisure hours, you will duly consider the unjust laws that now disgrace your statute books,—that you will unite with us against our national foe, Intemperance,—that you will lend us your influence to create a healthful public sentiment, that shall deny to drunkards the rights of husbands and fathers,—that shall give the drunkard's wife her property, without taxation, and her children, without fear of molestation. You would fain have women in the retirement of private life;—then protect her in her home. You love to look upon her as a sacred being;—then make her so in her holiest relations. . . . We, the women of the nineteenth century—your mothers, wives and sisters—ask you to throw around us a shield of defence against social tyranny and civil injustice—against a code of laws unworthy [of] Nero himself, so grievous are they in their bearing upon the poor and helpless of our sex. Alas! that such laws should now bear the sanction of our husbands, sires and sons. Alas! for this proud Republic, if its women, the repository of all that is noble and virtuous in national character, can command no higher honors, no purer homage, no juster laws at your hands.

Elizabeth C. Stanton

DOCUMENT 3

STANTON, "ADDRESS TO THE LEGISLATURE OF NEW YORK ON WOMEN'S RIGHTS," FEBRUARY 14, 1854

After their ouster from the women's temperance society, Stanton and Anthony began to work directly for women's legal rights in New York. In February, 1854, they held a convention in Albany to demand a revision of the state's legal code, and Elizabeth Stanton made a rare trip from Seneca Falls to address the legislature herself. This is the speech which caused her father such distress that he threatened to disown her; he eventually retracted his threat and helped her with the legal details. Stanton's speech contains all the basic elements of the legal program of the early women's rights movement. In addition to the vote, the right to sit on juries, and other rights of citizenship, she also demanded changes in the laws regulating those familial institutions—marriage, parenthood, widowhood—which structure the relations between men and women.

. . . GENTLEMEN, in republican America, in the nineteenth century, we, the daughters of the revolutionary heroes of '76, demand at your hands the redress of our grievances—a revision of your State Constitution—a new code of laws. Permit us then,

History of Woman Suffrage, Vol. 1, eds. Stanton, Anthony, and Matilda J. Gage (Rochester: Susan B. Anthony, 1881), pp. 595-605

as briefly as possible, to call your attention to the legal disabilities under which we labor.

1st. Look at the position of woman as woman. It is not enough for us that by your laws we are permitted to live and breathe, to claim the necessaries of life from our legal protectors—to pay the penalty of our crimes; we demand the full recognition of all our rights as citizens of the Empire State. We are persons; native, free-born citizens; property-holders, taxpayers; yet are we denied the exercise of our right to the elective franchise. We support ourselves, and, in part, your schools, colleges, churches, your poor-houses, jails, prisons, the army, the navy, the whole machinery of government, and yet we have no voice in your councils. We have every qualification required by the Constitution, necessary to the legal voter, but the one of sex. We are moral, virtuous, and intelligent, and in all respects quite equal to the proud white man himself, and yet by your laws we are classed with idiots, lunatics, and negroes; and though we do not feel honored by the place assigned us, yet, in fact, our legal position is lower than that of either; for the negro can be raised to the dignity of a voter if he possess himself of $250; the lunatic can vote in his moments of sanity, and the idiot, too, if he be a male one, and not more than nine-tenths a fool; but we, who have guided great movements of charity, established missions, edited journals, published works on history, economy, and statistics; who have governed nations, led armies, filled the professor's chair, taught philosophy and mathematics to the savants of our age, discovered planets, piloted ships across the sea, are denied the most sacred rights of citizens, because, forsooth, we came not into this republic crowned with the dignity of manhood! . . . Can it be that here, where we acknowledge no royal blood, no apostolic descent, that you, who have declared that all men were created equal—that governments derive their just powers from the consent of the governed, would willingly build up an aristocracy that places the ignorant and vulgar above the educated and refined—the alien and the ditch-digger above the authors and poets of the day—an aristocracy that would raise the sons above the mothers that bore them? Would that the men who can sanction a Constitution so opposed to the genius of this government, who can enact and execute laws so degrading to womankind, had sprung, Minerva-like, from the brains of their fathers, that the matrons of this republic need not blush to own their sons!

. . . we demand in criminal cases that most sacred of all rights, trial by a jury of our own peers. The establishment of trial by jury is of so early a date that its beginning is lost in antiquity; but the right of trial by a jury of one's own peers is a great progressive step of advanced civilization. No rank of men have ever been satisfied with being tried by jurors higher or lower in the civil or political scale than themselves; for jealousy on the one hand, and contempt on the other, has ever effectually blinded the eyes of justice. Hence, all along the pages of history, we find the king, the noble, the peasant, the cardinal, the priest, the layman, each in turn protesting against the authority of the tribunal before which they were summoned to appear. . . . And shall woman here consent to be tried by her liege lord, who has dubbed himself law-maker, judge, juror, and sheriff too?— whose power, though sanctioned by Church and State, has no foundation in justice and equity, and is a bold assumption of our inalienable rights. . . . Having seen that man fails to do justice to woman in her best estate, to the virtuous, the noble, the true of our sex, should we trust to his tender mercies the weak, the ignorant, the morally insane? It is not to be denied that the interests of man and woman in the present undeveloped state of the race, and under the existing social arrangements, are and must be antagonistic. The nobleman can not make just laws for the peasant; the slaveholder for the slave; neither can man make and execute just laws for woman, because in each case, the one in power fails to apply the immutable principles of right to any grade but his own.

Shall an erring woman be dragged before a bar of grim-visaged judges, lawyers, and jurors, there to be grossly questioned in public on subjects which women scarce breathe in secret to one another? Shall the most sacred relations of life be called up and rudely scanned by men who, by their own admission, are so coarse that women could not meet them even at the polls without contamination? and yet shall she find there no woman's face or voice to pity and defend? . . . His peers made the law, and shall law-makers lay nets for those of their own rank? Shall laws which come from the logical brain of man take cognizance of violence done to the moral and affectional nature which predominates, as is said, in woman? . . .

2d. Look at the position of woman as wife. Your laws relating to marriage—founded as they are on the old common law of England, a compound of barbarous usages, but partially modified by progressive civilization—are in open violation of our enlightened ideas of justice, and of the holiest feelings of our nature. If you take the highest view of marriage, as a Divine relation, which love alone can constitute and sanctify, then of course human legislation can only recognize it. Men can neither bind nor loose its ties, for that prerogative belongs to God alone, who makes man and woman, and the laws of attraction by which they are united. But if you regard marriage as a civil contract, then let it be subject to the same laws which control all other contracts. Do not make it a kind of half-human, half-divine institution, which you may build up, but can not regulate. Do not, by your special legislation for this one kind of contract, involve yourselves in the grossest absurdities and contradictions.

So long as by your laws no man can make a contract for a horse or piece of land until he is twenty-one years of age, and by which contract he is not bound if any deception has been practiced, or if the party contracting has not fulfilled his part of the agreement—so long as the parties in all mere civil contracts retain their identity and all the power and independence they had before contracting, with the full right to dissolve all partnerships and contracts for any reason, at the will and option of the parties themselves, upon what principle of civil jurisprudence do you permit the boy of fourteen and the girl of twelve, in violation of every natural law, to make a contract more momentous in importance than any other, and then hold them to it come what may, the whole of their natural lives, in spite of disappointment, deception, and misery? Then, too, the signing of this contract is instant civil death to one of the parties. The woman who but yesterday was sued on bended knee, who stood so high in the scale of being as to make an agreement on equal terms with a proud Saxon man, to-day has no civil existence, no social freedom. The wife who inherits no property holds about the same legal position that does the slave of the Southern plantation. She can own nothing, sell nothing. She has no right even to the wages she earns; her person, her time, her services are the property of another. . . .

There is nothing that an unruly wife might do against which the husband has not sufficient protection in the law. But not so with the wife. If she have a worthless husband, a confirmed drunkard, a villain, or a vagrant, he has still all the rights of a man, a husband, and a father. Though the whole support of the family be thrown upon the wife, if the wages she earns be paid to her by her employer, the husband can receive them again. . . .

But the wife who is so fortunate as to have inherited property, has, by the new law in this State, been redeemed from her lost condition. She is no longer a legal nonentity. This property law, if fairly construed, will overturn the whole code relating to woman and property. The right to property implies the right to buy and sell, to will and bequeath, and herein is the dawning of a civil existence for woman, for now the "femme covert" must have the right to make contracts. . . . The right to property will, of necessity, compel us in due time to the exercise of our right to the elective franchise, and then naturally follows the right to hold office.

3d. Look at the position of woman as widow. Whenever we attempt to point out the wrongs of the wife, those who would have us believe that the laws can not be improved, point us to the privileges, powers, and claims of the widow. Let us look into these a little. . . . Behold the magnanimity of the law in allowing the widow to retain a life interest in one-third the landed estate, and one-half the personal property of her husband, and taking the lion's share to itself! Had she died first, the house and land would all have been the husband's still. No one would have dared to intrude upon the privacy of his home, or to molest him in his sacred retreat of sorrow. How, I ask you, can that be called justice, which makes such a distinction as this between man and woman? . . .

4th. Look at the position of woman as mother. There is no human love so strong and steadfast as that of the mother for her child; yet behold how ruthless are your laws touching this most sacred relation. Nature has clearly made the mother the guardian of the child; but man, in his inordinate love of power, does continually set nature and nature's laws at open defiance. The father may apprentice his child, bind him out to a trade, without the mother's consent—yea, in direct opposition to her most earnest entreaties, prayers and tears.

He may apprentice his son to a gamester or rum-seller, and thus cancel his debts of *honor*. By the abuse of this absolute power, he may bind his daughter to the owner of a brothel, and, by the degradation of his child, supply his daily wants: and such things, gentlemen, have been done in our very midst. Moreover, the father, about to die, may bind out all his children wherever and to whomsoever he may see fit, and thus, in fact, will away the guardianship of all his children from the mother. The Revised Statutes of New York provide that "every father, whether of full age or a minor, of a child to be born, or of any living child under the age of twenty-one years, and unmarried, may by his deed or last will, duly executed, dispose of the custody and tuition of such child during its minority, or for any less time, to any person or persons, in possession or remainder." 2 R. S., page 150, sec. 1. Thus, by your laws, the child is the absolute property of the father, wholly at his disposal in life or at death. . . .

Again, as the condition of the child always follows that of the mother, and as by the sanction of your laws the father may beat the mother, so may he the child. What mother can not bear me witness to untold sufferings which cruel, vindictive fathers have visited upon their helpless children? Who ever saw a human being that would not abuse unlimited power? Base and ignoble must that man be who, let the provocation be what it may, would strike a woman: but he who would lacerate a trembling child is unworthy the name of man. A mother's love can be no protection to a child; she can not appeal to you to save it from a father's cruelty, for the laws take no cognizance of the mother's most grievous wrongs. Neither at home nor abroad can a mother protect her son. Look at the temptations that surround the paths of our youth at every step; look at the gambling and drinking saloons, the club rooms, the dens of infamy and abomination that infest all our villages and cities—slowly but surely sapping the very foundations of all virtue and strength.

By your laws, all these abominable resorts are permitted. It is folly to talk of a mother moulding the character of her son, when all mankind, backed up by law and public sentiment, conspire to destroy her influence. But when woman's moral power shall speak through the ballot-box, then shall her influence be seen and felt. . . .

Many times and oft it has been asked us, with unaffected seriousness, "What do you women want? What are you aiming at?" Many have manifested a laudable curiosity to know what the wives and daughters could complain of in republican America, where their sires and sons have so bravely fought for freedom and gloriously secured their independence, trampling all tyranny, bigotry, and caste in the dust, and declaring to a waiting world the divine truth that all men are created equal. What can woman want under such a government? Admit a radical difference in sex, and you demand different spheres—water for fish, and air for birds.

It is impossible to make the Southern planter believe that his slave feels and reasons just as he does—that injustice and subjection are as galling as to him—that the degradation of living by the will of another, the mere dependent on his caprice, at the mercy of his passions, is as keenly felt by him as his master. If you can force on his unwilling vision a vivid picture of the negro's wrongs, and for a moment touch his soul, his logic brings him instant consolation. He says, the slave does not feel this as I would. Here, gentlemen, is our difficulty: When we plead our cause before the law-makers and savants of the republic, they can not take in the idea that men and women are alike; and so long as the mass rest in this delusion, the public mind will not be so much startled by the revelations made of the injustice and degradation of woman's position as by the fact that she should at length wake up to a sense of it. . . .

But if, gentlemen, you take the ground that the sexes are

alike, and, therefore, you are our faithful representatives—then why all these special laws for woman? Would not one code answer for all of like needs and wants? Christ's golden rule is better than all the special legislation that the ingenuity of man can devise: "Do unto others as you would have others do unto you." This, men and brethren, is all we ask at your hands. We ask no better laws than those you have made for yourselves. We need no other protection than that which your present laws secure to you.

In conclusion, then, let us say, in behalf of the women of this State, we ask for all that you have asked for yourselves in the progress of your development, since the *Mayflower* cast anchor beside Plymouth rock; and simply on the ground that the rights of every human being are the same and identical. You may say that the mass of the women of this State do not make the demand; it comes from a few sour, disappointed old maids and childless women.

You are mistaken; the mass speak through us. A very large majority of the women of this State support themselves and their children, and many their husbands too. Go into any village you please, of three or four thousand inhabitants, and you will find as many as fifty men or more, whose only business is to discuss religion and politics, as they watch the trains come and go at the depot, or the passage of a canal boat through a lock; to laugh at the vagaries of some drunken brother, or the capers of a monkey dancing to the music of his master's organ. All these are supported by their mothers, wives, or sisters.

Now, do you candidly think these wives do not wish to control the wages they earn—to own the land they buy—the houses they build? to have at their disposal their own children, without being subject to the constant interference and tyranny of an idle, worthless profligate? Do you suppose that any woman is such a pattern of devotion and submission that she willingly stitches all day for the small sum of fifty cents, that she may enjoy the unspeakable privilege, in obedience to your laws, of paying for her husband's tobacco and rum? Think you the wife of the confirmed, beastly drunkard would consent to share with him her home and bed, if law and public sentiment would release her from such gross companionship? Verily, no! ... The drunkards' wives speak through us, and they number 50,000. Think you that the woman who has worked hard all her days in helping her husband to accumulate a large property, consents to the law that places this wholly at his disposal? Would not the mother whose only child is bound out for a term of years against her expressed wish, deprive the father of this absolute power if she could?

For all these, then, we speak. If to this long list you add the laboring women who are loudly demanding remuneration for their unending toil; those women who teach in our seminaries, academies, and public schools for a miserable pittance; the widows who are taxed without mercy; the unfortunate ones in our work-houses, poor-houses, and prisons; who are they that we do not now represent? But a small class of the fashionable butterflies, who, through the short summer days, seek the sunshine and the flowers; but the cool breezes of autumn and the hoary frosts of winter will soon chase all these away; then they too, will need and seek protection, and through other lips demand in their turn justice and equity at your hands.

STANTON AND ANTHONY, LETTERS, 1852–1859

These fifteen letters run from 1852, less than a year after Stanton and Anthony first met, to 1859, when Anthony was a paid organizer for the American Anti-Slavery Society and Stanton had just given birth to her seventh and last child. The letters show Anthony struggling to learn self-confidence and the "a, b, c, of the reformer";* they reveal the degree to which Stanton was caught between her political ambitions and her domestic realities; and they tell us a good deal about the characters of both women—Anthony's intensity and anxiety, Stanton's wit and brilliance. Overall, the letters give the impression that, from the very beginning of their collaboration, both women took a long-range perspective on the tasks of challenging traditional ways of seeing women's position and of building a women's rights movement. When their effort to turn the women's temperance movement in a feminist direction failed, Stanton consoled Anthony by reminding her that they had "other and bigger fish to fry."

These first three letters refer to: the organization of the New York State Women's Temperance Society in

These letters have been gathered from several sources: 1) the Elizabeth Cady Stanton manuscript collections at the Library of Congress and Vassar College; 2) Ida H. Harper, *The Life and Work of Susan B. Anthony* (Indianapolis: Bowen-Merrill Co., 1899); and 3) *Elizabeth Cady Stanton as Revealed in her Letters, Diary and Reminiscences*, eds. Theodore Stanton and Harriot Stanton Blatch (New York: Harper & Brothers, 1922). Stanton's children edited and on occasion censored their mother's correspondence. I have, where possible, replaced their versions with the unedited originals; these are noted.

* *Stanton Letters*, p. 39.

Rochester in April, 1852; Stanton's address, as the society's president, to the New York legislature in January, 1853, in which she called for the right of women
to divorce drunkards; and the defeat six months later of
the women's rights platform that she and Anthony had
advocated for the organization (see document 2).

Seneca Falls, April 2, 1852

My dear friend (Susan B. Anthony),

I think you are doing up the temperance business just right.
But do not let the conservative element control. For instance,
you must take Mrs. Bloomer's suggestions with great caution,
for she has not the spirit of the true reformer. At the first
woman's rights convention, but four years ago, she stood aloof
and laughed at us. It was only with great effort and patience
that she has been brought up to her present position. In her
paper, she will not speak against the fugitive slave law, nor in
her work to put down intemperance will she criticize the equiv-
ocal position of the Church. . . .

I will gladly do all in my power to help you. Come and stay
with me and I will write the best lecture I can for you. I have no
doubt a little practice will make you an admirable speaker.
Dress loosely, take a great deal of exercise, be particular about
your diet and sleep enough. The body has great influence upon
the mind. In your meetings, if attacked, be cool and good-
natured, for if you are simple and truth-loving, no sophistry can
confound you. As for my own address, if I am to be president it
ought perhaps to be sent out with the stamp of the convention,
but as anything from my pen is necessarily radical no one may
wish to share with me the odium of what I may choose to say. If
so, I am ready to stand alone. I never write to please any one. If
I do please I am happy, but to proclaim my highest convictions
of truth is always my sole object. . . .

I have been re-reading the report of the London convention of
1840. How thoroughly humiliating it was to us! . . . Men and

angels give me patience! I am at the boiling point! If I do not find some day the use of my tongue on this question, I shall die of an intellectual repression, a woman's rights convulsion! Oh, Susan! Susan! Susan! You must manage to spend a week with me before the Rochester convention, for I am afraid that I cannot attend it; I have so much with all these boys on my hands. But I will write a letter. How much I do long to be free from housekeeping and children, so as to have some time to read, and think, and write. But it may be well for me to understand all the trials of woman's lot, that I may more eloquently proclaim them when the time comes. Good night.

Stanton Letters, pp. 38–42, supplemented from Harper, *Life of Anthony*, Vol. 1, pp. 66–67

Seneca Falls, March 1st [1853]

Dear friend (Susan B. Anthony),

I do not know that the world is quite willing or ready to discuss the question of marriage. I feel in my innermost [soul] that the thoughts I sent your convention are true. It is in vain to look for the elevation of woman, so long as she is degraded in marriage. I say it is a sin, an outrage on our holiest feelings to pretend that anything but deep, fervent love and sympathy constitutes marriage. The right idea of marriage is at the foundation of all reforms. How strange it is, man will apply all the improvements in the arts and sciences to everything about him animate and inanimate, but himself. A child conceived in the midst of hate, sin, and discord, nurtured in abuse and injustice cannot do much to bless the world or himself. If we properly understood the science of life—it would be far easier to give to the world, harmonious, beautiful, noble, virtuous children, than it is to bring grown-up discord into harmony with the great divine soul of all. I ask for no laws on marriage. I say . . . remove law and a false public sentiment and woman will no more live as wife with a cruel, beastly drunkard, than a servant in this free country will stay with a pettish, unjust mistress. If law makers insist upon exercising their prerogative in some way on this question, let them forbid any woman to marry until she is twenty one. Let them fine a woman fifty dollars for every child she conceive by a Drunkard. Women have no right to saddle the state with idiots to be supported by the public. Only look at the statistics of the idiot asylums, nearly all the offspring of Drunkards. Woman must be made to feel that the transmitting of immortal life is a most solemn responsible act and never should be allowed, except when the parents are in the highest condition of mind and body. Man in his lust has regulated this whole question of sexual intercourse long enough. Let the mother of mankind whose prerogative it is to set bounds to his indulgence rouse up and give this whole question a thorough fearless examination. . . . My letter . . . will call attention to that subject, and if by martyrdom I can advance my race one step I am ready for it. I feel this whole question of woman's rights turns on the point of the marriage relation, and sooner or later it will be the question for discussion. I would not hurry it on, neither would I avoid it. . . .

Library of Congress, Stanton Papers [edited version in *Stanton Letters,* pp. 48–49]

Seneca Falls, June 20, 1853

Dear Susan,

Say not one word to me about another convention. I forbid you to ask me to send one thought or one line to any convention, any paper, or any individual; for I swear by all the saints that whilst I am nursing this baby I will not be tormented with suffering humanity. I am determined to make no effort to do anything beyond my imperative home duties until I can bring about the following conditions: 1st, Relieve myself of housekeeping altogether; 2nd, Secure some capable teacher for my children; 3rd, See my present baby on her feet. My ceaseless cares begin to wear upon my spirit. I feel it in my innermost soul and am resolved to seek some relief. Therefore, I say adieu to the public for a time, for I must give all my moments and my thoughts to my children. But above all this I am so full of dreams of the true associative life that all the reforms of the day beside that seem to me superficial and fragmentary. You ask me if I am not plunged in grief at my defeat at the recent convention for the presidency of our society. Not at all. I am only too happy in the relief I feel from this additional care. I accomplished at Rochester all I desired by having the divorce question brought up and so eloquently supported by dear little Lucy Stone. How proud I felt of her that night! We have no woman who compares with her. Now, Susan, I do beg of you to let the past be past, and to waste no powder on the Woman's State Temperance Society. We have other and bigger fish to fry.

Stanton Letters, pp. 50–52

The following two letters concern Stanton's important women's rights speech to the New York legislature, delivered in February, 1854 (see document 3).

Seneca Falls, December 1, 1853

Dear Susan,

Can you get any acute lawyer—perhaps Judge Hay is the man—sufficiently interested in our movement to look up just eight laws concerning us—the very worst in all the code? I can generalize and philosophize easily enough of myself; but the details of the particular laws I need, I have not time to look up. You see, while I am about the house, surrounded by my children, washing dishes, baking, sewing, etc., I can think up many points, but I cannot search books, for my hands as well as my brains would be necessary for that work. If I can, I shall go to Rochester as soon as I have finished my Address and submit it ... to [Reverend William H.] Channing's criticism. But prepare yourself to be disappointed in its merits, for I seldom have one hour undisturbed in which to sit down and write. Men who can, when they wish to write a document, shut themselves up for days with their thoughts and their books, know little of what difficulties a woman must surmount to get off a tolerable production.

Stanton Letters, pp. 54–55

Seneca Falls, January 20, 1854

Dear Susan,

My Address is not nearly finished; but if I sit up nights, it shall be done in time. I fear, however, it may not suit the committee, for it does not suit me. But make no arrangements with reference to my coming to Rochester, for I cannot say when I can come, if even I may come at all. Yesterday one of the boys shot an arrow into my baby's eye. The eye is safe, but oh! my fright when I saw the blood come and the organ swell, and witnessed her suffering! What an escape! Imagine if I had been in Rochester when this happened! Then, to-day, my nurse has gone home with a felon on her finger. So you see how I am bound here. In haste.

Stanton Letters, pp. 55–56

> The following three letters reveal, on the one hand, the pressures, responsibilities, and outright prejudice that held Stanton to domestic life so long; and, on the other hand, her love of politics and desire to become a public speaker and reformer. In 1855, Henry Stanton was helping to form the Republican party, and Elizabeth was filled with enthusiasm for this new political movement.

Peterboro, September 10, 1855

Dear Susan,

I wish that I were as free as you and I would stump the state in a twinkling. But I am not, and what is more, I passed through a terrible scourging when last at my father's. I cannot tell you how deep the iron entered my soul. I never felt more keenly the degradation of my sex. To think that all in me of which my father would have felt a proper pride had I been a man, is deeply mortifying to him because I am a woman. That thought has stung me to a fierce decision—to speak as soon as I can do myself credit. But the pressure on me just now is too great. Henry sides with my friends, who oppose me in all that is dearest to my heart. They are not willing that I should write even on the woman question. But I will both write and speak. I wish you to consider this letter strictly confidential. Sometimes, Susan, I struggle in deep waters. . . . I have sent six articles to the *Tribune*, and three have already appeared. I have promised to write for the *Una*. I read and write a good deal, as you see. But there are grievous interruptions. However, a good time is coming and my future is always bright and beautiful. Good night. . . .

Stanton Letters, pp. 59–60

Seneca Falls, November 4, 1855

Dear Susan,

I am rejoiced to say that Henry is heart and soul in the Republican movement and is faithfully stumping the state once more. I have attended all the Republican meetings and have had Senator John P. Hale staying with us. The day he was expected I met a Republican editor in the street. "Well, I suppose we are to hear Hale to-night," I remarked. "*We*," he replied, "we do not wish to spare any room for ladies; we mean to cram the hall with voters." "I have done my best to be a voter," was my response, "and it is no fault of mine if unavailable people occupy your seats. So I for one am determined to go and hear Hale." I went to the meeting with Mr. Hale and Henry, and we found a dozen women already there. . . .

Stanton Letters, pp. 62–63

Seneca Falls, Thursday Evening, January 24, 1856

Dear Friend (Susan B. Anthony),

. . . Well, another female child is born into the world! Last Sunday afternoon, Harriot Eaton Stanton—oh the little heretic thus to desecrate that holy day—opened her soft blue eyes on this mundane sphere. Maggie's joy over her little sister is unbounded. I am very . . . happy that the terrible ordeal is passed and that the result is another daughter. But I feel disappointed and sad at the same time at this grievous interruption of my plans. I might have been born an orator before spring, you acting as midwife. However, I feel that it will not be in vain that I am held back. My latent fires shall sometime burst forth. . . .

Library of Congress, Stanton Papers

In her interesting letter of May, 1856, Anthony described the various reactions of conservative women, in particular the wife of the noted evangelical minister Charles G. Finney, and Catherine Beecher herself, to women's rights. The speech Anthony was planning to give to the New York State Teacher's Convention caused her great anxiety and was the subject of the subsequent three letters.

Rochester, May 26, 1856

Dear Mrs. Stanton,

Taking it for granted that you are at home more, I'll say a word to you by way of "exhortation and prayer." I ought to be more pious than formerly, since I traveled all the way from Seneca Falls to Schenectady in company with President [of Oberlin] Finney and Lady and heard [William Lloyd] Garrison, [Theodore] Parker and all of us Woman's Rights actors duly trounced as *"Infidels."* I told him our cause *was Infidel* to the *popular Theology* and *popular interpretation* of the Bible. Mrs. Finney took me to another seat and with much earnestness enquired all about, what we were doing and the growth of our movement. Said she, you have the sympathy of a large proportion of the educated women with you. In my circle I hear the movement much talked of and earnest hopes for its spread expressed. But these women dare not speak out their sympathy. . . .

I attended the Anniversary of the "American Woman's Education Association" headed by Catherine E. Beecher. . . . Some parts of the Secretary's report were very fine [but] I said [to her] I would rather see the weight of your influence exerted to open the doors of the existing colleges to woman. Far greater good would be done for woman by such work, than by the establishment of separate Colleges. Said she, that is my mind exactly. Isn't it strange that such women as these, Miss Beecher, Mrs. [Caroline] Kirckland, Mrs. [Ann] Stevens, S[arah] J Hale, etc., etc., are so stupid. Yet so *false* as to work for any thing secondary, any thing other than their *highest* conviction. . . .

I am now just done with house fixing and ready to commence operations on that Report [to the New York State Teacher's Convention]. Don't you think it would be a good plan to first state *what* we mean by educating the sexes together, then go in to show how the few institutions that profess to give *equal* education fail in the Physical, Moral and Intellectual departments, and lastly that it is folly to talk of giving to the sexes, *equal advantages*, while you *withhold* from them equal motive to improve those advantages. Do you please mark out a plan and give me as soon as you can. Oh, that I had the requisite power to do credit to womanhood in this emergency. Why is nature so *sparing* of her gifts? When will you come to Rochester to spend those days, I shall be most happy to see whenever it shall be, only let me know a few days before that I may be as much at leisure as may be. Amelia [a domestic servant] and the two babies of course and as many more as convenient. With love.

Vassar College Library, Stanton Papers

Home-getting, along towards 12 o'clock
Thursday night, June 5, 1856
. . . And, Mrs. Stanton, not a *word written* on that Address for Teacher's Convention. *This* week was to be *leisure* to me and lo, our *girl*, a *wife*, had a *miscarriage*, . . . and the Mercy only knows when I can get a moment; and what is *worse*, as the *Lord knows full well*, is, if I *get all the time* the *world has*, I *can't get up* a *decent document*. So, for the love of me and for the saving of the *reputation* of *womanhood*, I beg you, with one baby on your knee and another at your feet, and four boys whistling, buzzing, hallooing *Ma, Ma*, set yourself about the work. It is of

but small moment *who writes* the Address, but of *vast moment* that it be *well done.* I promise you to work hard, oh, how hard, and *pay you whatever you say* for your *time* and *brains,* but . . . *don't* say *No* nor *don't delay* it a moment; for I must have it all done and almost commit it to memory. . . . Now will *you load my gun,* leaving me only to pull the trigger and let fly the powder and ball?

Don't delay one mail to tell me what you *will do,* for I *must not* and *will not* allow these *schoolmasters* to say—See, these *women can't* or *won't* do anything when we do give them a chance. No, they sha'n't say that, even if I have to get a *man* to write it! But no man can write from *my standpoint,* nor no woman but *you,* for *all, all* would base their *strongest* argument on the *un*likeness of the *sexes.* Nette [Brown] wrote me that she should, were she to make the Address. And more than any other place does the *difference* of sex, if there is any, need to be *forgotten* in the school room. . . . Now do, I pray you, give heed to my prayer. Those of you who have the *talent* to do honor to poor—oh! how poor—womanhood, have all given yourself over to baby-making; and left poor brainless me to do battle alone. It is a shame. Such a body as I might be spared to rock cradles. But it is a crime for you and Lucy Stone and Antoinette Brown to be doing it. I have just engaged to attend a progressive meeting in Erie County, the first of September, just because there is no other woman to be had, but not because I feel in the least competent. Oh, dear, dear! If the spirits would only just make me a trance medium and put the right thing into my mouth. You can't think how earnestly I have prayed to be made a speaking medium for a whole week. If they would only come to me thus, I'd give them a hearty welcome. How I do wish I could step in to see you and make you feel all my infirmities—*mental, I mean.* . . . Do get all on fire and be as *cross* as you please. You remember, Mr. Stanton told how cross you always get over a speech. Good Bye

Library of Congress, Stanton Papers (an edited version is in *Stanton Letters,* pp. 64–66)

Seneca Falls, June 10, 1856

Dear Susan,

Your servant is not dead but liveth. Imagine me, day in and day out, watching, bathing, dressing, nursing, and promenading the precious contents of a little crib in the corner of the room. I pace up and down these two chambers of mine like a caged lioness, longing to bring to a close nursing and housekeeping cares. I have other work on hand too. . . . Is your speech to be exclusively on the point of educating the sexes together, or as to the best manner of educating women? I will do what I can to help you with your lecture. Let Lucy and Antoinette rest awhile in peace and quietness and think great thoughts for the future. It is not well to be in the excitement of public life all the time; do not keep stirring them up or mourning over their repose. You need rest too, Susan. Let the world alone awhile. We cannot bring about a moral revolution in a day or year. Now that I have two daughters, I feel fresh strength to work. It is not in vain that in myself I have experienced all the wearisome cares to which woman in her best estate is subject. Good night.

Stanton Letters, pp. 66–67

Seneca Falls, August 20, 1857

Dear Susan,

I did indeed see by the papers that you had once more stirred that part of intellectual stagnation, the educational convention. The *Times* was really quite complimentary. Henry brought me every item he could see about you. "Well," he would say, "another notice about Susan. You stir up Susan, and she stirs the world." What a set of fools those schoolmarms must be! Well, if in order to please men they wish to live on air, let them. I was glad you went to torment them. I will do anything to help you on. If I do nothing else this fall I am bound to aid you to get up an antislavery address. You must come here for a week or two and we will accomplish wonders. You and I have a prospect of a good long life. We shall not be in our prime before fifty, and after that we shall be good for twenty years at least. . . .

Stanton Letters, pp. 70–71

In her letter of September 29, 1857, Anthony described for Stanton a debate she had with the spiritualist-reformer Andrew Jackson Davis over "the likeness and unlikeness of the sexes." Anthony argued that the differences between men and women were socially created, the products of dress and the deliberate intent to attract the opposite sex, an assertion which her opponents charged was "gross" and "animal."

Collins Sept. 29, 1857

Dear Mrs. Stanton,

How I do long to be with you this very minute, to have one look into your very soul, and one sound of your soul stirring voice—

How are you, and how comes on the letter for the *National [Women's Rights] Convention?* It seems impossible to array our forces for effective action this Autumn. I, therefore, a few days since, wrote Lucy Stone, begging her to *Postpone* the Convention into *May next....* That Convention has been a heavy burden to me, the last two months. Nothing looked promising. Nobody seemed to feel any personal responsibility and [I], *alone,* feeling utterly incompetent to go forward, unless sure of reliable and effective speakers to sustain the Con., could but grope in the dark. But I now hope Lucy will say *amen* to any proposition.... I can't Remember whether I have answered your last letter or not. Be that as it may, I will remember how good a word it brought to me, and how it cheered me onward. Mrs. Stanton, I have *very weak* moments, and long to lay my weary head somewhere and nestle my full soul close to that of another in full sympathy. I sometimes fear that *I too* shall faint by the wayside, and drop out [of] the ranks of the faithful few.

There is so much, mid all that is so hopeful, to discourage and dishearten, and I feel *alone.* Still I know I am *not alone,* but that all the true and the good souls, both in and out of the body, keep me company, and that the Good Father more than all is ever a host in every good effort.

But you will see that this is one of my *tired* moments, so no more, but to the Cause thereof.

I left home the [?th] of Sept., and commenced Anti-Slavery work at Binghamton.... Had three weeks of cold hard labor among people not yet initiated into the first principles of true freedom. I returned home the 19th Sept. Found *company* there, and company *came* and *came*. Our folks were in the midst of a heavy *Peach* harvest, my mother was very feeble, the *Hibernian* unskilled, my *wardrobe* in need of repair, my brain and body in need of rest. For a week I was in such a home *whirl*. On Friday the 25th I left for the Collins Progressive Friends Meeting. Arrived Saturday A.M....

Mrs. D. from the Committee read a paper on Womans Rights going back to Woman's position in marriage as the starting point. *Mr.* Davis spoke first. He set forth his idea of the nature of the sexes and their relation to each [other]. Spoke truthfully and nobly of re-production, of the *abuses* in marriage etc, etc. But to his idea of the sexes, he said woman's inherent nature *is Love and Man's Wisdom.* That Love reaches out to Wisdom, Man, and Wisdom reaches out to Love, Woman, and the two meet and make a beautiful blending of the two principles....

My soul was on fire. This is but a *revamp* of the world's idea from the beginning, the very same doctrine that consigned woman from the beginning to the sphere of the affections, that subjugated her to man's wisdom. ... The question was *called for*. I *must out*, and said Mr. President, I must say a word, and I did say a word. I said *Women*. If you accept the theory given you by Davis, you may give up all talk of a change for woman: she is now where God and nature intended she should be. If it be a fact that the principle of Wisdom is indigenous in Man, and Love an exotic, then must wisdom *prevail*, and so with woman, must *Love prevail.*

Therefore woman must look to *man* for *Wisdom*, must ever feel it impossible for her to attain Wisdom equal to him. Such a doctrine makes my heart *sink* within me, said I. And did I accept it, I would return to my own Father's house, and never again raise my voice for woman's right to the control of her own person, the ownership of her own earnings, the guardianship of her own children. For if this be true, she ought not to possess those rights. She ought to make final appeal to the wisdom of her husband, father and brother. My word stirred the waters, and brought Davis to his feet again, but he failed to extricate himself from the conclusions to which his premises philosophically lead. Well Sunday, there were more than a *thousand* people congregated, hundreds more *out* than in doors. . . .

All day yesterday, the likeness and unlikeness of the sexes has been the topic of discussion. Phillip D. Moore of Newark N.J. took sides with me. Says my note at Waterloo, last spring, was the *first* he ever heard sounded on that side, and there he came forthwith to me and expressed his sympathy. Well on the Love and Wisdom side, we had [Aaron M.] Powell, George Taylor, Dr. Mary Taylor of Buffalo, and a Mr. Lloyd of Pa. The discussion has been loud and long, and how I wished that *you* could be here. I tell you, Mrs. Stanton, after all, it is very *precious* to the soul of man, that he shall *reign supreme in intellect,* and it will take Centuries if not ages to dispossess him of the fancy that he is born to do so.

Mr. Moore and the Listeners, two women and one man, sound, sensible people, say I sustained my position by *fact* and argument. The Female Doctor urged as a Physiological fact that *girl babies* have from their births less physical vigor, than the boy baby. Then she claimed that there is ever passing from the Woman out to Man a "female arrow," influence she meant, that thrills his soul, all unlike that of man to man etc. Well then here is a fact, a girl dressed in boy's clothes stands at a type case side by side with a young man for three years, and this "female arrow" is never perceived, at least not sufficiently to cause the recipient to suspect the *sex* at his side [is] other than his own.

Take that same being, array her in woman's dress, and to-morrow morning place her at the same case. While the tones of her voice, the move of her hand, the glance of her eye are all the same as yesterday, her presence causes the sensuous thrill to rush to his very fingers and toes ends. Now tell me the cause. Is the "arrow" in the being, does it go out to that young man from the brain, the soul, the femininity of that young woman, or is it in the flowing robes and waving tresses, in the *knowledge* of the *difference* of *sex. The latter I say.* At least to a very great extent. But, say our opponents, such an admission is so gross, so animal. Well I can't help that. *If it is fact,* there it is. To me it is not coarse or gross, it is simply the answering of the highest and holiest function of the physical organism, that is that of *reproduction.* To be a *Mother,* to be a *Father* is the last and highest wish of any human being, to *re-produce himself* or *herself.* The accomplish[ment] of this purpose is only through the meeting of the sexes. And when we come into the presence of one of the opposite sex, who embodies what to us seems the true and the noble and the beautiful, our souls are stirred, and whether we realize it or not, it is a thrill of joy that such qualities are reproducible *and* that we may be the *agents,* the *artists* in such re-production. It is the *knowledge* that the two together may be the instruments, that shall execute a work so *God like.*

But I have wearied you already, I fear, and surely have exhausted my moment of time. I must add that many women came to me and thanked me for the word I uttered in opposition to Davis. Said they, had you not spoken we should have gone home burdened in soul.

Oh Mrs. Stanton how my soul longs to see you in the great Battle field. When will the time come? You say in two or three years. God and the Angels keep you safe from all hindrances and keep you from all mountain barriers. If you come not to the rescue, who shall? . . .

Don't fail to write me. It always does me so much good to get a letter from you. A Kiss for Maggie and Hattie and Sadie [another servant] and a kindly word for the boys. . . .

Library of Congress, Stanton Papers

Stanton usually described most of her childbirth experiences as easy and undebilitating, but the birth of her seventh child left her weak and depressed. As she struggled to regain her strength, the conflict over slavery was reaching a climax. The raid on Harpers Ferry, Virginia, and the subsequent martyrdom of John Brown affected her as it affected all abolitionists; her cousin Gerrit Smith had supported Brown and nearly went mad in the following weeks.

April 2, (1859)

Dear Susan,

I have a great boy now three weeks old. He weighed at his birth without a particle of clothing 12¼ lb. My labour was long and very very severe. I never suffered so much before. I was sick all the time before he was born, and I have been very weak ever since. He seemed to take up every particle of my vitality soul and body. He is a great specimen so every body says. He looks like Gattie and Maggie. Think However! I am through the siege once more! . . .

Vassar College Library, Stanton Papers

April 10th (1859)

Dear Susan,

You need expect nothing from me for some time. I have no vitality of body or soul. All I had or was has gone with the development of that boy. It is now four weeks since my confinement and I can scarcely walk across the room. You have no idea how weak I am and I have to keep my mind in the most quiet state in order to sleep. I have suffered so much from wakefullness. I am always glad to hear from you and hope to see you on your way to N.Y. . . .

Vassar College Library, Stanton Papers

Seneca Falls, December 23, 1859

Dear Susan,

Where are you? Since a week ago last Monday, I have looked for you every day. I had the washing put off, we cooked a turkey, I made a pie in the morning, sent my first-born to the depot and put clean aprons on the children, but lo! you did not come. Nor did you soften the rough angles of our disappointment by one solitary line of excuse. And it would do me such great good to see some reformers just now. The death of my father, the worse than death of my dear Cousin Gerrit, the martyrdom of that grand and glorious John Brown—all this conspires to make me regret more than ever my dwarfed womanhood. In times like these, every one should do the work of a full-grown man. When I pass the gate of the celestial city and good Peter asks me where I would sit, I shall say, "Anywhere, so that I am neither a negro nor a woman. Confer on me, good angel, the glory of white manhood so that henceforth, sitting or standing, rising up or lying down, I may enjoy the most unlimited freedom." Good night.

Stanton Letters, pp. 74–75.

ANTHONY, DIARY OF A LECTURE TOUR WITH ERNESTINE ROSE TO WASHINGTON, BALTIMORE, AND PHILADELPHIA, 1854

After the presentation of Stanton's memorial and the women's rights petitions to the New York legislature in Albany, Anthony joined Ernestine Rose, the well-known feminist and freethinker, in a four-week lecture tour of the slave border cities. Thus began Anthony's fifty-year career as a traveling organizer for women's rights. Although she had been earning her own living and participating in temperance and teachers' organizations for several years, the trip broadened her horizons considerably. The diary gives an excellent picture of the world of antebellum reform in which Anthony was moving—its uncompromising moralism, individualism, impatience with "expediency," and eagerness to challenge time-honored beliefs. Anthony provides a marvellous portrait of Ernestine Rose, a woman every bit as intense as herself, who was painfully isolated, even from other reformers, by her atheism. The trip was Anthony's first direct encounter with slavery, and her observations of the effects of slavery on Southern society, the slaves themselves, and her own feelings are keen and moving.

Schlesinger Library, Susan B. Anthony Papers

MARCH 24, 1854. [Washington, D.C.] Directed tickets to Mrs. Rose Meeting on Political and Legal Rights of Woman this evening at Carusi's Saloon, to both Representatives and Senators, in all about 300 in number. Asked the Speaker of the House for the use of the Capitol on Sunday A.M. He referred me to Mr. Milburn the Chaplain. Called on him. He could not allow her to speak there because she was not a member of some religious society. I remarked to him that ours was a country professing Religious as well as Civil Liberty and not to allow any and every faith to be declared in the Capitol of the nation, made the profession to religious freedom a perfect mockery. Though acknowledging the truthfulness of my position he could not allow a person who failed to recognize the Divine, to speak in his place. . . .

March 25. Mrs. Davis called in evening. We went into the Parlor, and all hands, save me, joined in the dance. Tired and weary I slipped out at an early hour and laid my head upon my pillow.

March 26. Went to the Capitol and listened to Mr. Milburn on Home Life. He said many good things and many things that indicated gross ignorance, misrepresentation. Said "It is here in the home that *most* men and *all* women's chiefest duties lie."

. . . Called also at Gerrit Smith's and spent the evening, had a delightful conversation. Mrs. Smith is a most splendid woman, plays beautifully on the Piano and sings most sweetly. . . .

Mr. Smith said he wished to share with us in the pecuniary loss of one meeting and insisted on my accepting a Bill which I afterward learned to be a $20 bank note. Expressed himself *very glad* that Mrs. R. had come to Washington. . . .

March 29. Left Washington at ¼ to 9 o'clock for Mt. Vernon, where we arrived about 11 o'clock. The weather cold and windy, but more mild than the day before. The location of Washington's home is most beautiful and commanding, but oh the air of dilapidation and decay that every where meets the eye, the tottering out-buildings, the mark of slavery o'ershadows the whole. Oh, the thought that it was here, that he whose name is the pride of this nation was the *Slave Master*. The humorous, little buildings surrounding, or rather in rear of the great house plainly tell the tale—a Slave, Woman, the cook of the present owner, Grand Nephew of Gen. Washington, told me these buildings were the Servants' Quarters.

The tomb is humble indeed. It would seem that if the profession of reverence for the "Father of his Country" were *real*, that this home of Washington would be rescued from the curse of slave labor, and made to blossom in the sunshine of free labor. . . .

(P.M.) This noon, I ate my dinner without once asking myself, are these human beings who minister to my wants *Slaves* to be bought and sold and hired out at the will of a master? And when the thought first entered my mind, I said, even I am getting *accustomed* to *Slavery*, so much so that I ceased continually to be made to feel its blighting, cursing influence, so much so that I can sit down and eat from the hand of the bondman [*sic*], without being once mindful of the fact that he is such.

Oh Slavery, hateful thing that thou art, thus to blunt the keen edge of men's conscience, even while they strive to shun thy poisonous touch.

I learn to day that the present owner of Mt. Vernon is an *intemperate* man. This fact added to slave holding, accounts for the ruinous state of the Plantation.

A white woman here, a slave holder, says she frequently gets perfectly disgusted with Slavery, the *Licentiousness* between the White men and the Slave women is so universal and so revolting, *free* colored women will boast of rooming with a white man for a whole week. The Proprietor of this City Hotel hires slaves of their masters. . . .

March 30. Baltimore. . . . There is no promptness, no order, no anything about these Southerners. I have had Pro Slavery People tell me just go South once, and see Slavery as it is, and then you will talk very differently. I can assure all such, that contact with Slavery has not a tendency to make me hate it less. No, the ruinous effect of the institution upon the white man alone causes me to hate it. . . .

I came on to Baltimore on the 3 o'c P.M., called on Dr. J. E. Snodgrass firstly and then went in search of a private boarding house, finally decided to take rooms at Mrs. Waters, 49 Hanover.

Every thing is plain but so far seems cleanly. Learned from the chambermaid Sarah that she and other of the Servants were Slaves. It is perfectly astonishing to see what an array of Servants there is about every establishment. Three Northern girls, with the engineering of a Northern boarding house keeper would do all the work of one dozen of these men, women and children, whether slaves or free. Such is the baneful effect of slavery upon labor.

The free blacks who receive wages, expect to do no more work than do the *slaves.* Slave labor is the standard and it needs but a glance at Southern life to enable an Abolitionist to understand why it is that the Northern man is a more exacting slave master than is a Southern one. He requires of the slave an amount of labor equal to that he has been accustomed to get from the well paid Northern free laborer. . . .

April 2. A little colored boy came into our room with Sarah, the Chambermaid. Said Mrs. R. whose boy is that Sarah? He *belongs* to Mrs. Waters, Miss. Where is his mother? She is Cook in the kitchen Miss. Where is his Father? On the Eastern Shore, Miss. Is he a Slave? Yes, Miss. Does he come to see his wife? No, Miss, not since my mistress moved to the City. Has the Cook any more children? Yes, Miss, two more little boys younger than this. Oh, how did my blood run chill.

Before this I said to Sarah, are you *free* Sarah? No, Miss! Do you belong to Mrs. Waters? No Miss, she hires me of my Master for $8 per month. And don't you get any portion of it? No Miss, only my Master gives me my clothes. Does he keep you well clothed? Sometimes, Miss, and sometimes I gets short. And don't you have any pocket money of your own? Yes, Miss, what the ladies gives me. Sarah is a bright girl, fine expression of face. Oh how I long to probe her soul in search of that Divine spark that scorns to be a slave. But then would it be right for me by so doing to add to the burden of her wretched life?

April 4. Mrs. Rose meeting small. Sold only about 54 tickets. Some 60 free tickets present. The people are so *afraid* that some thing will be said on Slavery that they will not countenance the meeting, and more than that there is at the bottom a sad want of intelligence. Science and literature have no charms for them any more than the Reforms. . . .

April 6. I lectured this evening by invitation from the Marion Temperance Society of Baltimore. Had a full house. The meeting was called to order by the President of the Society and opened by prayer by an old man who made the stereotype prayer of Stephen S. Foster's Slave holder—"O Lord we thanks thee, that our lives have been cast in places and that we live in a land where every man can sit under his own vine and fig tree, and none dare to molest or make him afraid." Oh, how did my blood boil within me and then to go on with my lecture and not protest against a man's telling the Lord such terrible falsehoods. . . .

April 8. This is a delightful A.M., yesterday and day before have been beautiful spring days. This has been a week without rain. Went out to the Post Office, found no letter, feel very much disappointed at not hearing from home while here this week. Got the Morning Papers, and gave most of the Editors a copy of Mrs. Stanton's Address [to the New York legislature]. . . .

Mrs. R. and myself were talking of the *know nothing* organizations, when she criticized Lucy Stone and Wendell Philips [*sic*] with regard to their feelings toward foreigners. Said she had heard them both express themselves in terms of prejudice against granting to foreigners the rights of Citizenship.

I expressed disbelief as to either of them having that narrow, mean prejudice in their souls. She then said I was blinded and could see nor hear nothing wrong in that clique of Abolitionists. She thought she, being connected with no Society or association, either in religion or reforms, could judge all impartially. I then ventured to say that Kossuth's non committal course while in this country, it seemed to me, she did not criticise as she would an American. She thought she did, and could see reasons why he pursued the course he did. Yes, said I, you excuse him, because you can see the causes why he acted and spoke thus, while you will not allow me to bring forward the probable cause of Lucy's seeming fault. It seemed to *me* that *she* could not ascribe *pure motives* to any of our Reformers, and while to her it seemed that I was blindly bound to see no fault, however glaring. At length in the anguish of my soul, I said Mrs. Rose, there is not *one* in the Reform ranks, whom you think true, not one but whom panders to the popular feeling. She answered I can't help it, I take them by the words of their own mouths. I trust all until their words or acts declare them false to truth and right and continued she, no one can tell the hours of anguish I have suffered, as one after another I have seen those whom I had trusted betray falsity of motive as I have been compelled to place one after another on the list of panderers to public favor. Said I, do you know Mrs. Rose, that I can but feel that you place me too on that list. Said she, I will tell you when I see you untrue. A silence ensued. While I copied the verse from the hymn sung in Church this A.M., and subscribed it Susan B. Anthony, for her dear friend Ernestine L. Rose, as I handed it to her, I observed tears in her eyes. Said I Mrs. Rose, have I been wicked and hurt your feelings? She answered, no, but I expect never to be understood while I live. Her anguish was extreme. I too wept, for it filled my soul with anguish to see one so noble, so true (even though I felt I could not comprehend her) so bowed down, so overcome with deep swelling emotions. At length she said, no one knows how I have suffered from not being understood. [I said] I know you must suffer and heaven forbid that I should add a feather's weight to your burdens.

Mrs. Rose is not appreciated, nor cannot be by this age. She is too much in advance of the extreme ultraists even, to be understood by them. Almost every reformer feels that the odium of his own ultraisms is as much as he is able to bear and therefore shrinks from being identified with one in whose view their ultraism is sheer conservatism. This fact has been most plainly brought home to me. Every [one] says, "I am *ultra enough*, the mercy knows; I don't want to seem any more so by identifying myself with one whose every sentiment is so shocking to the public mind." . . .

April 11. Philadelphia. . . . Contrary to Mrs. R['s] expectation, Mrs. Mott expressed herself in favor of having a meeting, and Mr. Mott sallied out forthwith to secure a Hall, Spring Garden Institute for Thursday and Samson St. Hall for Friday evening. It seems quite good to me to have some one take the burden off my shoulders. . . .

April 13. I went to the Female Anti Slavery Society. In attendance was a young lady, Virginia ————, of Maryland. She and her sister had left them by their Father, *three* slaves worth $1000 each of whom they set at liberty. Beside these three, their Father left 13 slaves, all of whom save one they have been instrumental in freeing. This one is a Cooper, and belongs to their only brother, who is ill and not expected to live long. He has an offer of $800 for the slave but tells the girls, if they can give him $400 he will take it and thus set the last of the 16 at liberty. Virginia has raised over $200 and I hope she may succeed in getting the remaining $200. In consequence of their Slaves, she and her sister have been compelled to resort to day labor. She has a fine expressive face. It is indeed noble to see two such young girls make such a sacrifice of their all. . . .

April 14. Dined at James Motts. Abby Gibbons, Sarah Grimpke [*sic*], Thomas Curtis, Griffith Cooper and Eliah Capron and wife Rebecca were invited guests. . . . We had a . . . chat, spiritualism as usual being the principle topic. Mrs. Rose and Mr. Curtis believing the spirit inseparable from the body, of course, were on the unbelieving side while Sarah Grimpke was all enthusiasm in the faith. Eliah Capron doesn't believe, he *knows* there is a reality in spirit disembodied, communicating with the living. The rest of the company, with myself, seemed not to know whether or not there is any truth in these modern manifestations.

Mrs. R returned . . . immediately after dinner to rest for the meeting to be held at Samson's Street Hall. I remained and with Lucretia and Sarah Grimpke and myself on one side and Thomas Curtis on the other had an argument as to the probable future existence of the mind or soul or spirit of man. Not an argument could one of us bring other than an intuitive feeling that we were not to cease to exist when the body dies. While Mr. Curtis reasoned (as has Mrs. Rose often done with me) that all things in Nature die, or rather that the elements of all things are separated and assume new forms, then if the soul, the vital spark of man lives eternally so must the essence of the tree, the animal, the fern and the flower. There certainly is no argument to be brought against such reasonings. But if it be true that we die like the flower, leaving behind, only the fragrance . . . while the elements that compose us go to form new bodies, what a delusion has the race ever been in, What a dream is the life of Man. . . .

DOCUMENT 6

STANTON, "SPEECH TO THE ANNIVERSARY OF THE AMERICAN ANTI-SLAVERY SOCIETY," 1860

Stanton was invited to deliver this speech before the May, 1860, annual meeting of the American Anti-Slavery Society, six months after John Brown's raid on Harpers Ferry. While the speech is an attack on slavery and praises abolitionists, it also offers a series of connections between antislavery and women's rights. First, abolitionism's "universal" principles of truth and freedom had undermined the superstition and bigotry fostered by religious orthodoxy. In addition, women were treated as equals in the antislavery movement and abolitionist men defended their rights. Stanton also spoke of the "subjective" link between white women and slaves, both of whom knew oppression from the inside. Most powerfully, she described the condition of women under chattel slavery, emphasizing their sexual abuse and mental crippling in such a way that some of her audience could not tell if she was speaking of Black women or white. Undoubtedly, this ambiguity was intentional.

The Liberator, May 18, 1860, p. 78

THIS is generally known as the platform of one idea—that is negro slavery. In a certain sense this may be true, but the most casual observation of this whole anti-slavery movement, of your lives, conventions, public speeches and journals, show this one idea to be a great humanitarian one. The motto of your leading organ, "The world is my country and all mankind my countrymen," proclaims the magnitude and universality of this one idea, which takes in the whole human family, irrespective of nation, color, caste, or sex, with all their interests, temporal and spiritual—a question of religion, philanthropy, political economy, commerce, education and social life on which depends the very existence of this republic, of the state, of the family, the sacredness of the lives and property of Northern freemen, the holiness of the marriage relation, and the perpetuity of the Christian religion. Such are the various phases of the question you are wont to debate in your conventions. They all grow out of and legitimately belong to that *so-called* petty, insignificant, annoying subject, which thrusts up its head everywhere in Church and State—"the eternal nigger." But in settling the question of the negro's rights, we find out the exact limits of our own, for rights never clash or interfere; and where no individual in a community is denied his rights, the mass are the more perfectly protected in theirs; for whenever any class is subject to fraud or injustice, it shows that the spirit of tyranny is at work, and no one can tell where or how or when the infection will spread. . . .

It was thought a small matter to kidnap a black man in Africa, and set him to work in the rice swamps of Georgia; but when we look at the panorama of horrors that followed that event, at all the statute laws that were enacted to make that act legal, at the perversion of man's moral sense and innate love of justice in being compelled to defend such laws; when we consider the long, hard tussle we have witnessed here for near a century between the spirit of Liberty and Slavery, we may, in some measure, appreciate the magnitude of the wrong done to that one, lone, friendless negro, who, under the cover of darkness and the star-spangled banner, was stolen from his African hut and lodged in the hold of the American slaver. That one act has, in its consequences, convulsed this Union. It has corrupted our churches, our politics, our press; laid violent hands on Northern freemen at their own firesides; it has gagged our statesmen, and stricken our Northern Senators dumb in their seats; yes, beneath the flag of freedom, Liberty has crouched in fear.

That grand declaration of rights made by WILLIAM LLOYD GARRISON, while yet a printer's boy, was on a higher plane than that of '76. His was uttered with the Christian's view of the dignity of man, the value of the immortal being; the other but from the self-respect of one proud race. But, in spite of noble words, deeds of thirty years of protest, prayers and preaching, slavery still lives, the negro toils on in his weary bondage, his chains have not yet melted in the intense heat of the sun of righteousness; but in the discussion of this question, in grappling with its foes, how many of us have worked out our salvation; what mountains of superstition have been rolled off the human soul! I have always regarded Garrison as the great missionary of the gospel of Jesus to this guilty nation, for he has waged an uncompromising warfare with the deadly sins of both Church and State. My own experience is, no doubt, that of many others. In the darkness and gloom of a false theology, I was slowly sawing off the chains of my spiritual bondage, when, for the first time, I met Garrison in London. A few bold strokes from the hammer of his truth, I was free! Only those who have lived all their lives under the dark clouds of vague, undefined fears can appreciate the joy of a doubting soul suddenly born into the kingdom of reason and free thought. Is the bondage of the priest-ridden less galling than that of the slave, because we do not see the chains, the indelible scars, the festering wounds, the deep degradation of all the powers of the God-like mind? . . .

I do not believe that all history affords another such example as the so-called "Garrisonian Conspiracy"—a body of educated men of decided talent, wealth, rank and position, standing for a quarter of a century battling a whole nation, Church and State, law and public sentiment, without the shadow of ever wavering, turning or faltering, as if chained to the great Gibraltar-truth of human freedom and equality. This unheard-of steadfastness can only be accounted for in the fact that woman too is represented in this 'conspiracy.' Yes, the Marys and the Marthas have gathered round the prophets of our day. With noble words and deeds, and holy sympathy, they have cheered these exiles from the love and honor of their own false countrymen. At their family altars they have been remembered, and unseen spirits of the brave and good have hovered over them, and rejoiced in these true sons of earth.

Yes, this is the only organization on God's footstool where the humanity of woman is recognized, and these are the only men who have ever echoed back her cries for justice and equality. I shall never forget our champions in the World's Anti-Slavery Convention; how nobly [Wendell] Phillips did speak, and how still more nobly Garrison would not speak, because woman was there denied her rights. Think of a World's Convention and one half the world left out! Shame on the women of this nation who help to swell the cry of 'INFIDEL' against men like these! All time would not be long enough to pay the debt of gratitude we owe these noble men, who spoke for us when we were dumb, who roused us to a sense of our own rights, to the dignity of our high calling.

No the mission of this Radical Anti-Slavery Movement is not to the African slave alone, but to the slaves of custom, creed and sex, as well; and most faithfully has it done its work. . . . As we rejoice this day in our deliverance from the sad train of fears and errors that have so long crippled and dwarfed the greatest minds of earth. . . , let us seek a new and holier baptism for the work that lies for each of us in the future.

The last fear from which man may hope deliverance is the fear of man. To this glorious freedom did the immortal John Brown arrive. He feared neither man nor God; he was made perfect in love, the future was bright and beautiful to him! . . . Noble John Brown! thou wert true to thyself and thy race, and loyal to thy God. I ask no higher honor in the gift of this nation for any sons of mine than a gallows and a grave like thine! As these sons now gather round me, and ask questions about different nations, governments and laws, think you it is with pride I read to them our constitutions, statute laws, and late judicial decisions on great questions of human rights? Ah, no! . . . it is with the deepest sorrow that I check the budding patriotism in their young hearts—that I unveil to them our falsehood and hypocrisy, in the face of those grand and glorious declarations of freedom and equality which, when first proclaimed at the mouth of the cannon, raised us head and shoulders above the nations of the earth. It is all-important, in a republican government, that our laws be always on the side of justice. Here where we have neither Pope nor King, no royal family, crown or sceptre, no nobility, rank or class, nothing outward to cultivate or command our veneration, Law, the immutable principles of right, are all and everything to us.

See to it, you have the best interests of our Republic in your care, that your laws keep pace with public sentiment. If you would have us teach our sons a sacred reverence for law, so frame your constitutions and your codes that, in yielding obedience to their requirements, they are not false to the holy claims of humanity—that they degrade not the mothers who gave them life. No one can be more awake than I am to all the blessings of a republican form of government, nor, as a mother, more apprehensive lest her sons should confound liberty with license. Here, where individual responsibilities are so great, and the influence of one so all-powerful, I fain would have them lovers of law and order, and meekly to suffer wrong themselves, if need be, to preserve it; but when the panting fugitive throws himself on our generosity and hospitality, I dare not check the noble, God-given impulses of their natures to place the man above all law. Yes, I must ever teach them that man alone is divine; his words and works are fallible; his institutions, however venerable with age and authority, his constitutions, laws and interpretations of Holy Writ, may all prove false. That alone is sacred that can fully meet the wants of the immortal soul—that can stand the test of time and eternity. . . .

Eloquently and earnestly as noble men have denounced slavery on this platform, they have been able to take only an objective view. They can describe the general features of that infernal system—the horrors of the African slave trade, the agonizing sufferings of the middle-passage, the auction-block, the slave-pen and coffle, the diabolism of the internal traffic, the cruel severing of family ties, the hopeless degradation of woman; all that is outward they can see; but a privileged class can never conceive the feelings of those who are born to contempt, to inferiority, to degradation. Herein is woman more fully identified with the slave than man can possibly be, for she can take the subjective view. She early learns the misfortune of being born an heir to the crown of thorns, to martyrdom, to womanhood. For while the man is born to do whatever he can, for the woman and the negro there is no such privilege. There is a Procrustean bedstead ever ready for them, body and soul, and all mankind stand on the alert to restrain their impulses, check their aspirations, fetter their limbs, lest, in their freedom and strength, in their full development, they should take an even platform with proud man himself. To you, white man, the world throws wide her gates; the way is clear to wealth, to fame, to glory, to renown; the high places of independence and honor and trust are yours; all your efforts are praised and encouraged; all your successes are welcomed with loud hurrahs and cheers; but the black man and the woman are born to shame. The badge of degradation is the skin and sex—the "scarlet letter" so sadly worn upon the breast. Children, even, can define the sphere of the black man, and the most ignorant Irishman hiss him into it, while striplings, mere swaddlings of law and divinity, can talk quite glibly of woman's sphere, and pedant priests at the altar discourse most lovingly of her holy mission to cook him meat, and bear him children, and minister to his sickly lust.

In conversation with a reverend gentleman, not long ago, I chanced to speak of the injustice done to woman. Ah! said he, so far from complaining, your heart should go out in thankfulness that you are an American woman, for in no country in the world does woman hold so high a position as here. Why, sir, said I, you must be very ignorant, or very false. Is my political position as high as that of Victoria, Queen of the mightiest nation on the globe? Are not nearly two millions of native-born

American women, at this very hour, doomed to the foulest slavery that angels ever wept to witness? Are they not doubly damned as immortal beasts of burden in the field, and sad mothers of a most accursed race? Are not they raised for the express purposes of lust? Are they not chained and driven in the slave-coffle at the crack of the whip of an unfeeling driver? Are they not sold on the auction-block? Are they not exposed naked to the coarse jests and voluptuous eyes of brutal men? Are they not trained up in ignorance of all laws, both human and divine, and denied the right to read the Bible? For them there is no Sabbath, no Jesus, no Heaven, no hope, no holy mission of wife and mother, no privacy of home, nothing sacred to look for, but an eternal sleep in dust and the grave. And these are the daughters and sisters of the first men in the Southern states: think of fathers and brothers selling their own flesh on the auction-block, exposing beautiful women of refinement and education in a New Orleans market, and selling them, body and soul, to the highest bidder! And this is the condition of woman in republican, Christian America, and you dare not look me in the face, and tell me that, for blessings such as these, my heart should go out in thankfulness! No, proud priest, you may cover your soul in holy robes, and hide your manhood in a pulpit, and, like the Pharisee of old, turn your face away from the sufferings of your race; but I am a Christian—a follower of Jesus—and "whatever is done unto one of the *least* of these my sisters is done also unto me." Though, in the person of the poor trembling slave mother, you have bound me with heavy burthens most grievous to bear, though you have done all you could to quench the spark of immortality, which, from the throne of God, brought me into being . . . yet can I still speak to him. . . . I have asked the everlasting hills, that in their upward yearnings seem to touch the heavens if I, an immortal being, though clothed in womanhood, was made for the vile purposes to which proud Southern man has doomed me, and in solemn chorus they all chanted, NO! I have turned my eyes within, I have asked this bleeding heart, so full of love to God and man, so generous and self-sacrificing, ever longing for the pure, the holy, the divine, if this graceful form, this soft and tender flesh was made to crawl and shiver in the cold, foul embrace of Southern tyrants; and in stifled sobs, it answered, NO! Think you, oh Christian priests, meekly I will take your insults, taunts and sneers? To you my gratitude is due for all the *peculiar blessings* of slavery, for you have had the morals of this nation in your keeping. Behold the depths into which you have plunged me—the bottomless pit of human misery! But perchance your head grows dizzy to look down so far, and your heart faint to see what torture I can bear! It is enough.

But . . . I rejoice that it has been given to woman to drink the very dregs of human wretchedness and woe. For now, by an eternal law of matter and of mind, when the reaction comes, upward and upward, and still upward, she shall rise. Behold how far above your priestly robes, your bloody altars, your foul incense, your steepled synagogues she shall stand secure on holy mounts, mid clouds of dazzling radiance, to which, in your gross vision, you shall not dare even to lift your eyes! (Applause.)

PART TWO
1861–1873

THE issue which dominated reform politics after the Civil War was Black suffrage. The abolition of slavery left Southern Blacks in an extremely unsettled position, neither slave nor free. They were vulnerable to attacks by their former masters— "legal" attacks like the postwar Black codes, and violent, illegal ones, like the terrorism of the Ku Klux Klan. Friends of the freedmen contended that the very meaning of emancipation would be eroded if southern Blacks did not have the political power to protect themselves against the establishment of virtual slavery in another form. Abolitionists, fresh from the victory of emancipation, joined with their allies in the Republican party, known as "Radicals," to make the cause of Black suffrage their foremost postwar goal.

The emergence of Black suffrage as the central issue in Reconstruction politics very much influenced the struggle for woman suffrage. The fact that the debate on the ex-slaves' legal status focused on Black suffrage helped to destroy whatever doubts remained among feminists that the suffrage was the key to the legal position of women as well. Women like Mary Livermore and Julia Ward Howe, who supported women's rights in the 1850s but had been hesitant about asking for the vote, became active proponents of woman suffrage soon after the war. Indeed, almost without anyone noticing the change, "women's rights" was replaced by "woman suffrage" as the designation of the movement for equality for women.[1] Reconstruction was generally a period of intense popular concern with politics and political equality. The political aspect of the movement for women's emancipation, the essence of which was the demand for enfranchisement, grew in significance accordingly. Because Stanton and Anthony were so closely identified with woman suffrage, their claim to leadership within feminism was particularly strengthened during Reconstruction.

The ideological orientation of the drive for Black suffrage was "natural rights," or, as it was called during Reconstruction, "equal rights." Radicals' ultimate claim for Black suffrage was that the freedman had the same natural right to life, liberty and property as the white man, and therefore equal need of political power to protect those rights. Other reform movements, for instance the postwar labor movement, drew heavily on this equal rights ideology.[2] Feminists counted on the universalistic thrust of the Radicals' equal rights approach to Black suffrage to bring the rights of women, alongside those of the freedmen, into Reconstruction debate. Natural rights ideology had long been fundamental in feminist thought. In some sense it reached a climax during Reconstruction. The characteristic woman suffrage argument of this period rested proudly and starkly on the notion of the common, if abstract, humanity of all persons, Black and white, male and female. "[Y]ou are not legitimately called on to make any special arguments for women and negroes as if they were anomolous beings outside all law," Stanton contended. "The same arguments made . . . for the last century for the extension of the suffrage to all white men . . . are all the arguments we have to make for women and negroes."

During Reconstruction, the demand for woman suffrage moved from the state legislatures, where it had been focused in the 1850s, to the U.S. Congress, where postwar debates on Black suffrage were taking place. "Up to this hour we have looked to State action only for the recognition of our rights," Anthony explained, "but now, by the results of the war, the whole question of suffrage reverts back to Congress and the U.S. Constitution."[3] In 1865, she and Stanton petitioned Congress for woman suffrage for the first time. This new preference for national over state action was ideological as well as strategic. Feminists were part of a whole generation of reformers who lost their prewar suspicion of the federal government for its role in harboring slavery in their postwar admiration for the power of a Constitutional amendment to abolish slavery. They now believed that the federal government could become a major force for increasing democratization and radical social reform. Indeed, a strong national state seemed to these postwar reformers the best protection for individual rights and universal equality.

"States' rights," on the other hand, was associated in their minds with the Confederate rebellion, slavery, and an attack on the Constitutional rights of life, liberty, and property. Thus Stanton and Anthony wanted national citizenship, not only because it was more efficient than state by state action, but because it seemed more consonant with their claim that women had the same natural rights, particularly to political power, as men.

The American Equal Rights Association

In cooperation with Lucy Stone, Lucretia Mott and others, Stanton and Anthony reorganized the women's rights movement in 1866 to bring it more into conjunction with the drive for Black suffrage. They formed the American Equal Rights Association (AERA), the object of which was to combine the demands for Black and woman suffrage into a single campaign for universal adult suffrage. The AERA's basic task was to convince abolitionists and Radicals that their own equal rights logic should lead them to advocate woman suffrage along with Black suffrage as the basis of Reconstruction (see document 7). "Has not the time come to bury the black man and the woman in the citizen?"[4] Stanton proclaimed at the founding convention.

AERA's first and in some ways most significant campaign was over the framing of the Fourteenth Amendment. The Fourteenth Amendment was designed to offer minimal protection for the freedmen's political rights by requiring that, as a condition for readmission, the former Confederate states enfranchise their ex-slaves or have their congressional delegations cut proportionately. The Amendment deliberately excluded women from its provisions by specifying "male" citizens as the basis for calculating congressional representation. The AERA petitioned Congress and protested to abolitionists and Radicals. "Abolitionists have demanded suffrage for women for the last ten years, and why do they ignore the question now? . . ." Stanton asked. "When it is proposed to introduce the word male into the Federal constitution, when the whole nation is upheaved and men are everywhere discussing the foundation principles of government, is not their duty to lift the people into the true idea and protest against all partial legislation?"[5] But the AERA's protests got virtually no hearing. Radicals, fearful that a link with woman suffrage would further weaken the demand for Black suffrage, refused to read their petitions in Congress, and the Fourteenth Amendment, with the word "male," was passed in June, 1866.

After the passage of the Fourteenth Amendment, it became increasingly clear that the AERA formula for reconciling Black suffrage and woman suffrage was doomed. Radicals and abolitionists refused to "trammel" their demand for Black suffrage with women's enfranchisement, and urged feminists to hold back until the freedmen's rights were secured. Feminists either had to defer their demands to Black suffrage or oppose the enfranchisement of Black men in the name of women's emancipation. The AERA floundered on this dilemma and feminists split into two camps. One group, under the leadership of Lucy Stone and Henry Blackwell, accepted the priority of Black suffrage, as well as Radicals' promises they would eventually work for women's enfranchisement. Stanton and Anthony, believing that they had already taken the measure of Republican antifeminism, were determined to agitate for woman suffrage without the aid of Radicals or abolitionists, or any expectation of Republican party support. Having made this decision, they began to build women's rights into something it had never been before, a movement which gained its power primarily from the support of women rather than from the aid of other reformers.

The most emotional aspect of the collapse of the AERA for Stanton and Anthony was their disillusionment with their long-time male allies among abolitionists and Radicals (see document 8). For twenty years Stanton and Anthony had helped to guide the women's rights movement in conjunction with the movement for Black emancipation; then, just at the moment that the champions of the Black man's freedom achieved a real degree of political influence, Stanton and Anthony found they could no longer count on their support for woman suffrage. For a long time, they railed against "the best men," abolitionists like Charles Sumner, Wendell Phillips, and Frederick Douglass, men in whom they had once had absolute political faith. Their sense of betrayal was immense and gave new force to their conviction that until sexual equality was established, women put their faith in men at their peril. "We would warn the young women of the coming generation against men's advice as to their best interests, their highest development," Stanton wrote. "She must not put her trust in man in this transition period since, while regarded as his subject, his inferior, his slave, their interests must be antagonistic."[6]

Anthony and particularly Stanton reacted to the conflict between Black and woman suffrage in a racist fashion, despite their abolitionist backgrounds. Political forces beyond their control had made it impossible to unite the demands of women and the freedmen, but Stanton and Anthony took the further step of opposing feminism to Black suffrage. On the one hand, they argued that white women, educated and virtuous, were more deserving of the vote than the ex-slaves. On the other hand, they attempted to build feminism on the basis of white women's racism. At times, Stanton even fueled white women's sexual fears of Black men to rouse them against Black suffrage and for their own enfranchisement. Stanton's appeal to such arguments peaked during the 1869 debate over the Fifteenth Amendment, which fully enfranchised Black men. After the Amendment's ratification, her outright racism subsided, but the more subtle habit of seeing women's grievances from the viewpoint of white women had been firmly established within the suffrage movement.

The Revival of Feminist Militance

Although the process by which Stanton and Anthony disaffiliated themselves from abolitionists was difficult and often emotionally gruelling, the dominant mood with which they confronted their political prospects in the late 1860s was hopeful. Their breakaway was accompanied by a militant feminist spirit and the commitment to organize an independent movement of women on which the demand for woman suffrage would be based. "Woman must lead the way to her own enfran-

chisement and work out her own salvation with a hopeful courage and determination that knows no fear nor trembling."[7] In
1868, Stanton and Anthony established a boldly radical feminist newspaper, which they named *The Revolution*. There had
been talk in feminist circles for some time of such an enterprise,
but it was not until Stanton and Anthony became entirely independent of abolitionist influence that such a newspaper became a reality. *The Revolution*'s motto was "men their rights
and nothing more; women their rights and nothing less."
"While we would not refuse man an occasional word in our col-
umns," the editors wrote, "yet as masculine ideas have ruled the
race for six thousand years, we especially desire that THE
REVOLUTION shall be the mouth piece for women."[8] In fact,
there were always men involved in the paper, most prominently
George Francis Train, who co-founded it, and Parker Pillsbury,
who shared the editing with Stanton and Anthony. In *The Revolution*, Stanton finally found room for the wide range and full
radicalism of her ideas and knowledge of women. She wrote
about cooperative housekeeping and marriage reform, divorce
and prostitution. Anthony threw herself into the management
and had hopes of producing a newspaper run entirely by
women. Her psychological and financial involvement with the
paper was enormous. She personally assumed the entire $10,000
debt it accumulated in the two years she was editor. When she
was finally forced to give up the paper she mourned her loss in-
tensely, and for many years after imagined reviving it.[9]

Soon after the establishment of *The Revolution*, Stanton and
Anthony founded the National Woman Suffrage Association
(NWSA).[10] Formed in May, 1869, the NWSA was both a national society of woman suffragists and a local New York City
group that discussed all aspects of women's emancipation, social
and economic, as well as political. Although many NWSA
members did not share Stanton's and Anthony's hostility to
Black suffrage, they did share their desire to have an organization which could represent a radical and comprehensive feminism. As they had in regard to *The Revolution*, Stanton and
Anthony each had quite different relations to the NWSA. Although a leader in its formation, Stanton held to the prewar re-

formers' suspicion of organizations. Her service to the NWSA
was more often than not at Anthony's insistence. Rather her
contribution to suffragism in this period was as a traveling lec-
turer and publicist for the radical ideas for which the NWSA
stood. Anthony, on the other hand, finally found in the NWSA
a field for her particular political genius. She was a consummate
organization builder and dedicated herself to creating an enduring feminist organization. More than any other single figure, she
sustained the NWSA for the next quarter of a century over
some very low times, so that when the suffrage movement
began to expand again in the 1890s it had leaders, resources, ex-
pertise, and a history.

The feminist revival of the late Reconstruction period affected the substance as well as the form of the woman suffrage
movement. In 1866 and in 1867, when their watchword was
"universal suffrage," Stanton and Anthony had emphasized
principles of universal equality in their speeches. After the collapse of the AERA, however, they began to make a much more
particular case for woman suffrage, basing their arguments on
the actual grievances of women's lives. Stanton was interested
in the sexual exploitation of women, the nature of marriage, and
the need for divorce reform. Anthony's concerns were with the
economic realm—the low wages, lack of mobility, and general
powerlessness of working women. They extended their natural
rights principles to these areas, and tried to link the demand for
political equality with changes in women's economic and sexual
conditions. Between them, they began to produce a bold and
comprehensive portrait of the exploitation of women. Perhaps
nothing else so characterized their activity in late Reconstruction as the expansion of the demand for woman suffrage into a
radical and multifaceted feminism.

Sex and Vork

Stanton's contribution to the call for sexual liberation for
women was as important as her pioneering role in demanding
woman suffrage. She was by no means the first nineteenth-cen-

tury woman to speak out on these matters, but she approached them with unusual forthrightness and clarity. She had first spoken on questions of marriage and sexuality in the 1850s, in connection with temperance. The examination of marriage, divorce, and sexuality in the women's rights movement was interrupted before the Civil War because the slavery issue came to supersede all other reform concerns and because influential male abolitionists argued that the issue of marriage affected women and men equally and therefore did not belong on the women's rights platform.[11]

When she and Anthony freed themselves from abolitionist influence after the war, Stanton returned enthusiastically to her investigations of women's sexual and marital discontent. She wrote at length on these questions in *The Revolution*. In 1868, she and Anthony organized a mass meeting of women to protest the murder sentence of Hester Vaughn, an immigrant domestic servant who had been raped by her employer, become pregnant and given birth, and then found guilty of infanticide. In 1870, they organized a similar meeting in conjunction with the notorious McFarland-Richardson affair, in which an abusive husband who had fatally shot his ex-wife's lover was found innocent of murder on the grounds of insanity and then awarded custody of their child (see document 9). A third such meeting was held to protest efforts to bring prostitution under state regulation in New York.[12]

Stanton also spoke to small private groups of women on sex and marriage during this period. Everywhere she lectured on suffrage in the evenings, she held parlor meetings of women only on "marriage and maternity" in the afternoons.[13] Her central point was that women ought to be able to control their own sexual lives, a right which she called "individual" or "self" sovereignty. She struggled against the stifling euphemisms of the nineteenth century to mount a feminist attack against the laws and customs which institutionalized marital rape by granting men the right of sexual access to their wives whenever they wanted them. "The fundamental falsehood on which . . . the decision of the court, the defense of the prisoner, and his bloody deed are based," Stanton declared at the McFarland-Richardson protest meeting, "[is] the husband's right of property in the wife."

Stanton's ideas on sex and marriage reflected the material conditions of nineteenth-century women's lives, including her own, namely the realities of many children and long years of motherhood. Although Stanton believed that women had the same capacity for sexual passion as men, and although she was critical of the fact that "the subject of marriage is usually discussed as if the interests of the children were everything and those of grown persons nothing," she invariably focused more on the question of how and when women would conceive than on their sexual pleasure as such.[14] She was one of the pioneers of the nineteenth-century approach to women's sexual rights characterized by historian Linda Gordon as "voluntary motherhood," which asserted a woman's right to refuse her husband intercourse except when she wanted to have a baby.[15]

Philosophically, Stanton's ideas about sexual freedom for women were based on the ideas of natural rights, which she insisted were as applicable to sex and marriage as to government and economics. She argued that the values of equality, independence, and enlightened self-interest could be extended from the public sphere, where they were the standards for civil life, to domestic relations, which were still shaped by feudal standards of hierarchy and obedience to higher authority (see document 10). "The same law of equality that has revolutionized the state and the church is now knocking at the door of our homes," she declared, "and sooner or later there too it must do its work." Her position on divorce also reveals the natural rights basis of her sexual radicalism. She advocated the reform of divorce laws and the liberalization of public opinion to make it easier for women to leave loveless marriages and to remarry if they chose. She wanted marriage to become just like any other contractual relation, which either party had equal freedom to dissolve. She thought that the sacrament of marriage, a holy and indissoluble relation, was a fiction designed to reconcile women to something that men had never considered permanent and which they had abandoned at will.

At first Stanton's insistence that feminists declare for individual freedom and equality in marriage as well as in politics was not well received. The notion that woman should have "sovereignty" over her sexuality, that her own wishes should take precedence over her husband's or that of any other external authority, seemed even to some feminists to spell the end of marriage and the family. There was "a good deal of fear about saying 'sole and absolute right over her own person,'" Anthony wrote in her diary after a debate on marital equality at a NWSA meeting in 1870.[16] By the mid-1870s, however, sexual topics were frequently discussed among feminists, and there was much more boldness in speaking about prostitution, marital abuse, and involuntary pregnancy. "To [Stanton's] lectures . . . is due a healthier tone of public sentiment on the marriage question," Paulina Wright Davis wrote. "It is slowly beginning to be felt that in that relation, there is a vast amount of legalized prostitution, bearing the semblance of virtue, which is rotten below the fair exterior."[17]

Although Stanton played a key role in initiating discussions on sex and marriage within the feminist movement, she was often in the minority in those debates. Many nineteenth-century feminists differed with her on the question of divorce and wanted to hold men more firmly to their marital obligations rather than to make it easier for women to shed theirs. Their position was that easy divorce would hurt women, and that women's interests would best be served by making marriage truly permanent. According to her daughter, Lucy Stone believed that although Mrs. Stanton was "sincere in her antagonism to inequitable laws as between men and women," she mistakenly sought an "equal license accorded to both, instead of equal restraint imposed on both."[18] Liberalized divorce, Stone and others feared, would further weaken the family and contribute to the spread of the selfish and individualistic values that prevailed outside it, in the marketplace.

Stanton's arguments in favor of liberalized divorce were closely connected to the question of self-support for women, an issue that particularly concerned Anthony. Stanton connected the rise of divorce in her day to women's "growing independence," and Anthony pointed to the increasing number of wage-earning women.[19] During the Civil War years, the numbers and militance of working women had increased significantly, and the labor movement was forced to recognize and even to welcome women. Anthony was affected by and tried to contribute to this development. In 1868 she helped to form a short-lived but pioneering organization of working women that tried to integrate feminist and trade union goals.[20] From then on, she maintained a strong sympathy and identification with wage-earning women. At a time when most middle-class women still disapproved of labor organizations and feared strikes, Anthony's sympathies were quite unusual. Like Stanton's concerns with women's sexual and marital emancipation, Anthony's interest in the woman wage-earner helped to broaden the scope of nineteenth-century feminism.

What Anthony wanted for working women was what working men had been demanding for themselves since the first factories were established—an "honorable independence," a wage adequate to support a respectable life, and work that led to dignity and self-respect (see document 11). The result of applying these goals to women, however, was similar to the impact of extending the demand for the vote from men to women: "freedom" had different implications for women than for men, and women faced different obstacles. In Anthony's hands, the ideology and vision of "free labor" became a feminist idea, as that of political democracy had become for Stanton. The regular labor movement was responding to men's experiences of seeing their work degraded and their artisan's independence eroded, when it demanded an honorable independence for them. Women, however, came to the factories from dependent positions within their families. They were not trying to recover something they had lost, but were demanding something they had never before enjoyed. The independence Anthony demanded on their behalf was not only from low wages and sweated labor but from the authority of husbands and fathers over their economically dependent wives and daughters. This was the spirit behind her speech, "Homes of Single Women," in which she described a new generation of self-supporting women who had achieved economic and therefore personal independence (see document 12). "As young women become educated in the industries of the world, thereby learning the sweetness of independent bread," she wrote with great optimism, "it will be more and more impossible for them to accept the Blackstone marriage limitation that 'husband and wife are one, and that one the husband.'"

The strength of Anthony's approach was that she linked her militant feminism to workingmen's political traditions through her attack on "dependence." In the face of the strong anti-woman sentiment of the labor movement, this was an important and difficult bond to forge. At the beginning of the speech she gave in San Francisco in 1871, she told the story of a brutal father who had prohibited his wife and daughter from coming to hear her. "I appeal to you men," she said to her audience, "If you were under such control of another man, would you not consider it absolute slavery?" In a strong union town like San Francisco, such pleas must have appealed to men, who may have harbored similar thoughts against their employers.

Anthony had a deep faith in wage labor, a belief she shared with the great majority of mid-nineteenth-century male labor leaders.[21] She saw the economy as a free enterprise and free labor system, participation in which meant economic independence and personal freedom. She believed that poverty could be eliminated and the excesses of the system controlled, to insure that hard-working individuals would rise to positions of relative security. Yet just as Anthony was developing the feminist case for equality for women in industrial society, this free labor ideology was beginning to show its inadequacies. The spread of factories, the erosion of skilled labor, and the deepening economic pressures on workers were eating away at the possibility for independence, especially among women and other unskilled factory laborers. Anthony did not understand these developments. Natural rights abstractions about independence, equality, and individual freedom permitted her to glorify the beneficial effects of "work"—another abstraction—for women. She described a visit she made to a working-class housewife, whom she urged to get a job so that she might help her children to rise.

When the woman took offense at the idea that times might be so hard that she, as well as her husband, should take a low paying, ten- to twelve-hour-a-day job, Anthony was at a loss to understand her response and could only credit it to the prejudice against work which she had encountered among women of her own class.

Stanton and Anthony quickly discovered that sex and work were much more deeply felt grievances among women than disfranchisement. When they talked about the terribly depressed conditions of working women or sexual abuse in and out of marriage, they spoke directly to the experiences which enraged women and forged their aspirations for freedom. "Women respond to my divorce speech as they never did to suffrage," Stanton wrote to Anthony. "Oh! How they flock to me with their sorrows."[22] "I had a splendid audience of ladies in St. Paul to hear my lecture on 'Marriage and Maternity,'" she wrote in *The Revolution*. "That subject seems to touch a deeper chord in the feminine soul than Suffrage, as few perceive how much the social status is affected by political equality."[23]

Yet they continued to insist on the primacy of the demand for woman suffrage and the importance of a political perspective on the emancipation of women. Anthony strenuously argued against the opinion that all working women needed was "bread, not the ballot." "While we would yield to none in the earnestness of our advocacy of these claims [to sexual and economic emancipation]," they wrote, "we make a broader demand for the enfranchisement of women, as the only way in which all her just rights can be permanently secured."[24] What seems like a contradiction in their analysis—whether politics, or sex and work, were at the root of women's oppression—dissolves when we examine what they meant by enfranchisement. They were living through a period of intense mass political activity, among the freedmen, working people, and in and around the Republican party, and they were demanding the right of women to engage in politics too. They assumed that in fighting for the vote, they were fighting, not merely for individual political rights, but for the possibility of collective political action among women. Thus, when Stanton spoke on women's position within marriage, she proceeded from an evocation of the sexual abuses women suffered to proposals for changes in marriage and divorce law. And when Anthony insisted that the vote would enable working women to raise their wages and win their strikes, she was only arguing for their right to combine politically to protect their interests as working men were doing.

Victoria Woodhull and Militant Suffragism

The militant spirit of late Reconstruction feminism soon spread to agitation for the vote itself, which had been stalled ever since it had become clear that the Republican party would not include woman suffrage in the Fourteenth or Fifteenth Amendments. The embodiment of militant suffragism in the last years of Reconstruction was the "notorious" Victoria Woodhull. Woodhull was a forceful advocate of equality between men and women and her feminism was quite similar to Stanton's. She was also a leader of the American wing of the International Workingmen's Association, formed in London by Karl Marx in 1864. In January, 1871, Woodhull appeared at a hearing of a congressional committee with a new and radical approach to woman suffrage.[25] Woodhull's argument was that women were already enfranchised by the Constitution: the Fourteenth and Fifteenth Amendments declared all persons born or naturalized in the United States to be national citizens, and all citizens to be protected by the Constitution in their rights; assuming that all women were people, and that suffrage was a right of citizenship, women must therefore be entitled to vote. Woodhull's argument suggested a much simpler strategy for woman suffrage than getting another Constitutional amendment; a congressional act or judicial decision would be sufficient to substantiate the argument and declare women enfranchised.

Woodhull's dramatic appearance before Congress, the first ever by a woman on behalf of woman suffrage, took Anthony and Stanton by surprise, but whatever suspicions they might have had about her quickly vanished. By all accounts, she was lucid and charismatic. "She is very charming," Anthony wrote in her diary, "utterly forgetful of difference of sex in her approach to *men*." [26] The Woodhull congressional argument was immediately adopted by the NWSA, and Woodhull was welcomed into suffragism's inner circle. It is instructive to note that two years before Woodhull made her arguments before a congressional committee, Missouri suffragist Virginia Minor had made a very similar case to the NWSA. [27] Minor was eventually the one who carried the Constitutional issues to the U.S. Supreme Court, but in 1869 she received almost no attention from suffragists, who were wedded to the idea that woman's path to the ballot must be just like the Black man's. Woodhull on the other hand was able to draw attention to the argument that women were already enfranchised, and to encourage the NWSA to look in new strategic directions.

This new Constitutional argument provided an activist approach to woman suffrage, asserting as it did that women did not need to ask for the vote but rather must find a way to take what was already theirs. Hopes for social change were so strong during Reconstruction, high-placed politicians indulged themselves so unrestrainedly in egalitarian rhetoric, and yet women's demands were so repeatedly and universally ignored, that many women had grown angry and impatient to have their political rights recognized. As Anthony explained before a group of congressmen, "Such tantalization endured by yourselves or any class of men would have wrought rebellion. . . . It is only the friendly relations that exist between the sexes that has prevented any such result from this injustice to women." [28] Privately Stanton said the same thing with less care and more passion. "[It] is enough to rouse one's blood to the white heat of rebellion against every 'white male' on the Continent. When I think of all the wrongs that have been heaped upon womankind, I am ashamed that I am not forever in a condition of chronic wrath, stark mad, skin and bone, my eyes a fountain of tears, my lips overflowing with curses, and my hand raised against every man and brother!" [29]

At the first congressional hearing held on woman suffrage after the NWSA adopted Woodhull's position, hundreds of women stormed the committee room, seeking admission. The

NWSA advised women not to wait to be given the suffrage, but to go to the polls, submit their ballots, and dare election officials to refuse them. "Women should attempt to qualify and attempt to vote. . . ," NWSA leaders announced. "This action not only serves the purpose of agitation of the question of suffrage, but it puts upon men, our brothers, the onus of refusing votes of their fellow citizens, and compels them to show just cause for such proceedings."[30] The notion that women should take the lead in their own enfranchisement corresponded to the mood of many women, and in the elections of 1871 and 1872, hundreds of women all over the country tried to vote.[31]

Like many others, Anthony assembled a group of women, including all her sisters and many of her friends, to try to vote in her home town of Rochester.[32] She had expected their votes to be refused and intended to sue the election officials on Constitutional grounds. Instead, the poll officials accepted her vote. The experience of voting literally thrilled her and she rushed home to write Stanton about it.[33] Two weeks later, a United States marshal came to her house and, citing a law passed to keep former Confederates from voting in federal elections, arrested her for "illegal voting." Anthony's arrest on federal charges represented an extraordinary response on the part of the government and suggests that suffragists' militance and their new Constitutional arguments were perceived by some in high places as a threat.

Placed in the spotlight by government persecution for her suffrage convictions, Anthony was at her best. After her arrest, she spoke in every district of the county in which she was to be tried, on the legal and Constitutional issues involved in her case (see document 13). The speech she gave focused primarily on questions of Constitutional law but within this framework she was able to communicate some sense of the political struggle of which her arrest was a part. On one side, she saw those who defended the principle, established by the Thirteenth, Fourteenth and Fifteenth Amendments, that the only legitimate object of a strong federal government was the protection and extension of equal rights to all citizens. On the other side was what she called the "political exigency of the Republican party," the efforts of its leaders to limit the democratic implications of the postwar amendments and to turn back the popular movements set loose by emancipation and Black suffrage. The U.S. District Attorney ruled that since Anthony's speaking would prejudice the jury, the venue of her trial must be changed to another county. In less than three weeks, she covered the second county so well that when the trial began the judge would not permit the jury to decide the case but directed it to find a verdict of guilty.[34] Because of a technicality firmly insisted on by the District Attorney, Anthony was unable to appeal the decision and, immensely frustrated, was forced to admit defeat.

Woodhull's own interest in the election of 1872 was not in the act of voting but in organizing a radical political alternative to the Republican party. In March or April, Woodhull and her friends in the First International met with leaders of the NWSA to discuss the desirability of a new reform party to challenge the Republicans' nearly total control over national politics. Although the initiative for a third party probably came from Woodhull, Stanton immediately seized the idea (see document 14). She had always believed that woman suffrage should be raised, not as an isolated issue, but as the center of a comprehensive program for the revolution of women's position, the reorganization of the relations between the sexes, and radical change throughout the society. Woodhull and the Internationalists shared this goal. They and the NWSA issued separate but carefully coordinated announcements of a joint convention, to be held in May, 1872, to consider a third party. While both announcements indicted the Republican party for "fostering land, railroad and money monopolies ... building up a commercial feudalism dangerous to the liberty of the people," the NWSA's call emphasized the centrality of the women's perspective and the importance of a feminist contribution to the new party. "As the women of the country are to take part for the first time in political action," it declared, "we propose that the initiative steps in the Convention shall be taken by them."[35] Accordingly, the NWSA arranged to hold a preliminary meeting the day before the general convention to clarify its own program.

The announcement of the joint convention precipitated a

conflict which had been brewing between Stanton and Anthony for some time.[36] The AERA experience had affected both of them profoundly, but in different ways. Much more than Stanton, Anthony had concluded that woman suffrage should never again be united in coalition with other reforms. Stanton on the other hand responded to the break with the abolitionists by searching for a more radical political framework in which to situate woman suffrage and feminism. For some time she had wanted to move beyond the suffrage demand to a more general political program for women. Thus, as Stanton became more and more enthusiastic about the third party effort, Anthony began to fear that the connection with Woodhull and the Internationalists would undercut the independence and dilute the feminism of the suffragists. She distrusted Woodhull because suffrage was not her primary goal and because her political comrades were men. She was not involved in planning the May conference and when she got the announcement written by Stanton, Matilda Joslyn Gage, Isabella Beecher Hooker, and Paulina Wright Davis, she urged them to abandon it. "Mrs. Woodhull . . . persistently means to run our craft into her port and none other," Anthony insisted. "She is wholly owned and dominated by men spirits."[37] Acting on her own behalf, Anthony tried desperately to keep the convention from occurring. She attempted to cancel the hall, and when she failed at that she went to the suffragists' preliminary meeting, declared it adjourned, and turned off the gas. She only succeeded in dispersing and disorganizing the suffragists, most of whom, including Stanton and Hooker, went to the next day's convention with the Internationalists anyhow.[38] "I never was so *hurt with folly of Stanton,*" Anthony wrote in her diary the day after the fiasco.[39]

A few weeks after the convention, Woodhull began to be the object of severe harassment. She was evicted from her home, the New York papers published scurrilous stories about her, and wealthy supporters of her paper, *Woodhull and Claflin's Weekly*, withdrew their money and forced her to stop publishing.[40] Angry at this harassment and determined to get herself back into the public eye, Woodhull revealed a scandal that had been gossip in reform circles for some time: the adulterous affair of America's most famous liberal minister, Henry Ward Beecher, with Elizabeth Tilton, wife of the prominent reform editor (and Beecher's best friend), Theodore Tilton.[41] Woodhull's goal in publicizing the scandal was to challenge the moral canon of "Respectability" which reformers like Beecher supported and advanced, and sexual radicals and utopian socialists like Woodhull and her friends repudiated.[42] Beecher was president of the NWSA's rival, the American Women Suffrage Association, while Tilton was friend and political adviser to Stanton and Anthony; in addition, Tilton had deserted the Republican party, to which Beecher was firmly attached. Although the personal complexities and political implications were endless and public interest in the scandal unquenchable, no major newspaper picked up the story and Woodhull was forced to publish a special issue of her own newspaper, every copy of which sold out within hours, to report it.[43] A federal warrant under the recently passed Comstock law was immediately sworn out for Woodhull's arrest, and on election eve 1872, Woodhull became the first person ever arrested under this statute. After her arrest, Woodhull's fortunes and probably her sanity declined steadily. When Anthony saw her four years later, she was astonished at what had become of her. "Mrs. W. has wholly changed from earnest simplicity to affected stage acting ... no connected train of thought."[44] While most accounts attribute Woodhull's arrest solely to her role in the Beecher/Tilton scandal, Woodhull herself thought that the Grant administration was threatened by her political radicalism. "I fear they intend ... to establish a precedent for the suppression of recalcitrant journals," she wrote to Anthony, and suggested a connection between her own indictment and Anthony's arrest and trial.[45] Subsequent events bore out Woodhull's suspicions. The Comstock law, which was passed with the support of the Republican party for the purpose of increasing the government's power to police public morality, was later used against freethinkers, sexual radicals, birth controllers, and a wide range of radicals, including feminists.

In a surprising turn of events, Stanton and Anthony ended up supporting the Republican party in the election of 1872 once

Woodhull had left the political scene. Anxious to bring rebel reformers back into the fold, the party offered a few well-placed concessions. To the labor movement, it conceded an eight-hour day for federal employees and an office of labor statistics. To feminists, it offered a small plank—Stanton called it a "splinter"—promising "respectful consideration" for women's demands for "additional rights."[46] Stanton supported the Republicans because of her intense hatred of the only other major Presidential candidate, Horace Greeley. "I had rather see Beezlebub President than Greeley," she wrote.[47] She did not believe the Republican overtures of friendship and was convinced that the forces of reform had already been defeated. "I do not feel jubilant over the situation," she wrote in response to Anthony's enthusiasm for the Republican support. "In fact, I never was so blue in my life."[48] Anthony, on the other hand, was increasingly convinced of "the immense gain to us to have the party in power commit itself to a respectful treatment of our claims," and was beginning to believe that the Republicans really did mean to support woman suffrage.[49] Despite her warning to Stanton that the Woodhull party might run woman suffrage into its "own port," she allowed herself to be flattered and fooled by Republican leaders, who wanted her endorsement only to increase the party's credibility with reformers. This demonstrates how inappropriate Anthony's belief in the necessity of keeping woman suffrage independent from entanglements was in a period of political upheaval and intense reform activity such as the early 1870s.

The Republican victory in 1872 solidified the party's political control, and, in a very basic way, signaled the end of an era of reform. After the election, the party showed no further interest in courting woman suffragists, and the "splinter" was never redeemed. In 1875, the U.S. Supreme Court ruled against the argument that the Fourteenth and Fifteenth Amendments enfranchised women. In the case of (Virginia) *Minor* vs. *Happersett*, the Court asserted that suffrage was not a right of national citizenship, but a privilege which each state granted to those whom it deemed fit.[50] The decision was not an attack on militant woman suffragism solely, but a reaction against the full

Reconstruction-era specter of a popular political movement. "The legal vindication of the natural right of all citizens to vote would . . . involve the destruction of civil government," a lower court judge ruled in a similar case. "The right of all men to vote is . . . fully recognized in our larger centers. . . . The result is political profligacy and violence verging on anarchy."[51] Once the Court ruled against suffragists' Constitutional arguments, the NWSA had no choice but to turn to the strategy of securing a separate amendment for woman suffrage, a goal which took almost a half century to achieve.

Radical Reconstruction was definitively ended in 1877, when all federal troops were withdrawn from the South, depriving the freedmen of the last vestiges of federal protection. In the same year, the U.S. Army was used for the first time against workers in an industrial labor dispute, a fitting indication that the political issues of the future would not be racial equality but class conflict.[52] The strength of the national government increasingly seemed committed to protecting big business and established power rather than individual rights and political democracy. Similarly, the principles of "natural rights" embodied in American law were undergoing a major reinterpretation. In 1886, the Supreme Court ruled that corporations could be considered "persons" before the law, and enjoyed the privileges of the Fourteenth Amendment and other Constitutional protections.

Natural rights ideas had always been at the center of Elizabeth Stanton's political philosophy. To some degree, the defeats of Reconstruction even strengthened her in this regard. Despite the fact that the 1875 *Minor* vs. *Happersett* decision demonstrated, in her words, "that the grand principles of equality are glittering generalities for women," in 1878 she was arguing with greater determination than ever for woman suffrage on the grounds that "mankind has a natural right, a natural instinct, and a natural capacity for self-government."[53] Yet she found it increasingly difficult to lead others into the feminist movement on the basis of these natural rights ideas. Her individualism, opposition to organized religion and other coercive moral systems, and her support for the liberalization of divorce laws, all of which derived from her natural rights beliefs, were less and less acceptable to the women's movement after the mid-1870s.

The formation of two important women's organizations in 1873 suggest the nature of the eventual move away from Stanton's kind of feminism: the Women's Christian Temperance Union, which defended women under the banner of "home protection"; and the Association for the Advancement of Women, precursor to the General Federation of Women's Clubs. Although both the WCTU and the AAW came to support woman suffrage, they did not emphasize natural rights arguments about egalitarianism but stressed instead the special needs and distinctive nature of women. The WCTU and the AAW heralded a new development in feminism, within which Stanton increasingly found herself marginal. This, and Anthony's quite different response to the growth and transformation of the late nineteenth-century women's movement, are the subjects of the next section.

NOTES

1. Ellen DuBois, *Feminism and Suffrage: The Emergence of an Independent Women's Movement in America, 1848–1869* (Ithaca: Cornell University Press, 1978), p. 54.

2. David Montgomery, *Beyond Equality: Labor and the Radical Republicans, 1862–1872* (New York: Vintage, 1967).

3. *History of Woman Suffrage*, Vol. 2, eds. Elizabeth Cady Stanton, Susan B. Anthony, and Matilda J. Gage (Rochester: Susan B. Anthony, 1881), pp. 171–172 (hereafter cited as *HWS*).

4. Ibid., p. 174. On the AERA, see DuBois, *Feminism and Suffrage*, chap. 2.

5. Stanton, "Reconstruction," unpublished manuscript speech, Elizabeth Cady Stanton Papers, Library of Congress.

6. *HWS*, Vol. 2, p. 268.

7. Ibid.

8. "*The Revolution* for 1870," *The Revolution*, December 6, 1869, p. 360.

9. See, for instance, Anthony to Lillie Devereux Blake, March 1, 1872, Blake Papers, Missouri Historical Society.

10. On the NWSA, see DuBois, *Feminism and Suffrage*, chap. 6.

11. On the prewar suspension of debate on marriage and divorce, see Elizabeth Cady Stanton, *Eighty Years and More: Reminiscences, 1815–1897* (New York: T. Fischer Unwin, 1898), pp. 218–20.

12. On the Hester Vaughn case, see DuBois, *Feminism and Suffrage*, pp. 145–47. The McFarland-Richardson episode is described in Alma Lutz, *Created Equal: A Biography of Elizabeth Cady Stanton, 1815–1902* (New York: The John Day Co., 1940), pp. 189–90. The protest meeting against the regulation of prostitution is mentioned in David Pivar, *Purity Crusade: Sexual Morality and Social Control, 1868–1900* (Westport, Conn.: Greenwood Press, 1973), p. 51.

13. Stanton to Martha Coffin Wright, June 19, 1871, Elizabeth Cady Stanton Papers, Library of Congress.

14. Stanton discusses women's sexual passion in her September 6, 1883, diary entry, in *Elizabeth Cady Stanton as Revealed in Her Letters, Diary, and Reminiscences*, eds. Theodore Stanton and Harriot Stanton Blatch (New York: Harper & Brothers, Publishers, 1922), p. 210 (hereafter referred to as *Stanton Letters.*) The quotations are from Stanton's 1869 speech on the McFarland-Richardson affair (see document 9).

15. Linda Gordon, *Woman's Body, Woman's Right: A Social History of Birth Control in America* (New York: Grossman, 1976), especially chap. 5.

16. Anthony, Diary, October 20, 1870, Susan B. Anthony Papers, Library of Congress.

17. Paulina Wright Davis, *A History of the National Woman's Rights Movement for Twenty Years, from 1850 to 1870* (New York: Journeymen Printers' Cooperative Association, 1871), p. 22.

18. Alice Stone Blackwell to Kitty Blackwell, March 8, 1883, National American Woman Suffrage Association Papers, Library of Congress.

19. Stanton made an explicit connection between divorce and self-support in a speech she gave in England in 1883, the manuscript of which is in the Elizabeth Cady Stanton Papers, Library of Congress.

20. This organization, the Working Women's Association, is discussed in DuBois, *Feminism and Suffrage*, chap. 5.

21. On the free labor ideology of Reconstruction-era labor leaders, see Montgomery, *Beyond Equality.*

22. Stanton to Anthony, June 27, 1870, *Stanton Letters*, p. 127.

23. Stanton, "Editorial Correspondence," *The Revolution*, April 14, 1870, p. 232.

24. "*The Revolution* for 1870," *The Revolution*, December 6, 1869, p. 360.

25. Woodhull's congressional argument is reprinted in *HWS*, Vol. 2, pp. 444–48. For a collection of her writings which emphasizes her political beliefs and natural rights philosophy see Madeline Stern, ed., *The Victoria Woodhull Reader* (Weston, Mass.: M & S Publishers, 1974).

26. Anthony, Diary, January 14, 1871, Susan B. Anthony Papers, Library of Congress.

27. *HWS*, Vol. 2, pp. 408–09.

28. Ida Harper, *The Life and Work of Susan B. Anthony*, Vol. 1 (Indianapolis: The Bowen-Merrill Company, 1899), p. 513.

29. Stanton to Martha Coffin Wright, March 21, 1870, Elizabeth Cady Stanton Papers, Library of Congress.

30. *HWS*, Vol. 2, p. 496.

31. Ibid , p 587, on protests in Washington, D.C.; Davis, *History of the National Women's Rights Movement*, p. 23, on California and New Jersey women voting.

32. *HWS*, Vol. 2, pp. 628–29.

33. Ibid., p. 935.

34. Ibid., p. 680.

35. The Internationalists' call to the joint convention is reprinted in Samuel Bernstein, *The First International in America* (New York: Augustus M. Kelly, 1962), p. 134. The NWSA's call is reprinted in *HWS*, Vol. 2, pp. 516–17.

36. See for instance the 1871 letter from Anthony to Stanton quoted in Lutz, *Created Equal*, pp. 207–08. The tension seems to have continued after the election. Stanton was not particularly sympathetic to Anthony after her arrest and relatively unenthusiastic about her organizing efforts around her trial; see Stanton to Matilda Gage, June 25, 1873, *Stanton Letters*, pp. 142–43.

37. Lutz, *Created Equal*, p. 217. The comment about spirits refers to Woodhull's spiritualism and her claim that spirits gave her the ideas for her congressional memorial.

38. A few weeks later, Hooker wrote to Anthony, "It is the last thing I ever dreamt of that I should be obliged to separate from you on a matter of radical policy, but when you pray that you may be able to work for the regular republican nominee, . . . I am praying against you." Hooker to Anthony, May 26, 1872, Susan B. Anthony Papers, Library of Congress.

39. Anthony, Diary, May 11, 1872, Susan B. Anthony Papers, Library of Congress.

40. The best biography of Woodhull is Emanie Sachs, *The Terrible Siren* (New York: Harper and Brothers, 1928).

41. See Robert Shaplen, *Free Love and Heavenly Sinners* (New York: Alfred A. Knopf, 1954).

42. Peter T. Cominos, "Late Victorian Sexual Respectability and the Social System," *International Review of Social History*, Vol. 8 (1963), pp. 18–48, 216–50.

43. *Woodhull and Claflin's Weekly*, November 2, 1872.

44. Anthony, Diary, November 21, 1876, Susan B. Anthony Papers, Library of Congress.

45. Woodhull to Anthony, January 2, 1873, Alma Lutz Collection, Huntington Library.

46. Stanton to Lucretia Mott, July 6, 1872, *Stanton Letters*, p. 139.

47. Stanton to Anthony, November 5, 1872, ibid., p. 140. The conflict between Stanton and Greeley dated back to 1867, when Greeley chaired the committee on suffrage of the New York Constitutional Convention. Greeley, who had long been considered a friend of women's rights, surprised feminists by ignoring 20,000 petitions they had collected, and reported against the inclusion of woman suffrage in the constitutional revision. Stanton never forgave him for the betrayal (see DuBois, *Feminism and Suffrage*, pp. 87–88).

48. Harper, *Life of Anthony*, Vol. 1, p. 420.

49. Anthony, Diary, July 26, 1872, as cited in ibid., p. 419.

50. *HWS*, Vol. 2, pp. 734–42.

51. Ibid., p. 599.

52. I want to thank Eric Foner for this observation.

53. Stanton, "National Protection for National Citizens," *HWS*, Vol. 3 (1886), pp. 80–93.

DOCUMENT 7

STANTON, "SPEECH AT LAWRENCE, KANSAS," 1867

Stanton and Anthony were among the half-dozen representatives of the American Equal Rights Association who went into Kansas in 1867 to campaign on behalf of two amendments to the state constitution—one on Black suffrage and the other on woman suffrage. Anthony stayed in Lawrence to give some much-needed organization to the teams of speakers canvassing the state, while Stanton went from town to town—the first extended political touring of her life—speaking on behalf of both referenda. The core of her speech was "the gospel of equality, that good time coming when all men and women, black and white, shall stand equal before the law," which she proclaimed with almost religious fervor. At the same time, Stanton recognized the limitation of natural rights as a reform ideology, that it was "selfish" and "slow," and she began to anticipate the kind of feminism which would emphasize women's special moral sensibility and eventually supersede natural rights arguments. Although local Republicans supported Black suffrage and opposed woman suffrage, neither referendum passed.

Library of Congress, Elizabeth Cady Stanton Papers

THE battles of the past, says Mazzini, have been fought for rights and on that selfish principle progress ever has been and must be slow. But when the most fortunate shall have to think of the multitude below them sunk in ignorance, poverty and vice, then will a divine power inspire those who would move the world. And this hour has come, and we see this divine power in this nineteenth century moving over the whole surface of society. . . . Look in our country how many men of wealth and family, high in the shining walks of life, have with a holy zeal given up luxury, ease, name and fame, and devoted themselves to the lifting up of the fallen and forsaken, to be mouths for the dumb, eyes for the blind and ears for those who could not hear.

And all these men have been led to the consideration of these moral questions by the women at their side. John Stuart Mill tells us in one of his works that his own wife first drew his attention to the importance of the enfranchisement of women and opened to him a new world of thought. Now while such men as Herbert Spencer, Garth Wilhelm Mazzini, Gasperin La Bridge are all writing up Republican institutions [and] the dignity of man, and all alike pointing to woman as the new element of the higher civilization, shall not woman in this republic clothe herself with new dignity and strength and take that lofty position that by right belongs to the mother of the race?

There is an old German proverb that says, "that every woman comes into the world with a stone on her head" and that is as true now as the day it was said. Your creeds, your codes, your conventionalisms have indeed fallen with crushing power on woman in all eyes. But nature is mightier than laws and customs, and in spite of the stone on her head, already behold woman close on your heels in the whole world of thought, art, science, literature and government. . . . [These] are so many protests against the degraded political condition of woman and so many proofs that she is destined everywhere to stand the peer of man.... What have all these old creeds and codes and customs amounted to? Have not true women stood up under all these crushing weights and walked forward as easily as did Sampson with the gates of the city? And now if you will only take the stone off her head she will be able to scale diviner heights—commune with the Gods and draw man up to her level, to lift him from the dust into which he is too prone to grovel. As in the degradation of woman, man has tasted sorrow, shame and death, so in her exaltation shall his moral and spiritual power gather new strength and hold the animal beneath his feet....

Since meeting you citizens of Lawrence three weeks ago, I have addressed audiences of the people of Kansas every day. I have looked in their earnest faces, felt the deep beatings of the great popular heart, in your cities and villages, in your pastures and on the highways. I have carefully noted the utterances of your pulpit and press and your leading men and women, and I feel assured that the people of Kansas are all right on both [Black and woman suffrage]. Here and there I have found some good republicans sitting anxious and distracted on the fence not knowing exactly which way to jump, and I have told these gentlemen if they would only take out their opera glasses and survey the opposing armies they would not be long in coming to a decision.

On the one side behold the ... forces divided into three distinct regiments with their banners waving in the breeze bearing the inscriptions anti-sabbath, anti-Temperance, anti-suffrage, waging a hopeless war against all those principles most sacred in republican institutions, against the liberal opinions of the nineteenth century. On the other side behold the heroic women of Kansas who for the last twenty years have stood sentinels at your doors in the darkest hour of danger.... Behold the leaders of your press and pulpit, your ablest editors and clergy, statesmen ... and the soul of old John Brown all teaching, preaching, and singing the gospel of equality, that good time coming when all men and women, Black and white, shall stand equal before the law, that triumphant day in November when your cannon shall startle the civilized world with the news that a genuine republic is at last realized in the very heart of this western continent. . . .

Your Legislature in submitting to you last winter the two propositions to strike the words white, male from your Constitution struck the key note of reconstruction. In the consideration of these propositions you are not legitimately called on to make any special arguments for women and negroes as if they were anomolous beings outside all law. The same arguments made by you for the last century for the extension of the suffrage to all white men, the same made by John Bright in England, the same made in Russia for the newly emancipated serfs are all the arguments we have to make for women and negroes. You are simply called to consider the rights of citizens of the republic. When you make negroes and women amenable to law, compel them to defend and support the state by war and taxation, you acknowledge their citizenship and are in justice bound to grant their rights parallel with their duties. We therefore appeal to the people of this state to vote thoughtfully and religiously on these two propositions.

The political wire-pullers of both parties endorse but one proposition. . . . Yet the fact that the most influential men of both parties as individuals favor both propositions is the most encouraging sign of the times showing that universal suffrage, which is the ultimatum of these propositions, is already accepted by the people and must form the basis of the liberal party of the not distant future. Just as freedom in the war was a "military necessity" and negro suffrage in peace a "political necessity," so in reconstruction is universal suffrage the moral necessity of the hour. As in our late political struggle the loyal element of the negro was needed to restore the balance of power, so in our legislation on all moral questions is the feminine element needed to secure success.

As the physical and moral necessities of the being ensure individual growth and development, so the commercial and political necessities of a nation compel each onward step of progress. When the great plough share of war roused this nation to the sin of slavery, few were ready for its death blow, so intertwined and incorporated was it with every branch of our government. But when defeat after defeat followed our armies and statesmanship stood at a deadlock, when dark clouds hung over the republic, in the depths of despair we learned the immutable law of justice. Then the nation rose in its majesty, emancipation was proclaimed, and man rejoiced in new found liberty. Then above the din of arms, the cannons' roar, the wail of mothers for their first born, rose soft and clear that divine symphony uttered on the cross and echoed round the world, "All men are created equal."

Then nerved for grand deeds, the people were ready for any onward step, but wily politicians who always have an eye to their personal aggrandizement, procrastinated . . . , and instead of grand measures based on principle, they have been professing partial measures based on policy, and the result is the problem of reconstruction is no nearer its solution to day than it was at the end of the war; and now the moral necessities of this hour press upon us and it is with these necessities we urge the people of this state to grapple to day. Your education, your judgment on the great principles of government are vital at this hour, as to you in Providence is given the opportunity to make the first experiment of a genuine republic. Remember the civilized world awaits your action to see if the principles of our Fathers are possible in government.

A witty Frenchman pictured the first conservative as one going about at the dawn of creation exclaiming with eyes and hands uplifted, "My God, my God, conserve the chaos." To the philosopher, who seeing the discord and disorder of our political, religious and social world, proposes some measures for establishing order and harmony, the objections of those about everything new, to every onward step, are not more absurd than the anxiety of this first conservative, lest in disturbing chaos something worse should come of it. . . . The philosophers and far seeing statesmen of our day, viewing the moral chaos that surrounds, say, "Let there be light. Let us have free discussion of everything that concerns the deepest, broadest and holiest interests of mankind." But the narrow conservative, in view of all the selfishness and corruption of our politics, the bigotry and dissensions in our church, the jealousies and heart burnings of our homes, in view of all this, lifts up his hands and eyes with horror at every step. . . .

STANTON, "GERRIT SMITH ON PETITIONS"

This article is Stanton's impassioned protest against abolitionists and Radical Republicans for refusing to help the American Equal Rights Association or support its demand for universal suffrage. Because men like Wendell Phillips and Stanton's cousin Gerrit Smith had turned the question of the vote into one of "precedence," Stanton retaliated by arguing that "Saxon" women's need for the franchise was even greater than the Black man's. To make her case she used every rhetorical weapon available to her, in particular white women's fear and hatred of Black men, whom they did not want to see enfranchised before them. This accounts for the quite extraordinary mixture of militant feminism and intense racism in most of Stanton's writings in 1868 and 1869.

Peterboro, December 30, 1868

My Dear Susan B. Anthony: I this evening receive your earnest letter. It pains me to be obliged to disappoint you. But I cannot sign the Petition you send me. Cheerfully, gladly can I sign a Petition for the enfranchisement of women. But I cannot sign a paper against the enfranchisement of the negro man, unless at the same time woman shall be enfranchised. The removal of the political disabilities of race is my first desire, of sex, my second. If put on the same level and urged in the same connection neither will be soon accomplished. The former will very soon be, if untrammelled by the other, and its success will prepare the way for the accomplishment of the other.

> With great regard your friend,
> GERRIT SMITH.

To the Senate and House of Representatives, in Congress Assembled:
The undersigned, citizens of the State of ——— earnestly but respectfully request that, in any change or amendment of the Constitution you may propose to extend or regulate Suffrage, there shall be no distinctions made between men and women.

The above is the petition to which our friend Gerrit Smith, as an abolitionist, cannot conscientiously put his name, while republicans and democrats are signing it all over the country. He does not clearly read the signs of the times, or he would see that there is to be no reconstruction of this nation, except on the basis of Universal Suffrage, as the natural, inalienable right of every citizen to its exercise is the only logical ground on which to base an argument. The uprising of the women on both continents, in France, England, Russia, Switzerland, and the United States all show that advancing civilization demands a new element in the government of nations.

As the aristocracy in this country is the "male sex" and as Mr. Smith belongs to the privileged order, he naturally considers it important, for the best interests of the nation, that every type and shade of degraded, ignorant manhood should be enfranchised, before even the higher classes of womanhood should be admitted to the polls.

This does not surprise us. Men always judge more wisely of objective wrongs and oppressions, than of those in which they are themselves involved. Tyranny on a southern plantation is far more easily seen by white men at the north than the wrongs of the women of their own households. . . . [I]n criticising such good and noble men as Gerrit Smith and Wendell Phillips for their apathy on Woman's enfranchisement at this hour, it is not because we think their course at all remarkable, nor that we have the least hope of influencing *them*, but simply to rouse the women of the country to the fact that they must not look to these men for their champions at this hour. But what does surprise us in this cry of "manhood suffrage" is that every *woman* does not see in it national suicide, and her own destruction. In view of the present demoralization of our government, bribery and corruption alike in the legislative, the executive and judicial branches, drunkenness in the White House, Congress, and every state legislature . . . what thinking mind can look for any improvement, in extending suffrage still further to the very class that have produced this state of things.

While philosophy and science alike point to woman, as the new power destined to redeem the world, how can Mr. Smith fail to see that it is just this we need to restore honor and virtue in government. When society in California and Oregon was chiefly male and rapidly tending to savageism, ship loads of women went out and restored order and decency to life. Would black men have availed anything among those white savages? There is sex in the spiritual as well as the physical, and what we need today in government, in the world of morals and thought, is the recognition of the feminine element, as it is this alone that can hold the masculine in check.

Again: Mr. Smith refuses to sign the petition because he thinks to press the broader question of "Universal Suffrage" would defeat the partial one of "Manhood Suffrage"; in other words, to demand protection for women against her oppressors, would jeopardize the black man's chance of securing protection against his oppressors. If it is a question of precedence merely, on what principle of justice or courtesy should woman yield her right of enfranchisement to the negro? If men cannot be trusted to legislate for their own sex, how can they legislate for the opposite sex, of whose wants and needs they know nothing! It has always been considered good philosophy in pressing any measure to claim the uttermost in order to get something. . . . Henry Ward Beecher advised abolitionists, right after the war, to demand "Universal Suffrage" if they wished to secure the ballot for the new made freedmen. "Bait your hooks," said he, "with a woman and perhaps you will catch a negro." But their intense interest in the negro blinded them, and they foresook principle for policy, and in giving woman the cold shoulder they raised a more deadly opposition to the negro than any we had yet encountered, creating an antagonism between him, and the very element most needed, especially at the south, to be propitiated in his behalf. It was this feeling that defeated "negro suffrage" in Kansas. . . .

Although that state always gives large republican majorities and "negro suffrage" was a party measure, politicians, party, press, were alike powerless before the deep settled indignation of the women at the proposition to place the negro above their own heads. Such was their feeling in the matter that the mass of the men everywhere pledged that if the women were not enfranchised, neither should the negro be. The result was that the vote for woman's suffrage, without party, press or thorough canvass of the state, lacked of a few hundred of the vote of the great republican party for negro suffrage. Had republicans and abolitionists advocated both propositions, they would have been triumphantly carried. What is true in Kansas will prove equally true for every state in this Union; there can be no reconstruction of this government on any basis other than universal suffrage. There is no other ground on which to debate the question. Every argument for the negro is an argument for woman and no logician can escape it.

But Mr. Smith abandons the principle clearly involved, and entrenches himself on policy. He would undoubtedly plead the necessity of the ballot for the negro at the south for his protection, and points us to innumerable acts of cruelty he suffers today. But all these things fall as heavily on the women of the black race, yea far more so, for no man can ever know the deep, the damning degradation to which woman is subject in her youth, helplessness and poverty. The enfranchisement of the men of her race, Mr. Smith would say, is her protection.

Our Saxon men have held the ballot in this country for a century, and what honest man can claim that it has been used for woman's protection? Alas! we have given the very heyday of our life to undoing the cruel and unjust laws that the men of New York had made for their own mothers, wives and daughters. Have Saxon women no wrongs to right, and will they be better protected when negroes are their rulers? Remember that all woman needs protection against to-day is man, read the following:

SUPPOSED INFANTICIDE

A young girl named Abson, who has for the past few months been an inmate of the Hudson County poorhouse, at Snake Hill, gave birth, four days ago, to a child of negro parentage, which was found dead in a bed yesterday morning, supposed to have been smothered by its mother.... About a year ago, at which time she was fourteen years of age, the girl was sent to work on a farm in ... New Jersey. During the absence of her employer's father, a negro on the farm effected her ruin, which, being uncovered, and she being enciente, she was sent to ... the Almshouse, where the child was born, and killed as stated. Coroner Warren will hold an inquest.

With judges and jurors of negroes, remembering the generations of wrong and injustice their daughters have suffered at the white man's hands, how will Saxon girls fare in their courts for crimes like this?

How do they fare in our own courts to-day, tried by Saxon fathers, husbands, brothers, sons? Hester Vaughn, a young English woman under sentence of death for the alleged crime of Infanticide, which could not be proved against her, has dragged the weary days of a whole year away in the solitude and gloom of a Pennsylvania prison, while he who betrayed her walks this green earth in freedom....

Such is "manhood suffrage." Shall we prolong and perpetuate injustice like this, and increase its power by adding more ignorance and brutality, and thus risk worse oppressions for ourselves and our daughters? Society, as organized to-day under the man power, is one grand rape of womanhood, on the highways, in our jails, prisons, asylums, in our homes, alike in the world of fashion and of work. Hence, discord, despair, violence, crime, the blind, the deaf, the dumb, the idiot, the lunatic, the drunkard, all that was 'inverted' and must be so, until the mother of the race be made dictator in the social realm. To this end we need every power to lift her up, and teach mankind that in all God's universe there is nothing so holy and sacred as womanhood. Do such men as Gerrit Smith and Wendell Phillips teach this lesson to the lower order of men who learn truth and justice from their lips, when they tell the most noble, virtuous and educated matrons of this republic, to stand back until all the sons of Adam are clothed with citizenship? Do they teach her self-respect when they tell her to hold her claims to virtue, honor and dignity in abeyance to those of manhood? . . .

Although those who demand "Woman's Suffrage" on principle are few, those who would oppose "Negro suffrage" from prejudice are many, hence the only way to secure the latter is to end all this talk of class legislation, bury the negro in the citizen, and claim the suffrage for all men and women, as a natural, inalienable right. The friends of the negro never made a greater blunder, than when, at the close of the war, they timidly refused to lead the nation, in demanding suffrage for all. If even Wendell Phillips and Gerrit Smith, the very apostles of democracy upon this continent, failed at that point, why should we wonder at the vacillation and confusion of mere politicians at this hour? . . . We have pressed these considerations so often on Mr. Phillips and Mr. Smith, during the last four years, that we fear we have entirely forfeited the friendship of the one, and diminished the confidence of the other in our good judgment; but time, that rights all wrongs, will surely bring them back to the standpoint of principle.

STANTON, "SPEECH TO THE MCFARLAND-RICHARDSON PROTEST MEETING," MAY, 1869

In 1869, Daniel McFarland was tried for the shooting of Albert Richardson, who was planning to marry McFarland's former wife, Abby Sage McFarland. A New York court found McFarland innocent by reason of insanity, and then granted him custody of the couple's twelve-year-old son. Richardson eventually died of his wounds, after a dramatic deathbed marriage to Mrs. McFarland. Stanton and Anthony organized a mass meeting of women in New York to protest the decision and took the opportunity to make a feminist analysis of contemporary marriage. Stanton believed that "the husband's right of property in his wife," his legal right to coerce her sexually, was the central problem in marriage. This analysis was considerably more acceptable to the majority of women than the solution Stanton proposed: liberalized divorce.

THE deep interest of the entire nation in the McFarland trial for the last month is due not to any particular regard for the man, or abhorrence of the legal punishment for such crime, but to the fact that the trial indirectly involves the solution of the

Library of Congress, Elizabeth Cady Stanton Papers

momentous questions of marriage and divorce, questions that underlie our whole social, religious and political life.

As I have never seen the faces of either Daniel McFarland or Abby Sage Richardson I have no personal prejudices or preferences to bias my judgment in this matter. I will not admit now what I confess I did feel in earlier life, a prejudice always in favor of my own sex, for with sons and daughters alike growing up my mother's heart has taught me to balance all questions with equal reference to both sexes. Nevertheless I have felt during the past month, as Boston abolitionists felt when Anthony Burns, the black man, the runaway slave, was condemned in their courts and marched through their streets, the sad helpless victim of a false American public sentiment, who having just tasted the sweets of liberty, was remanded by Massachusetts law to southern slavery.

As I sat alone late one night and read the simple truthful story of Abby Sage Richardson, the fugitive wife, I tried to weigh the mountain of sorrow that had rolled over that poor woman's soul, through these long years of hopeless agony, through the fiery ordeal of a public trial in our courts, the merciless hounding of the press, the garbled testimony and unjust decision setting a madman free to keep that poor broken hearted woman in fear for her life as long as he lives. As I pondered all these things in the midnight hour, and recalled the hideous insults through the person of Abby S. Richardson on the entire womanhood of the nation, I resolved that as I had devoted my life heretofore to the enfranchisement of woman, my future work should be to teach woman her duties to herself in the home.

. . . In declaring [McFarland] "not guilty" our courts virtually declare that Mrs. Richardson, although she has married another man whom she loves, is still the wife of the criminal whom for years she has loathed. McFarland should have been pronounced "guilty" . . . but as neither women or slaves can testify against their supposed masters, the effort was made to prove her divorce illegal and thus by declaring her still the wife of the defendant they excluded her evidence in the case. But in the face of this decision there is sympathy enough to day with

Mrs. Richardson to redeem the mighty multitude of wretched wives she represents from the most degraded type of slavery the world knows, that of wife to a bloated drunkard or diseased libertine! But sympathy as a civil agent is vague and powerless until caught and chained in logical . . . propositions, and coined into state law.

Let us then waste no energy or time in tears over the sufferings of any one woman or in anger at the cruel injustice of the courts and the press in this particular case, but learn what we can do to day towards an entire revision of the laws of New York on marriage and divorce; from the pleas, testimony, verdict and decision in the late trial, see what all women need for their protection and where to strike the right blow.

To begin then with the ugly present fact and go back step by step to the foundation question, how comes it that a man who by our courts has been declared so insane that he may commit murder without being morally responsible to the state is let loose on society to repeat such depradations while the helpless victim of his hate and lust still lives and is liable at any moment to be sacrificed by his hand? . . . Although by the revised statutes of this state the mother is the equal guardian of her child to day, yet in the late trial we have the anomaly of a criminal acquitted on the ground of insanity, walking out of court with his child by his hand, its natural protector, while the mother of sound mind capable of supporting it, is denied the custody of its person. We have too a murderer with the crown and sceptre of American citizenship fully restored to him, though adjudged incapable of bearing the moral responsibilities of a man. . . .

The fundamental falsehood on which the opinions of the press, the decision of the court, the defense of the prisoner and his bloody deed are based [is] "the Husband's right of property in the wife." The old common law of the barbarous ages reflected in our statutes controls the public sentiment of the nineteenth century, though the real character and position of woman has entirely changed, from the thoughtless ignorant toy or drudge of the past, to the enlightened, dignified moral being of to day. These one sided degrading statutes on marriage and divorce which at this hour our sons are reading in their law schools are daily educating them into low, gross ideas of their mothers, sisters, future wives; preparing them to contemplate with stolid indifference the hideous features of our present marriage institution; and to call that sacred that every pure woman feels to be unnatural and infamous.

Another demand that the women of this state should make of our Legislature is an entire revision of our laws on marriage and divorce making man and woman in all respects equal partners, and when by the cold indifferent or base conduct of either party the contract is practically annulled the state should declare it so. . . .

[I hope] that my appeals may strengthen the bond of sisterhood between us, showing that while some have suffered, some prayed and others talked, we have all alike been working to the same end. While the stricken heart broken woman, to day a target for the nation's scorn, has through struggle and humiliation given us a glowing but painful picture of the depths of degradation a wife may be called to endure and thus touched a new chord of sympathy of the multitudes she represents, others of us not crushed or perplexed with domestic discord and tyranny, or cumbered with thoughts of our daily bread, have been solving the problem of woman's wrongs and revising for her benefit the statute laws of many of the states.

Though we are still in deep waters be not discouraged. The evils we are suffering to day must needs be in this transition period of woman from slavery to freedom. Not one tear has been shed, one prayer uttered, one word spoken in vain. Even these protracted divorce trials, with all their sickening details, are giving women new courage to sunder the ties they loathe and abhor and slowly but surely educating public sentiment to a true marriage relation. Thus far we have had the man idea of marriage. Now the time has come for woman to give the world the other side of this question.

When the calendars of our courts are crowded with divorce cases and such details of private life are continually paraded before the public in all our daily journals, when there are 1600 divorce cases in Massachusetts in one year and as many in proportion in Illinois, Indiana and Connecticut, we who have sons and daughters growing up to be happy or miserable in their relations have a deep interest in finding the cause of all this social confusion and suggesting some remedy.... I bring you today what I think; it is but the opinion of one woman ... and as in every soul there is bound up some truth and some error, may you have the wisdom to accept the truth I utter and throw the error like chaff to the winds.

I think divorce at the will of the parties is not only right but that it is a sin against nature, the family, the state for a man or woman to live together in the marriage relation in continual antagonism, indifference, disgust. A physical union should in all cases be the outgrowth of a spiritual and intellectual sympathy and anything short of this is lust and not love.... Charlotte Bronte said ... "Though the only road to freedom be through the gates of death those gates must be passed for freedom is indispensable." John Stuart Mill says, "The subject of marriage is usually discussed as if the interests of children were everything, those of grown persons nothing." ... Mrs. McFarland's married life from her own confession of loathing and abhorrence was nothing more or less than legalized prostitution, as Richter said, "no better than a work of adultery," and every pure woman must feel that when she sundered that tie she took the first step towards virtue and self respect....

As every divorce helps to educate other wives similarly situated into higher ideas of purity, virtue, self respect, the more publicity given to the success of each case, the better. As the highest happiness of society and the individual always lie in the same direction, a woman with a ready pen and tongue should not fear criticism, opposition, or persecution or accept personal freedom except through a fair debate of the higher position she intends to take, that thus she may help to mould public sentiment in harmony with her opinions and enable society to sanction her action. Another good effect of trying to take the world with us is that we shall move with greater deliberation. This is my idea of true freedom, not to coquette with unjust law, thrust it to one side or try to get beyond its reach, but to fight it where it is, and fight it to the death. Let the women of this state rise in mass and say they will no longer tolerate statutes that hold pure virtuous women indissolubly bound to gross vicious men, whom they loathe and abhor, and we shall soon have a complete codification of our laws.

The Protestant world has never regarded marriage as an indissoluble tie. Therefore it is no great stretch of the civil or religious conscience of our rulers to multiply the causes for divorce with advancing civilization.

STANTON, "HOME LIFE," c. 1875

> This speech on marriage and divorce, which Stanton
> gave on lecture tours around the country throughout
> the 1870s, was a probing and analytical account of the
> link between indissoluble marriage and the subjugation
> of women. She was especially interested in the role of
> religion in protecting "male headship," a theme which
> became very important in her later writings and which
> proved at least as disturbing to other feminists as her
> defense of liberalized divorce. In the McFarland-Rich-
> ardson speech, written at the height of Reconstruction
> political radicalism, Stanton emphasized laws and legal
> change. By contrast, morality, motherhood, and the
> shaping of children's characters, themes which became
> increasingly important in the post-Reconstruction
> women's movement, were her concerns in this speech,
> even down to its title—"Home Life."

. . . THE political phase of the woman's rights movement has
been so thoroughly discussed in England and this country, and
has already realized so many practical results, that it looks as if
the suffrage battle were nearly fought and won. . . . Hence those
who feel a deeper interest in the more vital questions of this reform—the social problems—should now give their earnest
thought and speech in such directions.

We are in the midst of a social revolution, greater than any

Library of Congress, Elizabeth Cady Stanton Papers

political or religious revolution, that the world has ever seen,
because it goes deep down to the very foundations of society.
. . . A question of [great] magnitude presses on our consideration, whether man and woman are equal, joint heirs to all the
richness and joy of earth and Heaven, or whether they were
eternally ordained, one to be sovereign, the other slave. . . . Here
is a question with half the human family, and that the stronger
half, on one side, who are in possession of the citadel, hold the
key to the treasury and make the laws and public sentiment to
suit their own purposes. Can all this be made to change base
without prolonged discussion, upheavings, heartburnings, violence and war? Will man yield what he considers to be his legitimate authority over woman with less struggle than have Popes
and Kings their supposed rights over their subjects, or slaveholders over their slaves? No, no. John Stuart Mill says the gen-
erality of the male sex cannot yet tolerate the idea of living with
an equal at the fireside; and here is the secret of the opposition
to woman's equality in the state and the church—men are not
ready to recognize it in the home. This is the real danger appre-
hended in giving woman the ballot, for as long as man makes,
interprets, and executes the laws for himself, he holds the power
under any system. Hence when he expresses the fear that liberty for woman would upset the family relation, he acknowl-
edges that her present condition of subjection is not of her own
choosing, and that if she had the power the whole relation
would be essentially changed. And this is just what is coming to
pass, the kernel of the struggle we witness to day.

This is woman's transition period from slavery to freedom
and all these social upheavings, before which the wisest and
bravest stand appalled, are but necessary incidents in her
progress to equality. Conservatism cries out we are going to destroy the family. Timid reformers answer, the political equality
of woman will not change it. They are both wrong. It will entirely revolutionize it. When woman is man's equal the marriage relation cannot stand on the basis it is to day. But this
change will not destroy it; as state constitutions and statute laws
did not create conjugal and maternal love, they cannot annul
them. . . . We shall have the family, that great conservator of

national strength and morals, after the present idea of man's headship is repudiated and woman set free. To establish a republican form of government [and] the right of individual judgment in the family must of necessity involve discussion, dissension, division, but the purer, higher, holier marriage will be evolved by the very evils we now see and deplore. This same law of equality that has revolutionized the state and the church is now knocking at the door of our homes and sooner or later there too it must do its work. Let us one and all wisely bring ourselves into line with this great law for man will gain as much as woman by an equal companionship in the nearest and holiest relations of life. . . . So long as people marry from considerations of policy, from every possible motive but the true one, discord and division must be the result. So long as the State provides no education for youth on the questions and throws no safeguards around the formation of marriage ties, it is in honor bound to open wide the door of escape. From a woman's standpoint, I see that marriage as an indissoluble tie is slavery for woman, because law, religion and public sentiment all combine under this idea to hold her true to this relation, whatever it may be and there is no other human slavery that knows such depths of degradations as a wife chained to a man whom she neither loves nor respects, no other slavery so disastrous in its consequences on the race, or to individual respect, growth and development.

The question to day with the Protestant world is not whether marriage is an indissoluble tie, a holy sacrament of the church, but as a civil contract for how many and what reasons it may be dissolved. In the beginning sacred and profane history alike show that this relation had not even the dignity of contract. The whole matter rested in the hand of the individual man, who took or put away his wife at pleasure. [There] it remained for centuries . . . until by a Papal act of encroachment, the power and arbitrament of divorce were wrested from the master of the family, and marriage became a sacrament of the church.

. . . Let us see how [marriage] is viewed by Protestants in our own country judging from their codes and canons. A new feature in the constitution of marriage in our day is the growing recognition of woman as a party to the contract, having an equal right with man to take and put away. Gov. Jewett of Connecticut told me . . . that there were a third as many divorces as marriages in one year in that state and that a majority of the applications were made by women. It is this new element that embitters the discussion for what is considered a legitimate love of freedom in man, is rank rebellion in woman; and yet the tendency in church and state is to secure her greater latitude than she ever enjoyed before. . . .

By the laws of several states in this republic made by Christian representatives of the people divorces are granted to day for . . . seventeen reasons. . . . By this kind of legislation in the several states we have practically decided two important points: 1st That marriage is a dissoluble tie that may be sundered by a decree of the courts. 2nd That it is a civil contract and not a sacrament of the church, and the one involves the other. . . .

A legal contract for a section of land requires that the parties be of age, of sound mind, [and] that there be no flaw in the title. . . . But a legal marriage in many states in the Union may be contracted between a boy of fourteen and a girl of twelve without the consent of parents or guardians, without publication of banns. . . . Now what person of common sense, or conscience, can endorse laws as wise or prudent that sanction acts such as these. Let the state be logical: if marriage is a civil contract, it should be subject to the laws of all other contracts, carefully made, the parties of age, and all agreements faithfully observed. . . .

Let us now glance at a few of the popular objections to liberal divorce laws. It is said that to make divorce respectable by law, gospel and public sentiment is to break up all family relations. Which is to say that human affections are the result and not the foundation of the canons of the church and statutes of the state. . . . To open the doors of escape to those who dwell in continual antagonism, to the unhappy wives of drunkards, libertines, knaves, lunatics and tyrants, need not necessarily embitter the relations of those who *are* contented and happy, but on the contrary the very fact of freedom strengthens and purifies the bond of union. When husbands and wives do not own each other as property, but are bound together only by affection, marriage will be a life long friendship and not a heavy yoke, from which both may sometimes long for deliverance. The freer the relations are between human beings, the happier. . . .

It is said that the 10,000 libertines, letchers and egotists would take a new wife every Christmas if they could legally and reputably rid themselves in season of the old one. . . . [This] objection is based on the idea that woman will always remain the penniless, helpless, resistless victim of every man she meets, that she is to-day. But in the new regime, when she holds her place in the world of work, educated to self-support, with land under her feet and a shelter over her head, the results of her own toil, the social, civil and political equal of the man by her side, she will not clutch at every offer of marriage, like the drowning man at the floating straw. Though men should remain just what they are, the entire revolution in woman's position now inaugurated forces a new moral code in social life. . . .

People say though it may be better for unhappy husbands and wives to part for their own happiness, yet the best interests of the children require an indissoluble union. The best interests of the children, the parents, the state all require that such ties should be religiously dissolved. It is a great thing to be well born, and no amount of love, care or education can ever compensate a child for the moral and physical weaknesses and deformities, the unhappy morbid conditions that result in its organization from coldness, indifference, aversion or disgust in the parents for one another. . . . It is sometimes the case that two people equally well organized desire divorce who like oil and water never move in the same currents. If such separate who shall have the children? In such cases a pleasant friendship would or might ensue where conjugal love was impossible and they could agree themselves on some satisfactory disposition of their children. . . .

It is objected that men and women would not exercise the deliberation and discrimination they now do if to marry were not considered a crime and the parties not doomed to suffer a life long penalty! As I have already shown, nothing could be more reckless than our present system, when merely to be seen walking together may be taken as evidence of intent to marry, and going through the ceremony in jest may seal the contract....

It is objected that the Bible is opposed to divorce.... I do not propose to go into the Bible argument.... On this as on every subject, the Bible can be quoted on both sides.... All this talk about the "indissoluble tie," and the sacredness of marriage irrespective of the character and habits of the husband, is for its effect on women. She never could have been held the pliant tool she is to day but for the subjugation of her religious nature to the idea that in whatever condition she found herself as man's subject, that condition was ordained by Heaven....

Women would not live as they now do in this enlightened age, in violation of every law of their being, giving the very hey-day of their existence to the exercise of one animal function, if subordination to man had not been made through the ages the cardinal point of their religious faith and daily life. It requires but little thought to see that the indissoluble tie was one of the necessary steps in this subjugation.... The indissoluble tie was found to be necessary in order to establish man's authority over woman. The argument runs thus: ... in the case of parent and child, husband and wife, as these relations cannot be dissolved, there must be some ultimate authority to decide all matters in which they cannot agree, hence man's headship....

Man waits today for woman's soul to meet him on the heights of science, philosophy, poetry and art where he has so long dwelt alone.... His isolation in the soul and intellect is the sad wail in nature that cannot be satisfied with simply a union of the flesh. The great and good in all ages have felt these yearnings for the higher truer marriage. Men have philosophised and poetized about it, legislated on it, but never touched the kernel of the question, because it is a relation that concerns man and woman equally and its corner stone must be laid in the freedom and equality of both parties. Many noble men and women who have suffered in their marriage relation have called aloud for its dissolution.... But suppose the tie dissolved, what then? Nothing but to form others equally unsatisfactory; for so long as woman remains man's subject, ever in the valley of humiliation, while he enjoys the purer atmosphere on the mountain tops and in hours of ease comes down to her, they meet only in their grosser natures. He is bereft of half his power, and she sad and dissatisfied because she knows she is cheated of her birthright to rise to the same sublime heights. . . .

What a record of heartlessness and indifference some of our greatest men have left of their domestic life. Dr. Franklin, that old utilitarian kite-flyer, went to Europe leaving his wife behind him and never saw her face for eleven years. She had shared his poverty, practiced his poor Richard maxims . . . , bred children and nursed them . . . while Benjamin enjoyed the splendors of a court, velvet coaches, good dinners and choice society. Of course, when he came back the poor drudge was no match for the philosopher. . . . That her heart rebelled in her solitude and neglect is manifest in the headstrong acts of her children. He quarreled with his sons and disinherited one of them: thus were the mother's wrongs revenged. A just retribution for every injustice to woman is sure to come in the vice and crime of her children to the third and fourth generation. The less said of Franklin's private character the better. William Franklin, Governor of New Jersey, was his natural son and how many more of the same sort he had probably Franklin himself never knew. . . . Undazzled by the glories of Franklin stoves and lightening rods, one sees much to disapprove in the life of the great philosopher!! . . .

Instead of leaving every thing in the home to chance as now, we should apply science and philosophy to our daily life. I should feel that I had not lived in vain if faith of mine could roll off the soul of woman that dark cloud, that nightmare, that false belief that all her weaknesses and disabilities are natural, that her sufferings in maternity are a punishment for the sins of Adam and Eve and teach her that higher gospel that by obedience to natural laws she might secure uninterrupted health and happiness for herself and mould future generations to her will. When we consider all a mother's influence over her child, antenatal as well as educational, we see her power is second only to that of God himself. . . .

There is no such sacredness and responsibility in any other

human relation as in that of the mother. Give her then a voice in the laws that regulate our social conditions, that we may learn how to live, how to marry, how to educate ourselves and children for the reproduction, not only of the mortal but immortal part of our natures. There is a good deal said rather deploringly about the small families of the American people. When we begin to weigh the momentous consequences of bringing badly organized children into the world, there will be fewer still. To simply propagate our kind is a mere animal function that we share in common with the beasts of the field, but when in self-denial, a pure chaste beautiful life, obedient to every law of soul and body, a mother can give the world one noble, healthy, happy man or woman, a perpetual blessing in the home, the church and the state, she will do a better work for humanity than in adding numbers alone with but little regard for quality. . . .

Home life to the best of us has its shadows and sorrows, and because of our ignorance this must needs be. . . . The day is breaking. It is something to know that life's ills are not showered upon us by the Good Father from a kind of Pandora's box, but are the results of causes that we have the power to control. By a knowledge and observance of law the road to health and happiness opens before [us]: a joy and peace that passeth all understanding shall yet be ours and Paradise regained on earth. When marriage results from a true union of intellect and spirit and when Mothers and Fathers give to their holy offices even that preparation of soul and body that the artist gives to the conception of his poem, statue or landscape, then will marriage, maternity and paternity acquire a new sacredness and dignity and a nobler type of manhood and womanhood will glorify the race!!

ANTHONY, "SUFFRAGE AND THE WORKING WOMAN," 1871

In this speech, different versions of which she delivered from the late 1860s through the 1890s, Anthony demanded that women be granted the twin rewards of American republicanism: equal opportunity to compete for wealth and advancement; and the ballot to protect them against injustice. The experience of recently emancipated and enfranchised Black men seemed to substantiate Anthony's case that the vote and "free labor" could bring honor and respect to previously despised classes. Anthony's relation to the wage-earning women for whom she spoke was ambiguous. On the one hand, she was clearly familiar with and sympathetic to their struggles and knew a good deal about the trade unions they had formed and the strikes they had waged. On the other hand, she understood them from the perspective of a middle-class woman, for whom work meant independence. She did not really understand the miserable and ill-paid work that many of them faced, and could only understand their aversion to wage-labor as "feminine" prejudice.

I COME to night . . . as a representative of the working women. I lay down my doctrine that the first step for the alleviation of their oppression is to secure to them pecuniary independence. Alexander Hamilton said 100 years ago "take my right over my

---

San Francisco Daily Evening Bulletin, July 13, 1871

subsistence and you possess absolute power over my moral being." That is applicable to the working women of the present day. Others possess the right over their subsistence. What is the cause of this? I will tell you. It is because of a false theory having been in the minds of the human family for ages that woman is born to be supported by man and to accept such circumstances as he chooses to accord to her. She not like him is not allowed to control her own circumstances. The pride of every man is that he is free to carve out his own destiny. A woman has no such pride.

A little circumstance happened at this hall last night which illustrates this. A mother and daughter came to the ticket office to purchase tickets, when they were confronted by a man who exclaimed, "Didn't I forbid you to come here to-night?" He had a heavy cane in his hand which he flourished over them, and finally drove them away from the hall.

I appeal to you men. If you were under such control of another man would you not consider it an absolute slavery? But you say that man was a brute. Suppose he is a brute, he is no more of a brute than the law permits him to be.

But to go back. Is it true that women are supported by men? If I was to go home with you all to-night, I should find ample proof of falsity. I should find among your homes many who support themselves. Then if I should go into your manufactories . . . I should find hundreds and thousands who support themselves by the industry of their own hands. In Boston there are 10,000 women engaged in shoemaking. You say these are extreme cases. So they are, but it is in these large cities that the hardship and wrong is most apparent. . . .

If you will take the stand with me on the main thoroughfares of New York, on the Bowery, at the ferries, you will see troops and troops of women going to their daily work. There are not quite so many as there are men, but the men think it is not disreputable to work. Not so with woman. If she makes an effort to support herself, she always makes an effort to conceal it. The young girl has her satchel as though going to the depot, or has her books as though going to school.

Some years ago we had a Woman's Benevolent Society in

New York and appointed a committee to visit all over the city among the poor. The committee visited among others a family of rag pickers. . . . In one little garret was a mother and five little children. The committee appealed to the mother to allow them to put her in a way to support her children and send them to school. They pleaded with her for some time without avail and finally she straightened herself up and exclaimed, "No indeed, ladies. I'll have you to understand my husband is a gintleman and no gintleman allows his wife to go out to work." [Laughter]

That society is wrong which looks on labor as being any more degrading to woman than to man.

It was no more ridiculous for the rag picker's wife to scout the idea of going to work out than it is for the daughter of a well-to-do farmer to scout the idea of supporting herself. . . .

I am proud of San Francisco that she is an exception to the rule, and that she has raised a woman to the position of Principal of one of the cosmopolitan schools with a full salary of $1,-200 a year. But if to-morrow, the same model girl, whom I have just referred to, were to marry a banker and live a life of idleness, with horses, carriages, and house finely furnished, able to take her trip to Europe and with all the advantages wealth could purchase, though her husband were a drunkard, a libertine and a vile and depraved wretch, the woman would never again receive pity. Now we want this rule changed.

The first result of this false theory is this: no woman is even educated to work. Sons are educated while daughters are allowed to grow up mere adornments, and when the hour of necessity comes, then comes cruelty in the extreme. The woman has to skill her hands for labor, and has to compete with men who have been skilled from boyhood; and not only this but when she has attained ability to compete with them and to do just as well in every respect she is placed at work, if at all, on half pay. Society dooms her always to a subordinate position, as an inferior. . . .

Nowhere can woman hold head offices and the reason is this, politicians can't afford to give an office to one who can't pay back in votes. If in New York the women could decide the fate of elections, don't you think they could afford to make women County Clerks or Surrogate Clerks or even Surrogate Judges? Said a Surrogate Judge to me, "Miss Anthony, I was almost converted by your lecture last night. I have one son and one daughter. The son is at college." I asked him, "Is your son possessed of the requisite ability to place him in your position?" "No," he replied; "he will spend his days in a garrett daubing paints on a canvass. But my daughter has a splendid legal mind, and understands already much of my duties. What a pity she was not a boy!" Only think, a brain wasted because it happens to be a woman's. For this reason one half the brain in the world remain undeveloped. How will we remedy this? Give woman an equal chance to compete with men, educate her and surround her with the same legal advantages. Every one knows that the great stimulus for activity is to be paid for in having that activity recognized by promotion.

How will the ballot cure the evil? You tell me the ballot is not going to alleviate this. I will tell you how it is going to alleviate it. Never have the disfranchised classes had equal chances with the enfranchised. What is the difference between the working classes of the United States and Europe? Simply that, here the workman has the ballot and there he has not. Here, if he has the brains or energy, his chances are quite equal with the son of the millionaire. That is American Republicanism—the ballot in the hand of every man. [Applause] . . . See how it works. Take the St. Crispins for example. . . . Well these three hundred St. Crispins strike against a reduction of wages, and not only they, but twenty other St. Crispin Societies, and not only they but other workmen. Now, suppose the New York *World* denounced those men, and the Democratic party manifested prejudice, not only those 300 men would vote against the party but all the other societies: the hod carriers, brick layers, the masons, the carpenters and the tailors would vote solidly against the party which opposed them, and that party would go to the wall.

No political party can hope for success and oppose the interests of the working class. You can all see that neither of the great parties dared to put a plank in the platform directly opposed. Both wrote a paragraph on finance, but nobody knew what it meant. They did this not because of a desire to do justice to the workingmen, but simply because of the power of the workingmen to do them harm. . . .

Now what do women want? Simply the same ballot. In this city, they, the women hat and cap makers, 2,000 of them, made a strike and held out three weeks, but finally they were forced to yield. Their employers said "Take that or nothing," and although "that" was *almost* "nothing" they had to take it or starve. Until two weeks ago I never heard of a successful strike among women. I'll tell you why this was successful. The employers of the Daughters of St. Crispin at Baltimore undertook to cut their wages down, and the Daughters struck. They were about to be defeated when the men St. Crispins came to the rescue and said to the employers, "If you don't accede we will strike," and they carried their point. How happened the workmen to do this? Because they are beginning to see that as long as women work, the capitalists are able to use them to undermine the workmen. . . .

In '68 the collar laundry women organized into a trades union. Their wages had once been but from $6 to $8 per week, but they gradually got them raised to $11 to $21 per week. You may all say that this is very good wages and so it was, compared with what they had been getting, but they thought they were poorly paid in proportion to the profits of their employers, and struck for an advance. Their employers said they must put a stop to this. Give women an inch and they will take an ell. The women called the men trades unions into counsel. The men said "Now is your time to make a strike; you are organized and your employers will come to terms." So one May morning in '69 the 1,000 women threw down their work. For three long months these women held out. They exhausted all their money. From all over the United States trade unions sent money to help them to carry the day. But their employers laughed at them; not a single paper advocated their cause, and they had to yield.

Not long ago I met the President of the organization and I asked her "If you were men you would have won?" "O yes," she said, "the men always win when they strike." "What was the cause of your defeat?" She said: "I guess it was the newspapers. They said if the women were not satisfied, they had better get married." [Laughter] "What made the newspapers oppose you?" "I guess our employers paid them money." "How much?" "I think $10,000." I asked her if the five hundred collar workers had had votes, would the newspapers dared to have opposed them? She said they would not. When the men strike, the employers try to bribe the newspapers in just the same way, but the newspapers dare not sell. The political editor of a party paper puts the votes in one scale and the cash in the other, and the cash knocks the beam every time. [Laughter] Simply because those five hundred women were helpless and powerless and represented the whole half of a country who were helpless and powerless, they failed. . . .

Now let me give you an example for teachers. In a certain city in the East, the women teachers petitioned for an advance of salary. The School Board finding it necessary to retrench, instead of advancing their salaries deducted from the salaries of the women intermediate teachers $25 a month. They did not dare to reduce the salaries of the male teachers because they had votes.

I have a sister somewhat younger than I who has been in those schools for twenty years. [Laughter] Suppose six or seven women were members of the Board, do you believe the Board would have failed to receive that petition? . . .

A few years ago in this house a colored woman would not have been allowed a seat. Now the negro is enfranchised and what is the result? We see the black man walk the streets as proud as any man, simply because he has the ballot. Now black men are mayors of cities, legislators and office holders. Nobody dares to vent his spleen on negroes to-day.

We always invite the mayor and governor to our conventions, but they always have important business which keeps them from attending. The negro invites them and they come. Two years ago they did not. . . . To-day the conservative Republicans bid the negro good morning, and even the Democrats look wistfully at him.

I visited last year the Legislature of Tennessee. I inquired, "Who is that negro member?" I was answered that it was the honorable gentleman of Lynchburg, and that is the honorable gentleman of Hampton County, and that is the honorable gentleman of somewhere else. There were 20 of them. They did not occupy the black man's corner. They were seated with the white members. One black member was sitting on the same cushion on which sat his master three or four years ago.

I thought it would be nice to ask this Legislative body to attend my lecture; and when I extended my invitation, a gentleman asked that the courtesy of the Legislature be extended to me, and that I be allowed the use of the Legislative Hall. This called forth derisive laughter. The question was put on a suspension of the rules and was lost by a vote of 18 to 38. For the benefit of the Democracy, I will state that the negroes voted in favor of the suspension. A man stood near, who, from his appearance, might have been a slave-driver, and he launched out in a tirade of oaths and ended with, "If that had been a damned nigger who wanted the House, he could have had it." [Laughter] And so he could. . . . I believe that women have now the legal right to vote, and I believe that they should go to the polls and deposit their ballot, and if refused carry the officers and inspectors before the Supreme Court.

When we get the ballot those men who now think we are angels just before election will actually see our wings cropping out. [Laughter]

You say the women and the negro are not parallel cases. The negro was a down trodden race, but for the women there is no such necessity for they are lovely and beloved, and the men will guard them from evil. I suppose they will guard their own wives and daughters and mothers and sisters, but is every man as careful to guard another man's wife, daughter, mother and sister? It is not a question of safety to women in general. It is simply "Is she *my* property?" . . . You women who have kind brothers and husband and sons, I ask you to join with us in this movement so that woman can protect herself.

ANTHONY, "HOMES OF SINGLE WOMEN," OCTOBER, 1877

In this very interesting speech, Anthony combined the Victorian reverence for domesticity with her own intense commitment to economic independence for women. She described the first generation of fully self-supporting women, many of them her friends, whose economic independence was marked by a new level of personal freedom, in particular their ability to own their own homes. Anthony herself was part of an earlier generation; she lived with her parents and sister and did not establish her own household until she was seventy. Anthony believed that the difference between the women she described and the great masses of wage-earning women was only a matter of degree, and she offered these "exceptional women" as "models" for "the average woman we everyday meet." "Homes of Single Women" was not a popular speech, or one of Anthony's own favorites. She gave it very few times and thought it "stale, flat and unprofitable."*

A HOME of one's own is the want, the necessity of every human being, the one thing above all others longed for, worked for. Whether the humblest cottage or the proudest palace, a home of our own is the soul's dream of rest, the one hope that

Library of Congress, Susan B. Anthony Papers
* The quotation is from Katherine Anthony, *Susan B. Anthony: Her Personal History and Her Era* (New York: Doubleday, 1954), p. 337.

will not die until we have reached the very portals of the ever-lasting home.

Probably none of us will attempt to question the superiority of the time-honored plan of making a home by the union of one man and one woman in marriage. But in a country like ours where such considerable numbers of men, from choice or necessity, fail to establish matrimonial homes, there is no way of escape; vast numbers of women must make homes for themselves, or forego them altogether. In Massachusetts, alone, there are, to-day, 70,000 more women than men, wives and sisters of soldiers and sailors, miners and stockmen, lumber-men and mountain-men, who in their search for wealth have forgotten the loved of their youth. To these deserted women, necessity has proved the mother of invention. And as you pass from village to village, you will see lovely white cottages, wreathed in vines, nestled midst gardens of vegetables and flowers, fruit and shade trees, each a little Paradise save the presence of the historic Adam before whom woman reverently says, "God thy law, thou mine!!" For homes like these, the passer-by is wont to heave a pitying sigh, as there rises before him the sad panorama of crushed affections, blighted hopes, bereaved hearts. But these are homes of exceeding joy and gladness, compared with the myriads of ill-assorted marriage homes, where existence, by night and by day, is but a living death!!

It has been said that the man of the nineteenth century insists upon having for a wife a woman of the seventeenth century. It is perhaps nearer the truth to say that he demands the spirit of the *two* centuries combined in one woman: the activity and liberality of thought which characterize the present era, with the submission to authority which belonged to the past.... In woman's transition from the position of subject to sovereign, there must needs be an era of self-sustained self-supported homes, where her freedom and equality shall be unquestioned. As young women become educated in the industries of the world, thereby learning the sweetness of independent bread, it will be more and more impossible for them to accept the Blackstone marriage limitation that "husband and wife are one, and that one the husband." ...

... Even when man's intellectual convictions shall be sincerely and fully on the side of Freedom and equality to woman, the force of long existing customs and laws will impel him to exert authority over her, which will be distasteful to the self-sustained, self-respectful woman. The habit of the ages cannot, at once, be changed. Not even amended constitutions and laws can revolutionize the practical relations of men and women, immediately, any more than did the Constitutional freedom and franchise of Black men, transform white men into practical recognition of the civil and political rights of those who were but yesterday their legal slaves. Constitutional equality only gives to all the aid and protection of the law, while they educate and develop themselves, while they grow into the full stature of freemen. It simply allows equality of *chances* to *establish equality*.

Not until women shall have practically demonstrated their claim to equality in the world of work, in agriculture, manufactures, mechanics, inventions, the arts and sciences, not until they shall have established themselves in education, literature and politics and are in actual possession of the highest places of honor and emolument, by the industry of their own hands and brains, and by election or appointment; not until they shall have actually won equality at every point, morally, intellectually, physically, politically, will the superior sex really accept the fact and lay aside all assumptions, dogmatic or autocratic.

Meanwhile, "the logic of events" points, inevitably, to an *epoch of single women.* If women will not accept marriage *with subjection,* nor men proffer it *without,* there is, there can be, *no alternative.* The women who will *not be ruled* must live without marriage. And during this transition period, wherever, for the maintenance of self-respect on the one side, and education into recognition of equality on the other, single women make comfortable and attractive homes for themselves, they furnish the best and most efficient object lessons for men.

Fanny Fern, in her inimitable way, pictures the Modern "Old Maid" thus: "No, sir, she don't shuffle round in skimpy rainments, awkward shoes, cotton gloves, with horn side-combs fastening six hairs to her temples. She don't ... keep a cat, a

snuff box, or go to bed at dark, or scowl at little children, or
gather catnip, not a bit of it. She wears nicely fitting dresses and
becoming bits of color in her hair; and she goes to concerts and
parties and suppers and lectures, and she don't go alone, either!
She lives in a good house earned by herself, and she gives nice,
little teas in it. She don't work for no wages and bare toleration,
day and night; no sir. If she has no money, she teaches or she
lectures or she writes books or poems, or she is a book-keeper,
or she sets type, or she does anything but depend on somebody
else's husband; and she feels well and independent, in conse-
quence, and holds up her head with the best, and asks no favor,
and woman's rights has done it." . . .

Mary Clemmer very truly says, "The secret of the rare material success which attended the Cary sisters is to be found in the
fact that from the first they began to make a home." . . . The
sisters were deeply interested in the cause of equal rights to all;
and the subject of woman's enfranchisement was frequently the
topic of conversation. While at that time Mr. Greeley, almost always present, advocated warmly the right of women to equal
educational and industrial advantages, he stoutly opposed their
demand for suffrage. It was his habit to say, "The best women I
know do not want to vote." The charming Alice would as often
put the question to each of the distinguished women at her
table, "Do you want to vote, Miss Booth?" "Yes," and "Do you
want to vote Mrs. Allen?" "Yes." "Do you want to vote, Miss
Dickenson?" "Yes." And each and every one as invariably replied, "Yes." Yet at the very next reception, Mr. Greeley would
again repeat his stereotype "settler" of the question. . . . He died
in the delusion that "the best women do not want to vote." . . .

Another delightful home of women alone is that of Mary L.
Booth, the successful editor of *Harper's Bazaar*, and Mrs.
Wright, in a beautiful four story brown front on 59th Street. . . .
Of this co-partnership, Miss Booth is so purely a woman of literary pursuits and outside affairs, that she gives over all domestic details, and largely too all those of her own wardrobe, to the
care of Mrs. Wright, whom the world would call more feminine
in her character. Yet, I have been told that she was the wife of a
Captain of a ship, and that once, when on a voyage with her

husband, he was taken very ill, and his mates and other officers proving inefficient, she bravely took command, and brought the vessel safely into port. . . .

A woman's home all must love and honor is that of the President of the National Woman Suffrage Association, Dr. Clemence S. Lozier, a very mother in Israel to every woman struggling for an honest subsistence. For twenty and more years, her house has been the home of one or more poor young women studying medicine at the College she herself founded, and in the maintenance of which she has invested between fifteen and twenty thousand dollars of her own earnings. . . . She is often heard to say, in public and in private, "All my success, professionally, and financially, I owe to the 'Woman's Rights Movement.' It is but my duty, therefore, to help it, and thereby help all other women who shall come after me."

The marriage of Dr. Lozier's youth was a very happy, but brief one, her husband dying early, leaving her the mother of one child. Her second experiment was exceedingly unfortunate; the man not only leaving her to support herself and young son, by sewing and teaching and nursing, but he himself *fed* on the scanty earnings of her hands. . . . Mrs. Lozier's eye chanced to rest on a letter of Elizabeth Cady Stanton's read at the first New York State Women's Temperance Convention, held at Albany in 1852, urging the right of divorce for drunkenness, and clearly setting forth the crime of the mother who stamped her child with the drunkard's appetite for rum. That letter shocked Mrs. Lozier into her first thought, not only of her right, but her solemn duty to cease to be the *wife* of such a man. She quickly obtained a legal separation from bed and board, which was all the laws of New York, then or now, allow for drunkenness, [and] set about studying medicine. . . .

What numbers of the wayfaring advocates of reform, will with me bear grateful testimony to that haven of rest, that coziest home of the Mott sisters, in Albany, New York. . . . For thirty years and more, in that stolidly conservative old Dutch City, those two women stood almost the *sole* representatives of the then unpopular movements for Temperance, Peace, Anti-Slavery, and Woman's Rights. At different periods during those years, those sisters earned their living by teaching, boarding-house keeping, and skirt-manufacturing. They were the most self respecting women I ever knew, always ennobling whatever work they laid their hands on. . . .

Do any of you Gentlemen and Ladies doubt the truth of my picturings of the homes of unmarried women? Do any of you still cling to the old theory, that single women, women's rights women, professional women, have no home instincts? . . . All this is done from pure love of home; no spurious second-hand domesticity affected for the praise of some man, or conscientiously maintained for the comfort of the one who furnishes the money; nor because she has nothing else to busy herself about, but her one impelling motive is from the true womanly home instinct, unsurpassed by that of any of the women who "have all the rights they want."

. . . The charm of all these women's homes is that their owners are "settled" in life; that the men, young or old, who visit them, no more count their hostesses' chances in the matrimonial market, than when guests in the homes of the most happily married women. Men go to these homes as they do to their gentlemen's clubs, to talk of art, science, politics, religion and reform. . . . They go to meet their equals in the proud domain of intellect, laying aside for the time being at least, all of their conventional "small talk for the ladies."

But, say you, all these beautiful homes are made by exceptional women; the few women of superior intellect, rare genius, or masculine executive ability, that enables them to rise above the environments of sex, to lean on themselves for support and protection, to amass wealth, to win honors and emoluments. They are not halves, needing complements, as are the masses of women; but evenly balanced well rounded characters; therefore are they models to be reached by the average women we everyday meet. . . .

DOCUMENT 13

ANTHONY, "CONSTITUTIONAL ARGUMENT," 1872

In November, 1872, Anthony was arrested in Rochester for "illegal voting." For the next few months, in
preparation for her trial on these charges, she traveled
around Monroe County, New York, lecturing on the
principles by which she claimed the right to vote.
Anthony's argument, the outlines of which had been
established in 1871 by Victoria Woodhull, was that
suffrage was a right of citizenship and that all persons,
including women, were citizens; thus women's disfranchisement was merely a matter of "precedent and prejudice" and not Constitutional law. Inalienable natural
rights, irrespective of sex, was Anthony's major theme,
and the dominant political ideology of the period.
However, she made other arguments as well: that the
disfranchisement of women created "an aristocracy of
sex" which was more pernicious than other inequalities, and that marriage constituted "involuntary servitude" for women, which was forbidden by the Thirteenth Amendment.

*F*RIENDS *and Fellow-Citizens:*—I stand before you under indictment for the alleged crime of having voted at the last presidential election, without having a lawful right to vote. It shall be
my work this evening to prove to you that in thus doing, I not

Ida H. Harper, *Life and Work of Susan B. Anthony,* Vol. 2, pp. 977–92 only committed no crime, but instead simply exercised my citizen's right, guaranteed to me and all United States citizens by the National Constitution beyond the power of any State to deny.

Our democratic-republican government is based on the idea of the natural right of every individual member thereof to a voice and a vote in making and executing the laws. We assert the province of government to be to secure the people in the enjoyment of their inalienable rights. We throw to the winds the old dogma that government can give rights. No one denies that before governments were organized each individual possessed the right to protect his own life, liberty and property. When 100 to 1,000,000 people enter into a free government, they do not barter away their natural rights; they simply pledge themselves to protect each other in the enjoyment of them through prescribed judicial and legislative tribunals. They agree to abandon the methods of brute force in the adjustment of their differences and adopt those of civilization. . . . The Declaration of Independence, the United States Constitution, the constitutions of the several States and the organic laws of the Territories, all alike propose to *protect* the people in the exercise of their God-given rights. Not one of them pretends to bestow rights.

> All men are created equal, and endowed by their Creator with certain inalienable rights. Among these are life, liberty and the pursuit of happiness. To secure these, governments are instituted among men, deriving their just powers from the consent of the governed.

Here is no shadow of government authority over rights, or exclusion of any class from their full and equal enjoyment. Here is pronounced the right of all men, and "consequently," as the Quaker preacher said, "of all women," to a voice in the government. And here, in this first paragraph of the Declaration, is the assertion of the natural right of all to the ballot; for how can "the consent of the governed" be given, if the right to vote be denied? . . . The women, dissatisfied as they are with this form of government, that enforces taxation without representation— that compels them to obey laws to which they never have given their consent—that imprisons and hangs them without a trial by a jury of their peers—that robs them, in marriage, of the custody of their own persons, wages and children—are this half of the people who are left wholly at the mercy of the other half, in direct violation of the spirit and letter of the declarations of the framers of this government, every one of which was based on the immutable principle of equal rights to all. By these declarations, kings, popes, priests, aristocrats, all were alike dethroned and placed on a common level, politically, with the lowliest born subject or serf. By them, too, men, as such, were deprived of their divine right to rule and placed on a political level with women. By the practice of these declarations all class and caste distinctions would be abolished, and slave, serf, plebeian, wife, woman, all alike rise from their subject position to the broader platform of equality.

The preamble of the Federal Constitution says:

> We, the people of the United States, in order to form a more perfect union, establish justice, insure domestic tranquillity, provide for the common defence, promote the general welfare and secure the blessings of liberty to ourselves and our posterity, do ordain and establish this Constitution for the United States of America.

It was we, the people, not we, the white male citizens, nor we, the male citizens; but we, the whole people, who formed this Union. We formed it not to give the blessings of liberty but to secure them; not to the half of ourselves and the half of our posterity, but to the whole people—women as well as men. It is downright mockery to talk to women of their enjoyment of the blessings of liberty while they are denied the only means of securing them provided by this democratic-republican government—the ballot.

The early journals of Congress show that, when the committee reported to that body the original articles of confederation, the very first one which became the subject of discussion was that respecting equality of suffrage. . . .

James Madison said:

> Under every view of the subject, it seems indispensable that the mass of the citizens should not be without a voice in making the laws which they are to obey, and in choosing the magistrates who are to administer them. . . . Let it be remembered, finally, that it has ever been the pride and the boast of America that the rights for which she contended were the rights of human nature.

These assertions by the framers of the United States Constitution of the equal and natural right of all the people to a voice in the government, have been affirmed and reaffirmed by the leading statesmen of the nation throughout the entire history of our government. Thaddeus Stevens, of Pennsylvania, said in 1866: "I have made up my mind that the elective franchise is one of the inalienable rights meant to be secured by the Declaration of Independence." . . .

Charles Sumner, in his brave protests against the Fourteenth and Fifteenth Amendments, insisted that so soon as by the Thirteenth Amendment the slaves became free men, the original powers of the United States Constitution guaranteed to them equal rights—the right to vote and to be voted for. . . .

The preamble of the constitution of the State of New York declares the same purpose. It says: "We, the people of the State of New York, grateful to Almighty God for our freedom, in order to secure its blessings, do establish this constitution." Here is not the slightest intimation either of receiving freedom from the United States Constitution, or of the State's conferring the blessings of liberty upon the people; and the same is true of every other State constitution. Each and all declare rights God-given, and that to secure the people in the enjoyment of their inalienable rights is their one and only object in ordaining and establishing government. All of the State constitutions are equally emphatic in their recognition of the ballot as the means of securing the people in the enjoyment of these rights. . . .

I submit that in view of the explicit assertions of the equal right of the whole people, both in the preamble and previous article of the constitution, this omission of the adjective "female" should not be construed into a denial; but instead should be considered as of no effect. . . . No barriers whatever stand today between women and the exercise of their right to vote

save those of precedent and prejudice, which refuse to expunge
the word "male" from the constitution.

. . . When, in 1871, I asked that senator to declare the power of
the United States Constitution to protect women in their right
to vote—as he had done for black men—he handed me a copy of
all his speeches during that reconstruction period, and said:

> Put "sex" where I have "race" or "color," and you have here
> the best and strongest argument I can make for woman. There is
> not a doubt but women have the constitutional right to vote, and
> I will never vote for a Sixteenth Amendment to guarantee it to
> them. I voted for both the Fourteenth and Fifteenth under pro-
> test; would never have done it but for the pressing emergency of
> that hour; would have insisted that the power of the original
> Constitution to protect all citizens in the equal enjoyment of
> their rights should have been vindicated through the courts. But
> the newly-made freedmen had neither the intelligence, wealth
> nor time to await that slow process. Women do possess all these
> in an eminent degree, and I insist that they shall appeal to the
> courts, and through them establish the powers of our American
> magna charta to protect every citizen of the republic.

But, friends, when in accordance with Senator Sumner's
counsel I went to the ballot-box, last November, and exercised
my citizen's right to vote, the courts did not wait for me to appeal to them—they appealed to me, and indicted me on the
charge of having voted illegally. Putting sex where he did color,
Senator Sumner would have said:

> Qualifications can be in their nature permanent or insur-
> mountable. Sex can not be a qualification any more than size,
> race, color or previous condition of servitude. A permanent or
> insurmountable qualification is equivalent to a deprivation of the
> suffrage. In other words, it is the tyranny of taxation without
> representation, against which our Revolutionary mothers, as
> well as fathers, rebelled.

For any State to make sex a qualification, which must ever
result in the disfranchisement of one entire half of the people, is
to pass a bill of attainder, an ex post facto law, and is therefore a
violation of the supreme law of the land. By it the blessings of

liberty are forever withheld from women and their female posterity. For them, this government has no just powers derived
from the consent of the governed. For them this government is
not a democracy; it is not a republic. It is the most odious aristocracy ever established on the face of the globe. An oligarchy
of wealth, where the rich govern the poor; an oligarchy of
learning, where the educated govern the ignorant; or even an oligarchy of race, where the Saxon rules the African, might be
endured; but this oligarchy of sex which makes father, brothers,
husband, sons, the oligarchs over the mother and sisters, the
wife and daughters of every household; which ordains all men
sovereigns, all women subjects—carries discord and rebellion
into every home of the nation. This most odious aristocracy
exists, too, in the face of Section 4, Article IV, which says: "The
United States shall guarantee to every State in the Union a republican form of government." . . .

It is urged that the use of the masculine pronouns *he, his* and
him in all the constitutions and laws, is proof that only men
were meant to be included in their provisions. If you insist on
this version of the letter of the law, we shall insist that you be
consistent and accept the other horn of the dilemma, which
would compel you to exempt women from taxation for the support of the government and from penalties for the violation of
laws. There is no *she* or *her* or *hers* in the tax laws, and this is
equally true of all the criminal laws.

Take for example the civil rights law which I am charged
with having violated; not only are all the pronouns in it masculine, but everybody knows that it was intended expressly to
hinder the rebel men from voting. It reads, "If any person shall
knowingly vote without *his* having a lawful right." . . . I insist if
government officials may thus manipulate the pronouns to tax,
fine, imprison and hang women, it is their duty to thus change
them in order to protect us in our right to vote. . . .

Though the words persons, people, inhabitants, electors, citizens, are all used indiscriminately in the national and State constitutions, there was always a conflict of opinion, prior to the
war, as to whether they were synonymous terms, but whatever
room there was for doubt, under the old regime, the adoption of

the Fourteenth Amendment settled that question forever in its first sentence:

> All persons born or naturalized in the United States, and subject to the jurisdiction thereof, are citizens of the United States, and of the State wherein they reside.

The second settles the equal status of all citizens:

> No State shall make or enforce any law which shall abridge the privileges or immunities of citizens of the United States; nor shall any State deprive any person of life, liberty or property without due process of law, or deny to any person within its jurisdiction the equal protection of the laws.

The only question left to be settled now is: Are women persons? I scarcely believe any of our opponents will have the hardihood to say they are not. Being persons, then, women are citizens, and no State has a right to make any new law, or to enforce any old law, which shall abridge their privileges or immunities. Hence, every discrimination against women in the constitutions and laws of the several States is today null and void, precisely as is every one against negroes.

Is the right to vote one of the privileges or immunities of citizens? I think the disfranchised ex-rebels and ex-State prisoners all will agree that it is not only one of them, but the one without which all the others are nothing. Seek first the kingdom of the ballot and all things else shall be added, is the political injunction. . . .

I am proud to mention the names of the two United States judges who have given opinions honorable to our republican idea, and honorable to themselves—Judge Howe, of Wyoming Territory, and Judge Underwood, of Virginia. The former gave it as his opinion a year ago, when the legislature seemed likely to revoke the law enfranchising the women of that Territory that, in case they succeeded, the women would still possess the right to vote under the Fourteenth Amendment. The latter, in noticing the recent decision of Judge Cartter, of the Supreme Court of the District of Columbia, denying to women the right to vote under the Fourteenth and Fifteenth Amendments, says:

If the people of the United States, by amendment of their Constitution, could expunge, without any explanatory or assisting legislation, an adjective of five letters from all State and local constitutions, and thereby raise millions of our most ignorant fellow-citizens to all of the rights and privileges of electors, why should not the same people, by the same amendment, expunge an adjective of four letters from the same State and local constitutions, and thereby raise other millions of more educated and better informed citizens to equal rights and privileges, without explanatory or assisting legislation?

If the Fourteenth Amendment does not secure to all citizens the right to vote, for what purpose was that grand old charter of the fathers lumbered with its unwieldy proportions? The Republican party, and Judges Howard and Bingham, who drafted the document, pretended it was to do something for black men; and if that something were not to secure them in their right to vote and hold office, what could it have been? For by the Thirteenth Amendment black men had become people, and hence were entitled to all the privileges and immunities of the government, precisely as were the women of the country and foreign men not naturalized. According to Associate-Justice Washington, they already had:

Protection of the government, the enjoyment of life and liberty, with the right to acquire and possess property of every kind, and to pursue and obtain happiness and safety, subject to such restraints as the government may justly prescribe for the general welfare of the whole; the right of a citizen of one State to pass through or to reside in any other State for the purpose of trade, agriculture, professional pursuit, or otherwise; to claim the benefit of the writ of habeas corpus, to institute and maintain actions of any kind in the courts of the State; to take, hold, and dispose of property, either real or personal, and an exemption from higher taxes or impositions than are paid by the other citizens of the State.

Thus, you see, those newly-freed men were in possession of every possible right, privilege and immunity of the government, except that of suffrage, and hence needed no constitutional amendment for any other purpose. What right in this country has the Irishman the day after he receives his naturalization papers that he did not possess the day before, save the right to vote and hold office? The Chinamen now crowding our Pacific coast are in precisely the same position. What privilege or immunity has California or Oregon the right to deny them, save that of the ballot? Clearly, then, if the Fourteenth Amendment was not to secure to black men their right to vote it did nothing for them, since they possessed everything else before. But if it was intended to prohibit the States from denying or abridging their right to vote, then it did the same for all persons, white women included, born or naturalized in the United States; for the amendment does not say that all male persons of African descent, but that all persons are citizens.

The second section is simply a threat to punish the States by reducing their representation on the floor of Congress, should they disfranchise any of their male citizens, and can not be construed into a sanction to disfranchise female citizens, nor does it in any wise weaken or invalidate the universal guarantee of the first section.

However much the doctors of the law may disagree as to whether people and citizens, in the original Constitution, were one and the same, or whether the privileges and immunities in the Fourteenth Amendment include the right of suffrage, the question of the citizen's right to vote is forever settled by the Fifteenth Amendment. "The right of citizens of the United States to vote shall not be denied or abridged by the United States, or by any State, on account of race, color or previous condition of servitude." How can the State deny or abridge the right of the citizen, if the citizen does not possess it? There is no escape from the conclusion that to vote is the citizen's right, and the specifications of race, color or previous condition of servitude can in no way impair the force of that emphatic assertion that the citizen's right to vote shall not be denied or abridged. . . .

If once we establish the false principle that United States citizenship does not carry with it the right to vote in every State in this Union, there is no end to the petty tricks and cunning devices which will be attempted to exclude one and another class of citizens from the right of suffrage. It will not always be the men combining to disfranchise all women; native born men combining to abridge the rights of all naturalized citizens, as in Rhode Island. It will not always be the rich and educated who may combine to cut off the poor and ignorant; but we may live to see the hard-working, uncultivated day laborers, foreign and native born, learning the power of the ballot and their vast majority of numbers, combine and amend State constitutions so as to disfranchise the Vanderbilts, the Stewarts, the Conklings and the Fentons. It is a poor rule that won't work more ways than one. Establish this precedent, admit the State's right to deny suffrage, and there is no limit to the confusion, discord and disruption that may await us. There is and can be but one safe principle of government—equal rights to all. Discrimination against any class on account of color, race, nativity, sex, property, culture, can but embitter and disaffect that class, and thereby endanger the safety of the whole people. Clearly, then, the national government not only must define the rights of citizens, but must stretch out its powerful hand and protect them in every State in this Union.

If, however, you will insist that the Fifteenth Amendment's emphatic interdiction against robbing United States citizens of their suffrage "on account of race, color or previous condition of servitude," is a recognition of the right of either the United States or any State to deprive them of the ballot for any or all other reasons, I will prove to you that the class of citizens for whom I now plead are, by all the principles of our government and many of the laws of the States, included under the term "previous conditions of servitude."

Consider first married women and their legal status. What is servitude? "The condition of a slave." What is a slave? "A person who is robbed of the proceeds of his labor; a person who is subject to the will of another." By the laws of Georgia, South Carolina and all the States of the South, the negro had no right to the custody and control of his person. He belonged to his master. If he were disobedient, the master had the right to use correction. If the negro did not like the correction and ran away, the master had the right to use coercion to bring him back. By the laws of almost every State in this Union today, North as well as South, the married woman has no right to the custody and control of her person. The wife belongs to the husband; and if she refuse obedience he may use moderate correction, and if she do not like his moderate correction and leave his "bed and board," the husband may use moderate coercion to bring her back. The little word "moderate," you see, is the saving clause for the wife, and would doubtless be overstepped should her offended husband administer his correction with the "cat-o'-nine-tails," or accomplish his coercion with blood-hounds.

Again the slave had no right to the earnings of his hands, they belonged to his master; no right to the custody of his children, they belonged to his master; no right to sue or be sued, or to testify in the courts. If he committed a crime, it was the master who must sue or be sued. In many of the States there has been special legislation, giving married women the right to property inherited or received by bequest, or earned by the pursuit of any avocation outside the home; also giving them the right to sue and be sued in matters pertaining to such separate property; but not a single State of this Union has ever secured the wife in the enjoyment of her right to equal ownership of the joint earnings of the marriage copartnership. And since, in the nature of things, the vast majority of married women never earn a dollar by work outside their families, or inherit a dollar from their fathers, it follows that from the day of their marriage to the day of the death of their husbands not one of them ever has a dollar, except it shall please her husband to let her have it. . . .

A good farmer's wife in Illinois, who had all the rights she wanted, had made for herself a full set of false teeth. The dentist pronounced them an admirable fit, and the wife declared it gave her fits to wear them. The dentist sued the husband for his bill; his counsel brought the wife as witness; the judge ruled her off the stand, saying, "A married woman can not be a witness in matters of joint interest between herself and her husband." Think of it, ye good wives, the false teeth in your mouths are a joint interest with your husbands, about which you are legally incompetent to speak! If a married woman is injured by accident, in nearly all of the States it is her husband who must sue, and it is to him that the damages will be awarded. . . . Isn't such a position humiliating enough to be called "servitude?" That husband sued and obtained damages for the loss of the services of his wife, precisely as he would have done had it been his ox, cow or horse; and exactly as the master, under the old regime, would have recovered for the services of his slave.

I submit the question, if the deprivation by law of the ownership of one's own person, wages, property, children, the denial of the right as an individual to sue and be sued and testify in the courts, is not a condition of servitude most bitter and absolute, even though under the sacred name of marriage? . . . The facts also prove that, by all the great fundamental principles of our free government, not only married women but the entire womanhood of the nation are in a "condition of servitude" as surely as were our Revolutionary fathers when they rebelled against King George. Women are taxed without representation, governed without their consent, tried, convicted and punished without a jury of their peers. Is all this tyranny any less humiliating and degrading to women under our democratic-republican government today than it was to men under their aristocratic, monarchial government one hundred years ago? . . .

Is anything further needed to prove woman's condition of servitude sufficient to entitle her to the guarantees of the Fifteenth Amendment? Is there a man who will not agree with me that to talk of freedom without the ballot is mockery to the women of this republic, precisely as New England's orator, Wendell Phillips, at the close of the late war declared it to be to the newly emancipated black man? I admit that, prior to the rebellion, by common consent, the right to enslave, as well as to disfranchise both native and foreign born persons, was conceded to the States. But the one grand principle settled by the war and the reconstruction legislation, is the supremacy of the national government to protect the citizens of the United States in their right to freedom and the elective franchise, against any and every interference on the part of the several States; and again and again have the American people asserted the triumph of this principle by their overwhelming majorities for Lincoln and Grant.

The one issue of the last two presidential elections was

whether the Fourteenth and Fifteenth Amendments should be considered the irrevocable will of the people; and the decision was that they should be, and that it is not only the right, but the duty of the national government to protect all United States citizens in the full enjoyment and free exercise of their privileges and immunities against the attempt of any State to deny or abridge. In this conclusion Republicans and Democrats alike agree. Senator Frelinghuysen said: "The heresy of State rights has been completely buried in these amendments, and as amended, the Constitution confers not only National but State citizenship upon all persons born or naturalized within our limits." . . .

Benjamin F. Butler, in a recent letter to me, said: "I do not believe anybody in Congress doubts that the Constitution authorizes the right of women to vote, precisely as it authorizes trial by jury and many other like rights guaranteed to citizens."

It is upon this just interpretation of the United States Constitution that our National Woman Suffrage Association, which celebrates the twenty-fifth anniversary of the woman's rights movement next May in New York City, has based all its arguments and action since the passage of these amendments. We no longer petition legislature or Congress to give us the right to vote, but appeal to women everywhere to exercise their too long neglected "citizen's right." We appeal to the inspectors of election to receive the votes of all United States citizens, as it is their duty to do. We appeal to United States commissioners and marshals to arrest, as is their duty, the inspectors who reject the votes of United States citizens, and leave alone those who perform their duties and accept these votes. We ask the juries to return verdicts of "not guilty" in the cases of law-abiding United States citizens who cast their votes, and inspectors of election who receive and count them.

We ask the judges to render unprejudiced opinions of the law, and wherever there is room for doubt to give the benefit to the side of liberty and equal rights for women, remembering that, as Sumner says, "The true rule of interpretation under our National Constitution, especially since its amendments, is that anything *for* human rights is constitutional, everything *against* human rights unconstitutional." It is on this line that we propose to fight our battle for the ballot—peaceably but nevertheless persistently—until we achieve complete triumph and all United States citizens, men and women alike, are recognized as equals in the government.

DOCUMENT 14

STANTON, "PROPOSAL TO FORM A NEW PARTY," MAY, 1872

Stanton wrote the following document, which provides an especially clear summary of her political beliefs, in preparation for the May, 1872, convention, which the NWSA called along with the International Workingmen's Association to form a new party. "The politicians who are afraid that our support will not be given them say our cause is ... holy and should be kept ... high in the clouds," she defiantly proclaimed. "But now we propose to descend to the political business of life."* Stanton had two objectives she sought to reconcile: that the new party represent "woman's method and purpose in entering the political field," and that its platform be broad and liberal. Her idea of the "woman's departure in politics" included the full range of radical reforms of the period—abolition of capital punishment, the peaceful transition from wage labor to cooperation, international peace—to which she added her own distinctive concerns, notably her "protest against the union of church and state." Although Stanton believed in a strong and independent feminism, which would not be subservient to any other political perspective, she wanted the women's movement to develop a comprehensive reform program and combine with other reformers to secure it.

Library of Congress, Elizabeth Cady Stanton Papers
* The quotation is from Alma Lutz, *Created Equal: A Biography of Elizabeth Cady Stanton, 1815–1902* (New York: The John Day Co., 1940), p. 219.

THE Republican party is petrifying rapidly and is in nearly the same fossil state as the Whig party thirty years ago, when the Liberty party took the field. The democratic party is in a state of decomposition. Nothing is to be hoped of either for the ideas born of the war. . . . The way is therefore clear and the need imminent of a third party composed of the men and women of the future. The Republican party cannot live long on the thin diet of its past history, but the Ku Klux business has been a Godsend to it and will probably tide it over the approaching election and launch it on another four years career. But the clans are gathering who are to conquer the power to administer the government. . . .

The immediate issue now and the practical point is the May Convention. I feel sure it cannot be . . . a nominating convention: that must come later. There is a great deal of work to be done before that, and the May Convention has its supreme function in this preparatory work. The May Convention is called really by the National Woman's Suffrage Committee, although it will seek influential signers to the public call. Its work obviously is to marshall all the practical reforms which are pressing for settlement under the woman's banner, to unite all such reforms to send representatives to consider the (womanly) solution of the problem of government. . . . The convention should make a declaration (not resolutions) of woman's method and purpose in entering the political field. The distinctiveness of this from the masculine methods should be shown.

It should be the woman's departure in politics. Above all it should be shown that woman holds in her hands the only peaceful, constructive solution of the labor question, the temperance question, etc., etc. . . . The convention should be a woman's convention more important and practical than any ever hitherto held. If it were a general convention, woman would lose her place in the next campaign. . . .

I think the Convention should solemnly declare the dangers

to our government and society, in the want of woman's participation. It should arraign all the existing abuses of society from the woman's standpoint and propose her remedy. My interpretation of woman's method in dealing with public conflicts where there are good elements on both sides is reconciliation, but where there is unpardonable or unmitigated wrong *direct* action.

On the Labor question woman's word is to claim for labor a progressively increasing share of the profits of work, replacing wages so as to inaugurate the partnership of capital and labor, or else pure cooperative industry, labor partnerships or cooperations. This is peaceful and constructive and the only bridge over the gulph of revolution not far ahead.

In temperance woman will not I think theorize and violate individual freedom and responsibility by saying that a man shall not buy, or sell, or drink, but they will deal directly with drunkenness and with public drinking dens, closing up the latter as nuisances. The women I think will extend the mantle of charity and common sisterhood to prostitutes and save the horror by making the condition redeemable. (Thank God I never spoke a harsh word to a prostitute.) The condition of prisons, poor houses, and insane asylums, with all their outrages and oppressions, cries to heaven for redress. Men have been too faithless, heedless, penurious or what not to revolutionize these infamies. . . . Woman will demand a repeal at once of all vindictive punishments. The prisons are to be asylums not places of torture. Capital punishment must of course go by the board. Our courts must be reformed so that justice may be impartially administered to the poor as well as the rich. The whole police system where government comes violently in contact with the people and especially with the lowest social stratum must be revolutionized. The existing brutality in our cities is beyond words.

In education woman should demand an extension of our common school system at both ends, to infant schools and public colleges. The children of women dependent on daily labor should be cared for during the hours of labor, including the noon intermission. They should be accounted as little cadets of the state and should be furnished with ginger snaps milk etc. as well as with kindergarten 'objects'. (I do not propose to put the ginger snaps into the declaration of the convention).

The colleges for graduates of the high schools should educate say 200 of the brightest boys and girls in each congressional district and they should if necessary be cadets of the state and receive enough rations of salary to keep them alive as in West Point, a reward for faithful competitive study up through all the inferior grades.

As regards international peace, obviously the woman's mission is to recognize the bond of humanity between all the peoples, the human solidarity deeper and prior to the national. The purpose of the May convention should be to mark woman's advent in government, to make her claim to equal rights, and to show her different methods. Then, while claiming a share in the new political organization, recognize the place and share of others, asking to work with man equally. . . .

The labor movement ought to be specially mentioned in the call. The spiritualists are a religious not a political body and cannot be specifically mentioned. The marriage question should be referred to in the declaration only (I guess) incidentally with prostitution. In the Declaration there is one more thing, a protest against union of church and state, grants to sectarian schools, the bible in common schools and patronage of God by putting him in the American constitution.

PART THREE
1874–1906

Anthony and the Consolidation of the Women's Movement

The major context for the political role that Stanton and Anthony played in the last decades of the nineteenth century was the tremendous expansion in women's reform activities during the 1870s and 1880s. In the years after Reconstruction, middle- and upper-class American women formed and joined an extraordinary number of socially conscious, all-female organizations. These organizations ranged from the innumerable women's clubs that sprang up in every town and city to foster study and sociability, to the larger social reform organizations, especially the Women's Christian Temperance Union (1874), the Young Women's Christian Association (1871), and the Women's Educational and Industrial Union (1877).[1] The dilemma for suffragists was how to relate their concerns for sexual equality and political power to this proliferation of organized public activity among women. Many, like Mary Livermore, Caroline Severance, and Julia Ward Howe, pulled away from the suffrage movement and put their energies into other more popular women's reforms like temperance and pacifism. The response of Stanton and Anthony was different, from this approach and from each other. Anthony tried to unify all organized, reform-minded women around the demand for the vote, whatever their differences over other issues. Stanton, aiming for a more comprehensive political unity, insisted on challenging women whenever she thought they were being too conservative on the wide variety of political issues she believed concerned them.

In basic ways, the women's organizations of the 1870s and 1880s continued the prewar tradition of women's benevolent and moral reform activity. Their leaders tended to stress women's unique virtues and special responsibility to the community, rather than the identity of men's and women's public roles, which had been the distinguishing argument of women's rights.[2] They placed great emphasis on women's privileged responsibility for domestic life and the rearing of children, and on the moral superiority that they believed flowed from it.[3] Even the religious emphases of prewar women's benevolent activities were maintained in the women's organizations of the period, most of which, despite nominal nonsectarianism and formal independence from church control, were committed to the organization of society around "Christian" values. Traditional "womanly" virtues like self-sacrifice and responsibility for the unfortunate and dependent appeared in a broader light in the context of the rapid industrialization of American society and the social upheaval and human suffering it produced in this period. The responsibility that benevolent women had once felt for pauper widows and orphans they now expressed for the struggling young wage-earning women of the cities; and the criticisms they had formerly directed against secular and individualist tendencies were now aimed at the relentless drive for money and the reduction of "what was meant to be perennial and sacred" to a matter of price and profit.[4]

The relation between these postwar women's organizations and the suffrage movement was complex. The formation of organizations that emphasized the separate spheres of the sexes and the moral superiority of women in their conception of women's public role was both a reaction against and a product of the prominence to which the women's rights perspective had risen in the 1850s and 1860s. On the one hand, many of the leaders of the organizations conceived of them as conservative alternatives to the suffrage movement, and especially to the leadership of Stanton and Anthony. They particularly objected to what they considered excessively radical attacks on femininity and criticisms of the domestic and sexual conventions of bourgeois society.[5] Although there were women's organization leaders who themselves supported the vote, they shared these objections, and believed it was important to create societies where conservative, non-suffrage women could develop and grow.[6] As a result, support for the vote was rarely voiced in postwar women's organizations.

On the other hand, the militant feminism of suffragists changed the traditions of female reform. Unlike prewar societies, most of which were women's auxiliaries, postwar women's organizations were generally free of male control and preached the importance of independence and equality for women. They were assertive about women's capacity to do more than men expected of them and developed techniques for encouraging women to gain wider interests and new skills.[7] Perhaps most important, they no longer insisted that women's influence be limited to the domestic circle and did not consider public life exclusively masculine. Most of these organizations moved over time in the direction of political activity. The WCTU, for instance, soon abandoned prayer to advocate anti-liquor laws, and women's clubs concentrated on programs of municipal reform.[8] The fear of overstepping "woman's sphere," which had restrained women's reform organizations before the rise of the women's rights movement, had largely faded, and women were beginning to recognize the necessity of political action, which was a basic premise of suffragism.

Initially, Anthony was not very enthusiastic about the postwar proliferation of women's organizations and reform activities.[9] It was a cardinal article of faith for her that any work which did not focus on enfranchisement was fruitless for women to pursue. Gradually, however, she began to recognize that there was a great deal of pro-suffrage sentiment latent in the non-suffrage women's organizations. In this regard, the achievements of Frances Willard in the WCTU especially impressed her. Initially, the leaders of the WCTU had been explicitly opposed to woman suffrage. Willard, who was elected second president of the WCTU in 1879, was a suffragist. In 1881, she risked her presidency to advocate full political equality for women, and won the support of most of the members.[10] By the 1890s, WCTU women constituted the majority of suffrage activists in the West and Midwest. Willard's successes demonstrated that support for the suffrage could be made compatible with relatively conventional ideas about the role of women and that it was therefore possible to create a much larger and broader woman suffrage movement than had been built before.

With the example of Willard behind her, Anthony began to work toward the formation of a broad consensus in favor of woman suffrage among all organized, reform-minded women. In order to achieve this goal Anthony was willing to accommodate herself to, rather than to challenge, the conservative beliefs about women and the family that flourished among such women. She had to retreat from the various radicalisms with which her leadership of the suffrage movement had long been associated. "Our intention . . . is [simply] to make every one . . . believe in the grand principle of equality of rights and chances for women . . . ," she wrote, in 1884, in an effort to keep Stanton from raising a controversial issue at a suffrage convention. "Neither you nor I have the right . . . to complicate or compromise our question."[11] Anthony even had to abandon the tactical militancy, for which she had always had a strong personal attraction, because it was "unladylike" and offended women who accepted the rule of respectability.[12] Instead of a movement of women united around an explicit political program for the transformation of society and women's place in it, she began to envision the unification of all women, whatever their social or political beliefs, around their common womanhood and the single goal of political equality. Beginning in the mid-1880s, Anthony began to dedicate her considerable energies and powers of organization to the consolidation of the many postwar women's reform organizations into a single, unified "woman movement."

Under Anthony's leadership, suffragists took on the work of unifying the various women's organizations. In 1888, the National Woman Suffrage Association organized and sponsored a gala, week-long International Council for Women. The initial plan, formulated by Stanton in 1883, had been to convene an international meeting of suffragists, but, two years later, the NWSA voted to expand the council to include "women workers along all lines of social, intellectual or civil progress and reform."[13] Anthony enthusiastically supported the change, hoping that the NWSA's willingness to accommodate itself to the broad range of women's reform interests and their doubts about suffragism would eventually lead to a substantial increase in their support for woman suffrage. However, while she was willing to see the International Council expanded, and to put aside her longstanding belief that woman suffrage must have a privileged place in women's reform efforts, she refused to authorize an invitation that was so broad that it included women who were opposed to woman suffrage. Instead, she saw to it that the call to the Council expressed her own suffragist conviction that "those active in great philanthropic enterprises [will] sooner or later realize that so long as women are not acknowledged to be the political equals of men, their judgment on public questions will have but little weight."[14] Stanton's opening speech to the Council, which was written under Anthony's careful supervision, represented all the gains which women had made in the last half-century—in education, economic independence, reform work, and general self-esteem—as "the natural outgrowth of the suffrage agitation" (see document 16).

Anthony's hope for the International Council was that it would be a model of harmony and united womanhood. "I don't want a controversy or a lot of negations," she warned Antoinette Brown Blackwell, "but shall tell each one to give her strongest affirmation."[15] Her goal was to show that, despite women's different political loyalties and various reform affiliations, they could still unite around the fact of their common womanhood. In many ways, the Council embodied this vision of a universal sisterhood. American women representing more than fifty suffrage, temperance, social purity, and general reform organizations attended the Congress. Feminists from nine foreign countries including India also came, many brought at the NWSA's expense. Perhaps most important, the Council defined "representative women" more broadly than other women's congresses of the period. Although white women of the middle and upper classes predominated, other women's voices could be heard. Huldah Loud, head of the Women's Department of the Knights of Labor, was a featured speaker. Even the color bar was crossed as Frances Ellen Harper, a leading Black feminist, spoke in the session on temperance about the obligation of the rich to the poor.[16] The only crack in the Council's pacific surface came in the closing session, when Stanton predicted that unless the question of women's freedom received "serious consideration" from men in power, "like every other step in progress, it will eventually be settled by violence." "Awake to their own wrongs, as they have never been before . . . ," she suggested, "it requires no prophet to foretell the revolution ahead when women strike hands with Nihilists, Socialists, Communists, and Anarchists, in defense of the most enlarged liberties of the people." Many protested her association of the women's movement with revolutionaries. "Mrs. Stanton's words fell dead on the audience," Lucy Stone assured a friend. "They had no response whatsoever."[17]

Anthony was extremely proud of the International Council, which was one of the most ambitious projects that the NWSA ever undertook. It figures prominently in her authorized biography, in the *History of Woman Suffrage*, and in other quasi-official accounts of the suffrage movement. How enduring were its successes, however? The 1888 International Council undoubtedly enhanced the pride and sense of sisterhood felt by reform-minded women in the United States and abroad. In particular it inaugurated an era of organizational consolidation among American women. A permanent National Council of Women was formed, the first multi-reform national women's organization ever founded in the United States; its goals included equal pay for women, increased access to industrial and professional education, and a single moral standard for both sexes. The formation of the National Council of Women was followed within a year by the creation of a second national organization, the General Federation of Women's Clubs. Both the National Council and the General Federation encouraged the formation of state and local affiliates and did a great deal to increase and consolidate women's ability to control community institutions and affect state and municipal governments.[18]

However, these developments did not generate as much support for woman suffrage as Anthony had hoped they would. During the 1888 International Council, suffrage was treated very cautiously. The session in which it was discussed was cautiously titled "political conditions" and enfranchisement was not included in the Council's final statement of goals. The National Council of Women also refused to adopt woman suffrage as one of its principles. Indeed, this reluctance to endorse the demand for the vote was so pronounced that, on the occasion of the 1899 International Council, antisuffragists were invited to participate in the session on "political conditions," and suffragists withdrew from the organization. Historian Richard Evans points out that the creation of an International Council of Women did so little to advance the suffrage movement worldwide that by 1904 American suffragists had to form an entirely new organization for that purpose, the International Women Suffrage Alliance.[19] Nor did the General Federation of Women's Clubs support suffrage until 1914, on the very eve of victory.[20] Anthony was mystified and disappointed by the fact that the consolidation of American women's organizations, to which she had contributed so much, had not done more to benefit woman suffrage. "The Federation of Clubs ... can count forty thousand members ... the Christian Temperance Union ... can report a half-million members; I will tell you frankly and honestly that all we number is seven thousand," she explained in 1893. "... what a hindrance this lack has been. ... If we could have demonstrated to the Congress ... that we had a thorough organization back of our demand, we should have had all our demands granted long ago."[21]

Simultaneous with the International Council, and out of a similar spirit of harmony and the desire to draw together women's organizational power, the suffrage movement itself began to unite. Ever since the initial split in 1869 there had been many calls for the unification of the National Woman Suffrage Association, led by Stanton and Anthony, and the American Woman Suffrage Association, led by Lucy Stone and Henry Blackwell, but not until the late 1880s were there any initiatives from the leaders of either organization.[22] In 1887, Alice Stone Blackwell, daughter of Stone and Blackwell and corresponding secretary of the American, proposed a joint meeting to consider merger. In a later account of the period, she explained that the American became willing to merge with the National because "the question of easy divorce" and "persons ... of notorious immorality" were no longer welcomed on the National's platform.[23] Representatives of the National responded enthusiastically to her invitation, formed a committee to discuss unification, and invited the leaders of the American to participate in the International Council, which was the first time the two organizations had cooperated in many years.[24]

Within the National, Anthony was a leading force for merger. From the beginning of the negotiations process, she was convinced that "the best good for women's enfranchisement ... surely will come through the union of all the friends of woman suffrage into one great and grand National Association. ..."[25] Her enthusiasm was consistent with her general effort in this period to set aside political differences among women in order to create the largest possible unity around the demand for the vote. At no time during the negotiations did she question the desirability of the merger or seriously examine the terms in which it was being proposed. "I cannot think of any stipulation I wish to make the basis of union," she wrote, "save that we unite and after that discuss all measures. ..."[26] Her position surprised many in light of the intense hatred she had often expressed for the leaders of the American, especially for Lucy Stone. To herself and others, Anthony justified her reversal by contending that the American was anxious to affiliate with the National, which it now recognized as the stronger and more successful of the two organizations. "They have always been on the *defensive* ... ," she wrote to Olympia Brown, "... while we have gone on from triumph to triumph, until they see and feel and want to share our glory and power."[27] Inasmuch as most of the terms of the merger were set by the American, there was considerable self-deception involved in her claim that the American was dissolving itself into the National.

Despite Anthony's authority and her efforts to convince friends and recruits to "stand by Susan once more," she faced opposition within the National that delayed the merger for two years.[28] Leading opponents to the move included veteran suffragists like Olympia Brown and Matilda Joslyn Gage, and young activists such as Clara Colby and Harriette Shattuck. Linking all their objections was their fear that the essence of the National's approach to suffrage would somehow be lost through unification. They were concerned that merger would lead to the abandonment of the National's strategic focus on federal citizenship and the ideological message it carried of women's full and absolute equality with men. They feared that suffragists would concentrate instead on enfranchisement at the state level, or worse, on partial suffrages, like the school or municipal vote. They objected to the proposed plan of organization, which they charged would shift the focus of organizational activity from the national society to the state and local affiliates.[29] Opponents of the merger believed that a majority of the members of the National supported them, and moved that the issue be submitted to a vote of the whole organization, but the National's Executive Committee, which was controlled by pro-union forces, refused, and itself made the decision to merge with the American. "The executive sessions . . . were the most stormy in the history of the association," Ida Harper, Anthony's biographer, wrote, "and only the unsurpassed parliamentary knowledge of the chairman, May Wright Sewall, aided by the firm cooperation of Miss Anthony, could have harmonized the opposing elements and secured a majority in favor of union."[30] In February, 1890, the two organizations met in joint convention and declared themselves the National American Woman Suffrage Association (NAWSA).

Like the International Council, the unification of the suffrage movement reflected the belief that political and ideological differences among women were far less important than, and could be subordinated to, their common struggle for enfranchisement. "The time is past when the mass of the suffrage women will be compromised by any one person's peculiarities!" Anthony wrote Stanton in 1897. "We number over ten thousand women and each one has opinions . . . and we can only hold them together to work for the ballot by letting alone their whims and prejudices on other subjects."[31] Thus, although Anthony was personally antiracist, she opposed all efforts to raise the question of discrimination against Black women in the NAWSA because she feared it would anger Southern white suffragists.[32] This approach to unity within the feminist movement was paralleled by a strategy for winning support outside it that refused to make political distinctions among potential allies. This "nonpartisan" approach was explicitly articulated at the NAWSA's founding convention, during a session on "Our Attitude Toward Political Parties." "The sentiment was in favor of keeping strictly aloof from all political alliances," Anthony and Ida Harper wrote. "It was shown that suffrage can only be gained through the assistance of men in all parties."[33] The "nonpartisan" posture that Anthony helped to shape remained the official strategy of the NAWSA for the next thirty years, and was carried over, after the vote was won, into the NAWSA's successor, the League of Women Voters.

However, the strategy of nonpartisanship had its weaknesses. It put a great deal of pressure on suffragists not to do anything that would divide their movement or drive support away. The result was a suffrage organization that could not tolerate serious political dissent and forced it outside. Throughout its history, the NAWSA was plagued by a series of organizational secessions, beginning with the Women's National Liberation Association, formed by Matilda Gage in 1890, and culminating in the Congressional Union, which broke away from the NAWSA in 1913.[34] Moreover, nonpartisanship was at crucial points an illusion. Even while the NAWSA proclaimed that it held aloof from politics, its "nonpartisan" stance both encouraged and helped to obscure the conservative ideas that were coming to dominate it, not only about women's role but about social reform in general. The NAWSA's antiradical bias began to emerge in reaction to the growth of Populism in the 1890s. In South Dakota, Kansas, and other states where Populists instigated and led woman suffrage campaigns, Anthony and other NAWSA leaders, barely hiding their distaste for Populist radicalism, concentrated their energies on courting Republican support, and organized "nonpartisan" suffrage societies in which only Republican women participated.[35] Some political conflicts are impossible to avoid, and in these cases the NAWSA's "nonpartisanship" inclined it toward conservatism and away from those who challenged established power, encouraged conflict, and exposed and mobilized social discontent.

Stanton and the Future of Suffrage Radicalism

Elizabeth Stanton's relation to the late nineteenth-century women's movement was quite different and far more uneasy than Anthony's. In many ways she was the first victim of the NAWSA's emphasis on unity, hostility to dissent, and implicit conservatism. While Anthony devoted herself to the unification of all women around the demand for the vote, Stanton understood that there were profound political differences that support for woman suffrage and the common fact of gender could not obscure forever. In a movement that was growing in conservatism, she was still temperamentally very much a radical, eager as she had always been to lead women to the most comprehensive and challenging interpretation of what it meant to be free. She was elected first president of the NAWSA in 1890, not because she represented the spirit of consolidation and "affirmation" that had led to the merger—she did not—but because Anthony insisted that she must have the office and that "every woman . . . who has any love for Susan B. Anthony . . . don't vote for any human being but Mrs. Stanton." Even so, 40 percent of those voting refused to support Stanton, and she remained in office only two difficult years.[36]

The whole thrust of Stanton's leadership was a challenge to the idea, fast becoming the watchword of the suffrage movement, that what women wanted to do with the ballot was irrelevant to their struggle to win it. She raised disturbing questions about what women wanted out of the political process, both for their own emancipation and for the reform of society in general. From the beginning of her presidency, she dissented from Anthony's "nonpartisan" strategy for winning outside support, and challenged the idea that the drive for woman suffrage should—or could—be isolated from political developments in the larger society (see document 18). Inasmuch as "our demands are to be made and carried like other political questions, by the aid of and affiliation with parties," she insisted, "it is puerile to say 'no matter how we use the ballot the right is ours.' "[37] While Anthony had concluded from her Reconstruction-era experience that political alliances inevitably compromised suffragism, Stanton learned a different lesson. She believed that feminists must continue to make themselves part of a larger political movement, but must do so from a position of independent strength and ally with the most radical and democratic forces they could find. Accordingly, she was enthusiastic about the Populists in the early 1890s, and, by the end of the decade, had identified herself with the growing socialist movement in the United States.[38]

However, Stanton challenged suffrage unity less by promoting alliances with other political movements, than by questioning the suffragists' own political program for the emancipation of women. She recognized that suffragists disagreed about what constituted the "civil, political, religious, social, educational, industrial rights" of women, and how to use the ballot to gain them.[39] Her own perspective on women's emancipation was significantly more radical than that which was coming to dominate the women's movement, and to call into question this growing orthodoxy, she insisted on full and open debate. "The fact that we differ on all these points is the very reason we should discuss them," she explained some years later. "If to question . . . is heresy in this Association, the sooner it is rent in twain the better."[40]

Above all, it was Stanton's systematic critique of Christianity which led her to challenge the suffrage mainstream. Although she had always been an anticleric and an opponent of Calvinism, her criticisms of the Christian religion became much more important to her in her later years. She was especially influenced by the secularist movement which developed in the late 1880s in England, where her daughter lived and where she spent a great deal of time.[41] In England, the continued existence of an established church meant that non-Christians could not sit in Parliament and that "blasphemy," which included antigovernment remarks, was a civil crime. Thus, the secularist demand for the complete separation of church and state was still a powerful political issue. Stanton knew and admired the leaders of British secularism—George Holyoake, Charles Bradlaugh, and especially Annie Besant, who like Stanton tried to combine freethought, sexual radicalism, and feminism. Stanton's studies in this period were profoundly shaped by intellectual currents closely associated with British secularism, such as Positivism, Biblical criticism, and the anthropological study of primitive societies.[42]

Like other secularists, Stanton argued that organized religion had a conservative impact on society; it led to tolerance for superstition, inculcated a spirit of submission to authority, looked to divine rather than human action, and encouraged charity rather than rebellion as a response to human suffering. Her particular emphasis, however, was feminist, and she charged Christianity with a special animus toward women (see document 19). She marshaled impressive historical evidence to show that the status of women in pre-Christian societies had been high, and that the spread of Christianity had debased the position of women. She charged the Christian church with excluding women from the priesthood and denying their divinity, thus identifying the deity solely with the masculine element. However, despite the contribution that Christianity had made to their oppression, she observed that women remained "the chief supporters of the church today," victims of its doctrine of female inferiority. "It has been through the perversion of [woman's] religious sentiments," Stanton concluded, "that she has been so long held in a condition of slavery."[43]

In considering the hold that religion had over women, Stanton found part of the answer in the deflection of their sexual attraction for men into religious passion for Jesus.[44] Like other feminist freethinkers, her criticisms of Christianity's spiritual claims were closely related to her challenge to existing sexual morality. In contrast to those who believed that Christian ethics were at the root of sexual decency, she argued that Christianity identified women with sexual corruption and was responsible for the double standard which oppressed nineteenth-century women. At the deepest level, Stanton dissented from the belief that the best way to understand human sexuality was by determining what constituted a proper sexual morality. In general she was skeptical of the idea that a universal standard of morality could be ascertained, and she utterly rejected the notion that it had triumphed under modern Christianity. "There never has been any true standard of social morality, and none exists to day," she insisted. ". . . What constitutes chastity changes with time and latitude; its definition would be as varied as is public opinion on other subjects."[45]

Back in the United States, Stanton's conviction that religion was at the root of women's oppression ran headlong into the growing power of Christian ideology within the women's movement. The WCTU was the center of this "Christian feminism," and Frances Willard was its most articulate spokeswoman. Unlike Stanton, Christian feminists believed that the spread of Christianity had profoundly elevated the status of women. They encouraged women's religious convictions as a way to develop their social conscience and their pride in womanhood. They believed that a strong community consensus based on Christian ethics would help to protect women, and they feared that its disintegration would increase women's abuse and exploitation. Nor were these differences merely philosophical; they were political in the most concrete sense of the word. Christian feminism was part of a general late nineteenth-century political movement, which not only promoted religious values, but sought to introduce them into law. Christian reformers, men and women alike, agitated for a Constitutional amendment recognizing Christianity, won state and local laws enforcing Sunday closings, and advocated censorship, antidivorce, and various other social purity legislation to use the power of the state to enforce Christian morality.[46]

Stanton took every opportunity to challenge the "Christian party in politics," its crusades against sexual immorality, and the influence it was gathering within American feminism. At the founding convention of the NAWSA, she insisted on declaring her opposition to the "women [who] are taking an active part in pressing on the consideration of Congress many narrow sectarian measures," some of whom were sitting alongside her on the platform.[47] She also introduced a resolution condemning the efforts of the National Reform Association, a social purity organization that included many feminists, to secure a federal law to reduce the number of divorces by severely limiting the grounds on which they could be obtained.[48] At the

1891 convention, she took the extremely unpopular position of defending the Irish patriot Charles Parnell, who was being hounded by the British and American public because he was an adulterer.[49] And in 1892 she began a campaign that brought her into direct conflict with the WCTU and other Christian reform organizations, to keep the Chicago World's Fair open on Sundays.[50]

Stanton's secularism in particular and her radicalism in general made her very unpopular among many feminists. Although she won a small minority over to her freethought perspective, most influential suffragists rejected her ideas and her leadership.[51] As president of the NAWSA she had little real power and few allies. Anna Howard Shaw, Anthony's protégé and an ordained Methodist minister, strongly opposed Stanton's election as president. "If [Aunt Susan] will crowd Mrs. Stanton down our throats, well we won't have her if we can help it . . ." she wrote to a friend in 1890. "I have said from the first I will not work under and will work to defeat Mrs. S."[52] Carrie Chapman Catt, who eventually led the suffrage movement to victory, also neither liked Stanton, whom she met in 1890, nor respected Anthony's devotion to her.[53] Stanton's resolutions were often ignored and she took to hiding her authorship in hopes of getting them passed. She held her office reluctantly, offering to resign after the first year, and spent most of her time in England. Finally, in 1892, she succeeded in leaving her office. "It is not good for all our thoughts or interests to run in one groove," she wrote to Olympia Brown. "For this reason I resigned the office I held."[54] Once she had resigned, she no longer felt the need to spend so much time abroad and she returned to the United States, where she lived without interruption until she died. Anthony, who had been virtual leader of the NAWSA since its formation, succeeded her as its president, an office she held until 1900.

How shall we evaluate Stanton's impassioned commitment to the secularist cause? Anthony believed that Stanton, in her zeal against Christianity, was attacking the very beliefs which were bringing large numbers of late nineteenth-century women and men into woman suffrage and other reform movements.[55]

Anthony respected the sincerity and commitment of the many religiously-motivated women who were flocking into feminism, and thought it was folly to attack or antagonize them. She believed that the battle against religious superstition and clerical authority had been fought and won long before, and that Stanton was wasting her energies on an antiquated issue. Yet the Christian morality from which Stanton dissented did indeed run counter to the feminist commitment to individual self-determination for women, especially in sexual matters. Moreover, the spread of Christian ideology in this period was introducing weaknesses into the American reform tradition, even as it was helping otherwise to reinvigorate it. Reformers who were rooted in the Christian dedication to harmony and reconciliation found it difficult to admit the existence of differences that could not be reconciled, or conflicts that could not be avoided.[56] Moreover, the assumption of Christian reformers that their values reflected the moral consensus of the entire community was self-righteous. Their habit of deciding what was good for society by appealing to a set of absolute beliefs that were determined morally and not politically was ultimately undemocratic. Stanton's secularist distrust of Christianity helped her to understand this and to grasp something of the coercive and paternalistic approach that was becoming more important to American reform in this period, and would reach full flower with Progressivism.

Stanton's most famous speech, "The Solitude of Self," was delivered at the convention at which she resigned the presidency of the NAWSA (see document 20). It was her swan song as leader of suffragism, and in it she presented the philosophical core of her thought about women's emancipation, as well as the differences between her ideas and those which were coming to dominate the suffrage movement. Her basic message was "the infinite diversity in human character" and the necessity of equal rights for all individuals, themes which had always been central to her feminism. Her approach to women's emancipation, which stressed the liberation of each woman's unique capacities and inclinations, was being eclipsed by an emphasis on that which was allegedly common to all women, the attributes and

abilities that women, once freed of male influence, were expected to share. Stanton conceded the claims of gender, the fact
that women had common concerns as "mother, wife, sister and
daughter," and even more as a sex equal in importance to men.
However, in determining women's rights, both of these considerations were far less important to her than "the individuality of
each human soul," the human condition which simultaneously
distinguishes each of us from the other, and is common to us all,
women and men alike.

Stanton's individualism had its roots in the past, in classical
natural rights thought, but it looked forward as well, to aspects
of modern twentieth-century feminism, anticipating what Angelina Grimké had once described as "new forms of truth . . . to
test the faithfulness of the pioneer minds of the age."[57] The individual of whom Stanton spoke was not just a creature of political philosophy, but of psychology as well. The new note Stanton struck as she insisted on "the solitude of self" was
existential. Although she urged women to continue to fight for
equality in "the outer conditions of human beings," she also encouraged them to struggle for full development and independence in the "inner" aspects as well. Even as she was moving toward socialism, and realizing the importance of cooperation as a
principle of social organization, her bequest to the women of the
future stressed the psychological dimension of freedom and defended the importance of individual self-determination for
women.

Four years after Stanton's resignation, the breach between
her and other leading suffragists widened. In late 1895, she finally published *The Woman's Bible*, a feminist commentary on
the Old Testament. Since 1886, she had been planning an ambitious study of the Bible that would avoid treating it as a "fetish," but would assess what it had to say about women's position, "as [one would] any book of human origin."[58] She tried to
interest women of widely differing opinions to join the project,
which she hoped would provide a debate on whether the Bible
taught women's inferiority or their equality. Leading Christian
feminists, including Frances Willard, were intrigued by the
project but ultimately did not participate because they feared

their conservative constituencies would see it as an attack on the Bible and be offended by it.[59] Finally, in 1894, Stanton began *The Woman's Bible* on a much less ambitious scale. She was assisted mainly by other feminist freethinkers, but also by a few exceptionally courageous religious women, such as the Reverend Phoebe Hanaford. Each commentator, Christian or freethinker, considered various Biblical passages as they supported or contradicted her particular beliefs. In her own commentaries, Stanton praised those few parts of the Bible that she believed depicted women as courageous and self-respecting, and criticized the many passages which seemed to her to degrade women and teach men to have contempt for them.

Within the women's movement and especially in the NAWSA, the publication of *The Woman's Bible* raised a storm of protest. *The Washington Post* reported that Anthony tried to establish a "truce" between Stanton's critics and her supporters but failed. Instead, at the 1896 NAWSA convention, there was "animated and at times rather personal" debate over *The Woman's Bible*. Corresponding secretary Rachel Foster Avery denounced the book in her annual report. "[It is] a volume with a pretentious title . . . without either scholarship or literary value, set forth in a spirit which is neither that of reverence or inquiry," Avery declared. "I recommend that we take some action by resolution to show that the Association is not responsible for the individual actions of its officers." (Stanton was not an officer.) Many suffragists spoke in Stanton's defense, including Charlotte Perkins Stetson (later Gilman), who was attending her first national suffrage convention, and Lillie Devereux Blake, who exposed the fact that only a minority of the critics of *The Woman's Bible* had even read it. Despite their arguments, a resolution was introduced declaring the NAWSA a "nonsectarian"—not nonreligious—organization and disavowing any connection with *The Woman's Bible*. The resolution passed, fifty-three to forty-one.[60]

Anthony was profoundly disturbed by the convention's attack on *The Woman's Bible* (see document 19). She left the chair to join the debate and defended Stanton with great passion. Anthony rejected the resolution both because she believed that "the right of individual opinion" must be protected, and because she recognized that the convention's repudiation of "one who has stood for half a century the acknowledged leader of progressive thought . . . in regard to . . . the absolute freedom of women" was a victory for conservatism. Yet Anthony herself had built the organization that had turned against Stanton. Every one of the younger women she had recruited into suffrage work voted against *The Woman's Bible,* and several—Rachel Foster Avery, Harriet Taylor Upton, Anna Howard Shaw—spearheaded the drive to repudiate it. The entire affair caused Anthony "great agony of spirit," and she briefly considered resigning, but in the end she rejected the idea and returned to her vision of a single-minded, "nonpartisan" suffrage movement, free of "entanglements" and inhospitable to radicalism.[61]

Through all this, Anthony's personal attachment to Stanton remained strong. "I never expect to know any joy in this world equal to that of going up and down the land . . . engaging halls and circulating Mrs. Stanton's speeches," she said. "If I ever have had any inspiration, she has given it to me."[62] Yet, despite her tremendous respect for Stanton and her tendency to portray herself as her intellectual dependent, a mere "hewer of wood and drawer of water" for a great philosopher and stateswoman, Anthony had found her own way politically;[63] and this way, although it was sometimes difficult for her to acknowledge, was different from Stanton's. While Stanton believed (in Anthony's words) that "women should take up . . . public questions which so evidently need the combined wisdom of men and women in their solution," Anthony was convinced that this would "create animosities and alienate supporters of a cause which can achieve victory only through the assistance of all religious bodies and political parties."[64] When Anthony retired from the presidency of the NAWSA in 1900, and identified Carrie Chapman Catt as her successor, Stanton and other insurgents supported a rival candidate.[65] Despite their enduring friendship, Stanton and Anthony were no longer united by a common political perspective and had ceased to provide American feminism with the same kind of leadership.

The *Woman's Bible* incident greatly accelerated Stanton's

alienation from the suffrage movement in the last years of her life. She had always demanded the suffrage, both because she thought it was women's right, and because she believed women would be a liberal and democratic force in politics. Now, she wrote, "Much as I desire the suffrage I would rather never vote than to see the policy of our government at the mercy of the religious bigotry of such women. My heart's desire is to lift women out of all these dangerous and degrading superstitions, and to this end will I labor my remaining days on earth." Deposed from leadership and increasingly aware that she had very little time left, she searched for ways to get her ideas across to American women. "I want to publish and scatter many good things on all questions before I leave this planet," she wrote two years before her death.[66] In 1898 she published her autobiography, *Eighty Years and More*, which, she complained, the suffrage press did not adequately review. For years she had resisted Anthony's efforts to issue a volume of her speeches and writings, but now she searched desperately for financial backing for an edition. She wrote to Carnegie and Rockefeller for money, but got only $500 from the latter.[67] The volume never appeared. This last disappointment left her uncharacteristically bitter. "If my suffrage coadjutors had ever treated me with the boundless generosity they have my friend Susan, I could have scattered my writings abundantly," she wrote to Elizabeth Boynton Harbert, one of the few young suffragists who continued to support her. "They have given Susan thousands of dollars, jewels, laces, silks and satins, and me criticisms for my radical ideas."[68]

Stanton died in 1902, Anthony four years later (see document 21). After their deaths, they were remembered quite differently. Many devoted followers carefully preserved Anthony's memory, literally making her a suffrage saint. Her home was made into a museum, her papers were collected in repositories on the East and West Coasts, and the story of her life was told in several honorific biographies.[69] Stanton was nowhere near as glorified. Her children issued a single volume of her letters, but otherwise no effort was made to collect her writings or remember her to later generations of women. She was not even the subject of a full-length biography until 1940.[70] The extraordinary breadth of her historical contribution—her interest in divorce reform and her passionate secularism, as well as her advocacy of the vote—was largely forgotten. In general, Stanton was honored only for her earliest accomplishments, in particular the Seneca Falls convention, while Anthony was identified with the whole history—and eventual triumph—of the woman suffrage movement.

From one perspective, the uneven honor paid Stanton and Anthony is understandable. By the end of their lives, their common conviction about the importance of enfranchising women had developed into two quite different approaches to building the woman suffrage movement. Stanton's perspective had been defeated. Her insistence that suffragists have a common political program for social reform and women's emancipation had been discredited. Instead, Anthony's belief that no other issue must be allowed to intrude on the question of political equality for women had come to predominate. The twentieth-century suffrage movement pursued this strategic direction; suffrage leaders who followed Anthony succeeded in unifying enormous numbers of women around the demand for the vote and marshaling their power to overcome opposition and force the enfranchisement of women. Inasmuch as Stanton and Anthony advocated different paths for suffragism, Anthony's path triumphed, and enfranchisement was eventually won, the victory has been laid at Anthony's feet and it is her leadership that the historical record commemorates.

From another perspective, however, this is an inadequate interpretation, a distortion embedded in the record of the suffrage movement itself. Remembering Anthony while forgetting Stanton is an historical half-truth, a serious obstacle to assessing the full meaning of the woman suffrage movement. If Anthony's triumph is an index to the movement's successes, Stanton's defeat has a great deal to tell us about its failures. In particular, the defeat of Stanton can help us to understand why the woman suffrage movement did not do more to transform "the bonds of womanhood" into an enduring political force. More than any other leader of the woman suffrage movement, Stanton had urged that women's solidarity be based on an explicit political program for social reform and women's emancipation. The party platform she drafted in 1872 made this very clear, as did her stubborn insistence through the 1890s that suffragists acknowledge and debate their many political differences. This approach to women's solidarity was rejected in favor of reliance on the simple fact of gender to unite women politically. The consequences of this choice for the future of women were enormous. The political effectiveness of the women's movement organized on this basis proved extremely limited. Suffragism, which had begun as a product of political forces like the French Revolution, utopian socialism, and abolitionism, no longer understood itself primarily as part of a larger political effort to transform society and achieve true democracy. Similarly, it no longer connected itself with the radical transformation of the sexual order and the emancipation of women from coercive sexual stereotypes. Indeed, it was at the point that the suffrage movement was consolidated that a new term—"feminism"— had to be invented to distinguish the small minority who called for radical transformation in women's lives from the great majority of suffragists who intended no such challenge.[71] The common fact of gender proved politically meaningless once the sole political measure on which agreement had been reached, woman suffrage, was achieved, and at this point the organized women's movement rapidly dissolved. To compound the tragedy, suffragists' decision to rely on the biological fact of gender to unite women, rather than on more political factors, may well have helped to strengthen and rebuild coercive sexual stereotypes, thus contributing to the creation of a new version of "true womanhood" against which a future feminist movement would eventually emerge to protest.[72]

NOTES

1. On the Women's Christian Temperance Union, see Mary Earhart, *Frances Willard: From Prayers to Politics* (Chicago: University of Chicago Press, 1944). On the club movement and the Women's Educational and Industrial Union, see Karen Blair, *The Clubwoman as Feminist: True Womanhood Redefined, 1868–1914* (New York:

Holmes and Meier, 1980). Black women formed their own organizations, both because their interests were different and because they were excluded from white women's societies, but their clubs and temperance unions shared many of the same characteristics. See Gerda Lerner, "Early Community Work of Black Club Women," *The Journal of Negro History*, Vol. 59 (1974), pp. 158–67; and Cynthia Neverdon-Morton, "The Black Woman's Struggle for Equality in the South, 1895–1915," in *The Afro-American Woman: Struggles and Images*, eds. Rosalyn Terborg-Penn and Sharon Harley (Port Washington, N.Y.: Kennikat Press, 1978), pp. 43–57.

2. Margaret Fuller, who believed that it was important to develop the "female element" in society—she also called it "femality"—was a major influence on many club leaders, for instance Julia Ward Howe and Caroline Severance.

3. These themes were very prominent in the Association for the Advancement of Women, a national organization formed in 1873 by the New England Women's Club and New York's Sorosis to encourage the formation of women's clubs (see Blair, *Clubwoman*); the first meeting of the AAW focused on "Enlightened Motherhood" and "The Inviolable Home."

4. The quotation is from a speech on "The Inviolable Home," by Charlotte Beebe Wilbour, *Association for the Advancement of Women, Papers and Letters* (New York: Mrs. Wm. Ballard, Book & Job Printer, 1874), p. 71. The New England Women's Club, Young Women's Christian Association, Women's Educational and Industrial Union, and Sorosis all took an early interest in working girls. By the mid-1880s there was a distinct branch of the club movement, the Working Girls Societies, devoted entirely to these concerns.

5. See, for instance, "An Historical Sketch of the New England Women's Club," 1884, pamphlet, Julia Ward Howe Papers, Schlesinger Library: "Care was to be taken to give the organization such a form as should make it self-protective against disturbing elements, that thus it might become . . . a place where women should have opportunity for culture in dignified . . . discussion." Also see the very interesting exchange of letters in the *Chicago Tribune*, November 27, 1873, on the social arrangements best suited to coeducation. Frances Willard argued for the necessity of careful supervision of young women to protect their reputations, while Elizabeth Stanton advised against "cribbing and crippling their natural impulses, to make them what is called 'ladylike.' " Undoubtedly, the notoriety of free lover Victoria Woodhull and the Beecher-Tilton scandal exacerbated, but did not create, this concern about the moral character of feminists (see Part Two).

6. See for instance Abigail Scott Duniway, *Pathbreaking: An Autobiographical History of the Woman Suffrage Movement in the Pa-*

cific Coast States (Portland, Ore.: James, Herns and Abbott, 1914), chap. 12.

7. Club women, few of whom had any collegiate education, frequently researched and read original papers on literary and cultural topics (Blair, *Clubwoman*). Frances Willard of the WCTU was a spectacularly successful organizer, and stressed the importance of giving as many women as possible individual responsibility; see Frances Willard, *Women and Temperance* (Hartford, Conn.: Park Publishing Co., 1883), chap. 35.

8. Blair, *Clubwoman;* F. M. Whitaker, "Ohio WCTU and the Prohibition Amendment Campaign of 1883," *Ohio History,* Vol. 83 (1974), pp. 84–102.

9. "Miss Willard is doing noble work but I cannot coincide with her view. . . . Miss Willard, in fact, has a lever but she has no fulcrum upon which to place it," ("Female Suffrage: An Interview with Susan B. Anthony," *Chicago Tribune,* December 10, 1879, p. 3).

10. Barbara Leslie Epstein, *The Politics of Domesticity: Women, Evangelism and Temperance in Nineteenth-Century America* (Middletown: Wesleyan University Press, 1981). After Willard's victory, she and Anthony became frequent correspondents and close friends.

11. Harper, *Life of Anthony,* Vol. 2 (Indianapolis: Bowen-Merrill, 1899), p. 586. The issue was Fredrick Douglass' marriage to a white woman, which Stanton believed that the suffrage movement should defend.

12. Anthony believed that she was not invited to the founding meeting of the Association for the Advancement for Women in 1873, while Stanton was, because of her arrest and trial for illegal voting earlier that same year. When Anthony led a group of women onto the platform of the 1876 American Revolution Centennial, to protest their exclusion from the ceremonies and from the blessings of American democracy in general, Lucy Stone and others criticized the "sensational manner" in which she had acted (Stone to Stanton, August 3, 1876, Blackwell Family Papers, Library of Congress). Later in her life, Anthony seemed to take particular pleasure when honor was paid her by wealthy and respectable women.

13. International Council of Women, *Women in a Changing World: The Dynamic Story of the International Council of Women since 1888* (London: Routledge and Kegan Paul, 1966), p. 11.

14. Barbara Jean Stephens, "May Wright Sewall" (unpublished Doctoral dissertation, Ball State University, 1977), p. 101.

15. Harper, *Life of Anthony,* Vol. 2, p. 634; Anthony was especially pleased that "very many conservative associations have appointed delegates" (Anthony to Elizabeth Smith Miller, January 26, 1888, Smith Family Papers, New York Public Library).

16. *Report of the International Council of Women Assembled by the National Woman Suffrage Association* (Washington, D.C.: R.H. Darby, 1888).

17. Ibid., p. 436; Lucy Stone to Edwin Start, April 27, 1888, Alma Lutz Collection, Schlesinger Library. The Washington, D.C. Federated Labor Unions also protested what they understood to be Stanton's inclusion of trade unionists along with anarchists and communists in her list of revolutionaries (*Report*, p. 164).

18. William O'Neill, *Everyone Was Brave* (Chicago: Quadrangle Books, 1969), p. 149.

19. Richard J. Evans, *The Feminists* (London: Croom Helm, 1977), p. 251; also see Edith F. Hurwitz, "The International Sisterhood," in *Becoming Visible: Women in European History*, eds. Renate Bridenthal and Claudia Koontz (Boston: Houghton Mifflin Company, 1977), p. 332.

20. Blair, *Clubwoman*, p. 112.

21. Anthony, "Organization among Women as an Instrument in Promoting the Interests of Political Liberty," in *The World Congress of Representative Women*, ed. May Wright Sewall (Chicago: Rand, McNally & Co., 1894), pp. 463–66.

22. See for instance Martha Coffin Wright to Lucy Stone, December 21, 1874, Garrison Family Papers, Smith College; and Antoinette Brown Blackwell to Lucy Stone, January 9, 1886, Blackwell Family Papers, Schlesinger Library.

23. Alice Stone Blackwell, *Lucy Stone, Pioneer of Women's Rights* (Boston: Little, Brown and Company, 1930), p. 229.

24. "Negotiations Between the American and National Associations in Regard to Union," ed. Rachel Foster Avery, pamphlet, Boston Public Library; Rachel Foster Avery to Olympia Brown, January 6, 1888, Olympia Brown Papers, Schlesinger Library.

25. Anthony to Rachel Foster, cited in Harper, *Life of Anthony*, Vol. 2, p. 628.

26. Anthony to Foster, cited in Katherine Anthony, *Susan B. Anthony: Her Personal History and Her Era* (New York: Doubleday & Co., 1954), p. 390.

27. Anthony to Olympia Brown, March 11, 1889, Olympia Brown Papers, Schlesinger Library.

28. Anthony to Mrs. Osborn, February 5, 1890, Garrison Family Papers, Smith College.

29. Harriet H. Robinson and Harriette Robinson Shattuck, "The Union, 1889," unpublished manuscript notebook, Harriet Robinson Papers, Schlesinger Library; Olympia Brown, "A Statement of Facts," privately printed pamphlet, 1889, Olympia Brown Papers, Schlesinger Library. In 1893, after the merger had been effected, the suffrage association passed a resolution encouraging women to work for municipal and school suffrage (*History of Woman Suffrage*, Vol. 4, eds. Susan

B. Anthony and Ida H. Harper [Rochester: Susan B. Anthony, 1902],
p. 216; hereafter referred to as *HWS*).

30. Harper, *Life of Anthony*, Vol. 2, p. 632.

31. Anthony to Stanton, 1897, Clara Colby Papers, Huntington Library.

32. At the 1899 NAWSA convention Anthony opposed a resolution condemning racial discrimination in public transportation; this incident is cited in Aileen Kraditor, *Ideas of the Woman Suffrage Movement, 1890–1920* (New York: Columbia University Press, 1965), p. 172.

33. *HWS*, Vol. 4, p. 173.

34. *Women's National Liberal Union, A Report of the Convention for Organization, February 24–25, 1890* (Syracuse: Masters and Stone Printers, 1890); Inez H. Irwin, *The Story of the National Women's Party* (New York: Harcourt, 1921). In addition, Olympia Brown formed the Federal Suffrage Association in 1892 to promote a Constitutional amendment (Olympia Brown, "History of the Federal Suffrage Association," unpublished manuscript, Olympia Brown Papers, Schlesinger Library).

35. Dorinda Russen Reed, "The Woman Suffrage Movement in South Dakota" (State University of South Dakota: Governmental Research Bulletin no. 41, 1958); also see Anthony to Mr. Bowman, September 7, 1894, Ida Harper Papers, Huntington Library. In Kansas, the Populists endorsed woman suffrage and the Republicans, despite Anthony's best efforts, did not; reluctantly, she joined the Populist campaign, speaking only on behalf of woman suffrage, but she was mercilessly criticized by other Eastern suffragists nonetheless (Blackwell to Anthony, July 13, 1894, Blackwell Family Papers, Library of Congress).

36. Harper, *Life of Anthony*, Vol. 2, pp. 631–32.

37. In addition to her speech to the 1890 founding convention, which is reprinted below as document 18, Stanton addressed these questions in a written dissent to the discussion on political parties (Stanton, "What Should Be Our Attitude Toward Political Parties," unpublished manuscript, Elizabeth Cady Stanton Papers, Library of Congress); quotations are taken from both documents.

38. "I have just had an article in the *Sun* in which I recommend our friends to join the People's Party. If the Prohibitionists, the Populists, the labor organizations and the women would all unite, we should be in the majority" (Diary entry, August, 1894, *Elizabeth Cady Stanton as Revealed in Her Letters, Diary and Reminiscences*, eds. Theodore Stanton and Harriot Stanton Blatch [New York: Harper & Brothers, Publishers, 1922], p. 307). On socialism, to an 1898 NAWSA convention, she wrote, "Those who have eyes to see recognize the fact that the period for all . . . fragmentary reforms has ended. Agitation of the broader question of philosophical socialism is now in order. This

next step in progress ... is now being agitated by able thinkers and writers in all civilized countries" (manuscript letter, Susan B. Anthony Papers, University of Rochester).

39. Stanton, "What Should Be Our Attitude."

40. Stanton, "Open Letter to the Suffrage Convention, 1898," unidentified clipping, Elizabeth Cady Stanton Papers, Library of Congress.

41. Susan Budd, *Varieties of Unbelief: Atheists and Agnostics in English Society, 1850–1960* (London: Heinemann, 1977).

42. Stanton, *Eighty Years and More, Reminiscences, 1815–1897* (New York: T. Fischer Unwin, 1898), especially chaps. 22–26. Stanton's concerns with religion permeate her autobiography.

43. Stanton, "Has Christianity Benefited Woman?" *North American Review*, Vol. 140 (1885), pp. 389–99.

44. Stanton to Harriot Stanton, April 17, 1880, Elizabeth Cady Stanton Papers, Library of Congress.

45. Stanton, "Patriotism and Chastity," *Westminster Review*, Vol. 135 (1891), pp. 1–5; I wish to thank Mari Jo Buhle for bringing this article to my attention.

46. David Pivar, *Purity Crusade: Sexual Morality and Social Control, 1868–1900* (Westport, Conn.: Greenwood Press, 1973); Sidney Warren, *American Freethought, 1860–1914* (New York: Columbia University Press, 1943).

47. Stanton, "Address to the 1890 Convention" (see document 18). Frances Willard was active in the Prohibition party, which supported a Constitutional amendment and stricter blue laws; Mary Livermore, Julia Ward Howe, Antoinette Brown Blackwell, and others were very involved in the social purity movement and its efforts to restrict divorce legislation (Pivar, *Purity Crusade*).

48. *HWS*, Vol. 4, p. 165; also see Stanton, "Divorce Versus Domestic Warfare," *Arena*, Vol. 5 (1890), pp. 560–69.

49. See note 42 above.

50. Stanton, "Sunday at the World's Fair," *North American Review*, Vol. 154 (1892), pp. 254–56; in 1893, Stanton also produced a leaflet, "Open the World's Fair on Sunday," which she distributed widely.

51. Other freethinkers in the suffrage movement included Matilda J. Gage, Olympia Brown, Josephine Henry, and Clara Colby; also see *Heroines of Freethought*, by Sara Underwood, a friend of Stanton (New York: Charles B. Somerby, 1876).

52. Shaw to Lucy Anthony, January 20, 1890, Mary Earhart Dillon Collection, Schlesinger Library.

53. Carrie Chapman Catt to Alice Stone Blackwell, September 18, 1930, Carrie Chapman Catt Papers, Huntington Library; also see Katherine Anthony, *Susan B. Anthony*, p. 438.

54. Stanton to Olympia Brown, November 11, 1892, Olympia Brown Papers, Schlesinger Library.

55. Anthony to Olympia Brown, March 11, 1889, ibid.; Anthony to Stanton, July 24, 1895, Clara Colby Papers, Huntington Library.

56. Consider, by way of contrast, Stanton's approach to political conflict: "where there are good elements on both sides . . . reconciliation but where there is unpardonable or unmitigated wrong *direct action* (see document 14). Angelina Grimké's 1851 advice to Stanton, cited in the epigraph to this book, begins, "Conflict is essential to growth; don't be weary of it" (Angelina Grimké Weld to Stanton, reprinted in *The Lily*, October, 1851, p. 75).

57. Ibid.

58. Stanton to Elizabeth Boynton Harbert, September 15, n.y., Elizabeth Boynton Harbert Papers, Huntington Library.

59. Mary Livermore to Stanton, September 1, 1886, Elizabeth Cady Stanton Papers, Library of Congress; Lady Henry Somerset to Stanton, June 5, 1895, ibid.

60. *The Washington Post*, January 28, 1896, and January 29, 1896, clippings in the Susan B. Anthony Papers, Library of Congress; also "The Washington Convention," *Woman's Journal*, February 1, 1896, p. 1. Despite the suffragists' repudiation of *The Woman's Bible*, it went through three editions in the United States and England; in 1898, Stanton issued a second volume, covering the New Testament.

61. Harper, *Life of Anthony*, Vol. 2, pp. 855–57.

62. Ibid., p. 667. Anthony made her remarks in 1890, at the celebration of her seventieth birthday.

63. International Council of Women, *Second Quinquennial Meeting: Proceedings* (London: T. Fisher Unwin, 1900), p. 62.

64. Anthony, "Women's Half-Century of Evolution," *North American Review*, Vol. 175 (1902), p. 807.

65. Lois Banner, *Elizabeth Cady Stanton: A Radical for Women's Rights* (Boston: Little, Brown & Co., 1980), pp. 171–72.

66. Stanton to Elizabeth Boynton Harbert, June 7, 1900, Elizabeth Boynton Harbert Papers, Huntington Library.

67. Stanton to Harbert, September 30, 1902, ibid.

68. Stanton to Harbert, June 7, 1900, ibid.

69. On the West Coast, Anthony memorabilia were collected by Una Winter and housed initially at the Los Angeles Public Library and later at the Huntington Library. On the East Coast, collections were established by the Susan B. Anthony Memorial, Inc., and housed in Anthony's home, now a museum, and at the Rochester Public Library. The University of Rochester has since established its own collection. Biographies of Anthony include Ida Husted Harper, *The Life and Work of Susan B. Anthony* (3 volumes); Katherine Anthony, *Susan B. Anthony: Her Personal History and Her Era*; Rheta Childe

Dorr, *Susan B. Anthony: The Woman Who Changed the Mind of a Nation* (New York: Frederick A. Stokes, 1928); and Alma Lutz, *Susan B. Anthony: Rebel, Crusader, Humanitarian* (Boston: Beacon, 1959). In 1980, Congress passed a bill designating Stanton's home, the church where the first women's rights convention was held, and other sites in Seneca Falls, New York, as a national historical park for women's rights.

70. Alma Lutz, *Created Equal.*

71. Deborah Gorham, "Flora MacDonald Denison: Canadian Feminist," in *A Not Unreasonable Claim: Women and Reform in Canada, 1880s–1920s* (Toronto: The Women's Press, 1979), p. 591.

72. At the legislative level, protective labor laws, statutory rape laws, and possibly other forms of morals legislation were achievements of the early twentieth century women's movement which became targets of the modern feminist movement. This interpretive framework may help to explain the split within the women's movement of the 1920s over the Equal Rights Amendment.

DOCUMENT 15

LETTERS TO ANTHONY IN SUPPORT OF WOMAN SUFFRAGE, 1880

In 1880, Anthony launched a campaign to convince the
major parties, in particular the Republicans, to include
woman suffrage in their platforms for the upcoming
presidential election. She arranged for a giant woman
suffrage meeting to be held in Chicago on the eve of the
Republican convention, wrote letters and placed adver-
tisements in several reform newspapers inviting all
women who supported suffrage to attend, and suggested that "everyone who cannot go ... send a postal
card to the mass convention, saying she wants the Republicans to put a Sixteenth Amendment pledge in
their platform."* The following letters were among the
more eloquent of the several thousand Anthony received. Although she had requested only a statement of
support for the vote, many women took the opportunity to send her detailed personal accounts of their sufferings. Others included long lists of signatures which
they had collected. The fact that so many women responded to Anthony's call makes it clear that the political feminism she championed was by no means limited
to upper-class, educated white women, and that the
poor, the old, the illiterate, and the Black also felt their
grievances as women and associated them with disfranchisement.

Chicago Historical Society, National Woman Suffrage Association Correspondence Volume
* Ida Harper, *Life of Anthony*, Vol. 2, p. 515

I BELIEVE that women should be emancipated from the accursed bondage that has kept them down for hundreds of years; laws invented by rascally men in the dark ages; knowing the women were too smart for them if they only had a chance to show what they were capable of. But now I hope the time is coming when the women can put their foot down heavy on any man that dares to trample on their rights. Women must arise in all their strength to let men know that she is his equal in all that is great and good. If Bergh in N.Y. City, can be paid to punish men for their cruelty to dumb brutes, I go for a law that will give women the power to go throughout the land to search out the poor and oppressed women, and in every case where a man ill treats his wife, I want him carried off to the Insane Asylum in Indiana or some other infernal place. I am over 76 years old; have lived in different places; have seen man's cruelty to women many times; just because they delighted to show their power over them. It must be stopped. I should be glad to say something on that great occasion and hear others; but I am a poor woman and a widow; and could not get money to come to save my life so sent my name and childrens.

MRS. A. BEAUMONT, Illinois City, Illinois

i have a disire to vote from ms Jane E. Sobers free holder and tax payer when will we have our Rights and Justice in this world. i do not know some times what to think of some of the woman of our city they are a sleep they want to be roused up in Some way i for one have Bin Struggling hard with this world Scince 1874 all Lone By my Self. i have to be man and woman boath i have to be at the helamn and look out for the Brakers i am now 48 years old. have Bin the mother of 9 children and still struggling for my freedom. Are we to have the chinia man to governs us and the colard man it Looks as it was fast approaching.

i feel proud that we have some noble woman to help unnBar the Prison Doors for the Poor Down trodden honst hard working woman of this countery. i have Suffered inJustice from the Law of this my native city. wronged and Robbed of what Did by Rights Belong to me. So good Bye you have my hand and my hart. i only wish i have the power to help you though But I hope the day will come soon. . . .

JANE E. SOBERS, Philadelphia

Withholding from feminine humanity evry natural right from infancy to death, is man's natural propensity. It is so natural that it requires more than ordinary courage in one to favor equal rights legally or morally.

So much has the world been accustomed to subjecting females (human) to all sort of penances that even female children are forced to forego nearly evry pleasure encouraged in the *MALE* sex. Bah! My blood has been brought to boiling heat while reading the contemptable pusilanimious proceedings of the late great Methodist Conference. Even now my cheek burns with contempt and disgust for the foolish virgins who unsuspectingly support them.

Believe me, I cannot sue and plead for my *evry* natural right. But am bitter enough if it comes to that, to fight manfully for our liberty. I would, were it in my power make a destroying Angel of my self, and go from house to house and should I personally receive the treatment that I daily receive in common with other female human beings, *distroy* the man or woman who would utter against equal and unqualified rights and privileges. Words fail to convey the bitter hatred I have for the foul demagogues who would take from me the freedom they claim for themselves.

MRS. H. GRISWOLD, Leavenworth Kansas

I cannot be at the meeting although it is my greatest desire to be there. I am an old lady not able to make the journey. And what a sadness it brings over me when I look back when I was young and had to stay at home and work while my Brothers was away to school never had time nor means to educate my self. I have worked many a week for two dollars while my brothers got 2 or more a day and can this awful curse ever be wiped from our free country as they call it. What a sham is freedom. My mother, good old lady living yet most one hundred and never wrote her name in her life she said that boys must be educated so they could go out in the world smart men well they are what the world call smart judges and statesmen while I old lady not capable to do anything for my poor down troden sisters. I am so thankful there is so many capable to do something strike your best blows go to all their great conventions let them know you mean freedom if we never get it keep them stirred up that is some satisfaction if nothing more all this scribbling does not amount to much of course but I have give you my mind on the subject now you can laugh over my composition it will do that much good any way you will find my name in the list from Shellsburg Iowa was not able to write when I put it there poor show for a town of 600 inhabitants we had to work hard to get that many

ALZINA RATHBUN, Shellsburg, Iowa

Do I wish to vote? do the farm-house slaves of the north want to vote? This is a question involving a two sided problem. What has the Womens-rights movement done for us? Just this, if nothing more, raised the wages of women and girls, and opened places in shops and stores where girls may earn more in a month than the farmers wife can command in a year. Well this is good for the girls in some respects but it means death, after a short life of endless toil and care, for the poor Mother at home. Help cannot be had in the farm house, for love nor money. Our young people are all rushing to Town. "Make home attractive" says some town stomper with more guts than brains. Our homes are as pleasant as our means will admit of. The cause of this unwholesome sentiment is not in the make up of our homes, but in the endless unpaid toil of the farmer, his wife, and his children. All year round, up at four o'clock in the morning, and nine and ten o'clock at night still finds the farmer and his family hard at work and when the harvest is over, and the men-helps are paid off, the grocer bill settled, and the hands paid, the farmer's wife and children know there is not enough left of the years gains, to feed and clothe them as others are clothed and then what is the prospect on the farm, toil, toil, without hope, ... scoffed at and scorned by our city-cousins. So away they flee to the fine prospects in town, to its corruptions and evils, to its temptations and sins, and still they go to be lost in the wild whirl-pool of gayety and fashion.

Dear Sister who can slave this terrible ... state of affairs. I would not tie any woman down to this life of unpaid toil, but justice means justice to all; and it is an undeniable fact that the condition of the farmers and their poor drudging wives, is every year becoming more intolerable; we are robbed and crowded to the wall on every side, our crop [is] taken for whatever the middlemen are of a mind to give us, and we are obliged to give them whatever they have the force to ask for their goods or go without, and this all means so much more self-denial and suffering. So much toil, and less help for the farmer's wife. But do I want to vote; yes, I do, and I would like to be Robertspere—or the heads-man just one year or till the head of every murderer, and every sin-licensing states-man had rolled down from the guillotine. This slow murder and usurpation calls for just such a bloody, unmitigated remedy.

MRS. MARY TRAVIS, Fore's Bend, Minnesota

Through a friend, whose sympathy are with us, showed me the Mind and Matter a Liberal paper publish in Philadelphia. . . .

Your Call for all woman of These United States to sign a petition or postal Card to be sent to you, from Your Mass Meeting to be sent to the Republican Presidential Convention asking them to extend to us Woman some recognition of our rights. We are your Sister though Colored still we feel in our Bosom and want of Faternal love from our White Sister of the Country. Our White men of this State of Virginia, who rule us with a rod of iron, and show themselves on every occasion the same Crule Task Master, as ever, have introduce on the Statute books right to wipp woman for any poor Discretion, that she might be guilt of. During the early part of febuary a poor weak colored Woman who was in the Extremes wants, stole a Over skirt Value fifty Cent, for which the presiding Magistrate Named J.

J. Gruchfield, Did order the poor creature 72 lashes to be well laid on. 36 lashes at the time the Other 36 in a week time and the man or, brute, went himself and saw the whipping was executed. Captain Scott a Col man became indignant went to the jail to see the poor Creature, was refused admission at first but succeed at Last. O My God, what a sight he then saw. the poor Woman Breast was Cut wide open by the lash, her poor back cut to pieces I call some woman together went to the Governor and stated the Case. he forbid the further lashing of the poor woman because the Dr. Beal said she could not live to receive further whipping. Yet the woman still have to remain in jail 12 month for stealing one over skirt Value fifty Cent and have since then been enable to enroll quite a number of Woman to gather form a Club. Our Object is to petition Lecture and to do all things wich shall so soffen the heart of Mankind that they will see and must grant and respect our rights. Would and pray that the Mass Meeting may endorse or demand of the Republican Convention to be Held in Chicigo the rights of Woman to put an Amendment to the Constitution a Cumpulsory Education of Every state of this Union.

Pardon me for this long letter i must i feel let my feeling go out, so to you Dear Madam have i address you on Behalf of your Down Trodden Colored Sisters of Virginia.

LIVE PRYOR, Richmond, Virginia
President, Ladies Enterprise Club

If you have any papers or book that is of no use to you our society would feel grateful to receive them as we wish to form a library.

Although only a working woman, I have by hard work and close economy accumulated a small property that I find I have the privilege to pay taxes for, but have not right to vote for men that tax me. I also find that I am taxed for said property as much again as what many men are that have political influence. Last year I appealed against the enormous tax the assessor put on my property. But could get no resolution because I have no political influence. . . .

MRS. CALLOR, Jersey City, New York

I always come to the same conclusion, namely that our rotten marriage institution is the main obstacle in the way of womans freedom, and just as long as our girls are taught to barter the use of their bodys for a living, must woman remain the degraded thing she is. Of course the Ballot is the great lever to lift her into self esteem and independence. I am more than glad to see the women getting so in dead earnest in the matter.

MRS. L. M. R. POOL, Vermillion, Ohio

I thank God, for giving you the *moral courage* to insist, and persist, under such difficulties and discouragements, as you for so many years have, that woman should have some of the rights she for so many centuries has unjustly been deprived of; and may your life be spared, until you see *all women* in possession of the first great right, Suffrage!

With deepest Love and Gratitude, I am Yours.

(NAME ILLEGIBLE), Cleveland

P.S. I saw the notice of this call several days ago and intended to have answered immediately, but many things prevented, for I am a married woman and not free, by any means, from the cares that relationship brings: and, 56 years old. I have added this explanation, as this Monday morning, I find my hands almost too stiff to write.

May God speed this note, so one more name may be added to your list. My whole soul goes out to you with great *hopes* and *wishes*.

DOCUMENT 16

STANTON, "ADDRESS OF WELCOME TO THE INTERNATIONAL COUNCIL OF WOMEN," MARCH 25, 1888

The predominant theme at the 1888 International Council of Women was women's universal sisterhood. In her opening speech, Elizabeth Stanton spoke eloquently of the solidarity of women, and the common subordination and "universal sense of injustice" on which it was based. She also emphasized the central role that suffragism had played in "the general uprising of women" in the nineteenth century and the democratic tradition of which women's rights was a part. At the end of her speech, she speculated on the political positions that enfranchised women would take, but the unity of the Council did not extend that far, and many feminists disagreed with her, for instance on the importance of maintaining the separation of church and state. In the years after the International Council, Stanton found herself increasingly isolated and her leadership under attack precisely because she differed with other women reformers over which legal changes would emancipate women.

Report of the International Council of Women (Washington, D.C.: Rufus H. Darby, 1888), pp. 31–39

W<small>E</small> are assembled here to-day to celebrate the fortieth anniversary of the first organized demand made by women for the right of suffrage. . . . It has been our custom to mark the passing years by holding meetings of the suffrage societies on each decade, but for this we decided a broader recognition of all the reform associations that have been the natural outgrowth of the suffrage agitation in the Old World as well as the New.

In the great National and State conventions for education, temperance, and religion, even thirty years ago, woman's voice was never heard. The battles fought by the pioneers in the suffrage movement to secure a foothold for woman on these platforms have been eloquently described many times by Susan B. Anthony, Lucy Stone, and Antoinette Brown, and I hope during this Council they will be rehearsed once more, for the benefit of those who, while holding the vantage ground they secured, are afraid of the principles by which it was gained. The civil and political position of woman, when I first understood its real significance, was enough to destroy all faith in the vitality of republican principles. Half a century ago the women of America were bond slaves, under the old common law of England. Their rights of person and property were under the absolute control of fathers and husbands. They were shut out of the schools and colleges, the trades and professions, and all offices under government; paid the most meager wages in the ordinary industries of life, and denied everywhere the necessary opportunities for their best development. Worse still, women had no proper appreciation of themselves as factors in civilization. Believing self-denial a higher virtue than self-development, they ignorantly made ladders of themselves by which fathers, husbands, brothers, and sons reached their highest ambitions, creating an impassable gulf between them and those they loved that no magnetic chords of affection or gratitude could span. Nothing was more common forty years ago than to see the sons of a family educated, while the daughters remained in ignorance; husbands at ease in the higher circles, in which their wives were unprepared to move. Like the foolish virgins in the parable, women everywhere in serving others forgot to keep their own lamps trimmed and burning, and when the great feasts of life were spread, to them the doors were shut.

. . . In welcoming representatives from other lands here today, we do not feel that you are strangers and foreigners, for the women of all nationalities, in the artificial distinctions of sex, have a universal sense of injustice, that forms a common bond of union between them.

Whether our feet are compressed in iron shoes, our faces hidden with veils and masks, whether yoked with cows to draw the plow through its furrows, or classed with idiots, lunatics, and criminals in the laws and constitutions of the state, the principle is the same, for the humiliations of spirit are as real as the visible badges of servitude. A difference in government, religion, laws, and social customs makes but little change in the relative status of woman to the self-constituted governing classes, so long as subordination in all nations is the rule of her being. Through suffering we have learned the open sesame to the hearts of each other. There is a language of universal significance, more subtle than that used in the busy marts of trade, that should be called the mother-tongue, by which with a sigh or a tear, a gesture, a glance of the eye, we know the experiences of each other in the varied forms of slavery. With the spirit forever in bondage, it is the same whether housed in golden cages, with every want supplied, or wandering in the dreary deserts of life friendless and forsaken. Now that our globe is girdled with railroads, steamships, and electric wires, every pulsation of your hearts is known to us.

It is with great satisfaction we also welcome here to-day representatives of our own country-women from thirty-one different associations of moral and philanthropic reforms. . . . I think most of us have come to feel that a voice in the laws is indispensable to achieve success; that these great moral struggles for higher education, temperance, peace, the rights of labor, religious freedom, international arbitration, are all questions to be finally adjusted by the action of government, and without a direct voice in legislation, woman's influence will be eventually lost.

Experience has fully proved, that sympathy as a civil agent is vague and powerless until caught and chained in logical propositions and coined into law. When every prayer and tear represents a ballot, the mothers of the race will no longer weep in vain over the miseries of their children. The active interest women are taking in all the great questions of the day is in strong contrast with the apathy and indifference in which we found them half a century ago, and the contrast in their condition between now and then is equally marked. Those who inaugurated the movement for woman's enfranchisement, who for long years endured the merciless storm of ridicule and persecution, mourned over by friends, ostracized in social life, scandalized by enemies, denounced by the pulpit, scarified and caricatured by the press, may well congratulate themselves on the marked change in public sentiment that this magnificent gathering of educated women from both hemispheres so triumphantly illustrates.

Now even married women enjoy, in a measure, their rights of person and property. They can make contracts, sue and be sued, testify in courts of justice, and with honor dissolve the marriage relation when it becomes intolerable. Now most of the colleges are open to girls, and they are rapidly taking their places in all the profitable industries, and in many of the offices under Government. They are in the professions, too, as lawyers, doctors, editors, professors in colleges, and ministers in the pulpits. Their political status is so far advanced that they enjoy all the rights of citizens in two Territories, municipal suffrage in one State, and school suffrage in half the States of the Union. Here is a good record of the work achieved in the past half-century; but we do not intend to rest our case until all our rights are secured, and, noting the steps of progress in other countries, on which their various representatives are here to report, we behold with satisfaction everywhere a general uprising of women, demanding higher education and an equal place in the industries of the world. Our gathering here to-day is highly significant, in its promises of future combined action. When, in the history of the world, was there ever before such an assemblage of able, educated women, celebrated in so many varied walks of life, and feeling their right and ability to discuss the vital questions of social life, religion, and government? When we think of the vantage-ground woman holds to-day, in spite of all the artificial obstacles she has surmounted, we are filled with wonder as to what the future mother of the race will be when free to seek her complete development.

Thus far women have been the mere echoes of men. Our laws and constitutions, our creeds and codes, and the customs of social life are all of masculine origin. The true woman is as yet a dream of the future. A just government, a humane religion, a pure social life await her coming. Then, and not till then, will the golden age of peace and prosperity be ours. This gathering is significant, too, in being held in the greatest republic on which the sun ever shone—a nation superior to every other on the globe in all that goes to make up a free and mighty people— boundless territory, magnificent scenery, mighty forests, lakes and rivers, and inexhaustible wealth in agriculture, manufactures, and mines—a country where the children of the masses in our public schools have all the appliances of a complete education—books, charts, maps, every advantage, not only in the rudimental but in many of the higher branches, alike free at their disposal. In the Old World the palace on the hill is the home of nobility; here it is the public school or university for the people, where the rich and the poor, side by side, take the prizes for good manners and scholarship. Thus the value of real character above all artificial distinctions—the great lesson of democracy—is early learned by our children.

This is the country, too, where every man has a right to self-government, to exercise his individual conscience and judgment on all matters of public interest. Here we have no entangling alliances in church and state, no tithes to be paid, no livings to be sold, no bartering for places by dignitaries among those who officiate at the altar, no religious test for those elected to take part in government.

Here, under the very shadow of the Capitol of this great nation, whose dome is crowned with the Goddess of Liberty, the women from many lands have assembled at last to claim their rightful place, as equal factors, in the great movements of the nineteenth century, so we bid our distinguished guests welcome, thrice welcome, to our triumphant democracy. I hope they will be able to stay long enough to take a bird's-eye view of our vast possessions, to see what can be done in a moral as well as material point of view in a government of the people. In the Old World they have governments and people; here we have a government of the people, by the people, for the people—that is, we soon shall have when that important half, called women, are enfranchised, and the laboring masses know how to use the power they possess. And you will see here, for the first time in the history of nations, a church without a pope, a state without a king, and a family without a divinely ordained head, for our laws are rapidly making fathers and mothers equal in the marriage relation. We call your attention, dear friends, to these patent facts, not in a spirit of boasting, but that you may look critically into the working of our republican institutions; that when you return to the Old World you may help your fathers to solve many of the tangled problems to which as yet they have found no answer. You can tell the Czar of Russia and the Tories of England that self-government and "home rule" are safe and possible, proved so by a nation of upward of 60,000,000 of people. . . .

The question is continually asked, If women had the right of suffrage how would they vote on national questions? I think I might venture to say that the women on this platform would all be opposed to war. As to the much-vexed question of the fisheries we would say, in view of our vast Atlantic and Pacific coast, thousands of miles in extent, do let Canada have three miles of the ocean if she wants it. If the cod is the bone of contention, as it is the poorest of all fish, let the Canadians eat it in peace so long as we have oysters, shad, bass and the delicate salmon from our Western lakes and California. Upon other questions now up for consideration we should probably be of one mind. As to a treaty with Russia to send back her political prisoners to be tortured in her prisons and the mines of Siberia, our verdict would be no, no. America must ever be the great university in which the lovers of freedom may safely graduate with the highest honors, and under our flag find peace and protection. The able statement by Stepniak, the Russian nihilist, laid before our Senate, should be carefully read by all of us, that our influence may be used intelligently against all treaties, compromising, as they would, the honor of a nation upholding the right of free speech and free press in the criticism of their rulers by the people. As to international copyright, we should no doubt say let us have a law to that effect by all means, because it is fair and honest. Moreover, since we now have our own historians, philosophers, scientists, poets, and novelists and England steals as much from us as we do from her, it is evident that sound policy and common honesty lie in the same direction. As to the overflowing Treasury that troubles the conscience of our good President, our wisest women would undoubtedly say, pay the national debt and lighten the taxes on the shoulders of the laboring masses. As to the amendments of the Constitution now asked for by some reformers, and a body of the clergy, to recognize the Christian theology in the Constitution and introduce religious tests into political parties and platforms in direct violation of Article VI, clause 3, of the National Constitution, I think the majority in our woman suffrage associations would be opposed to all such amendments, as they would destroy the secular nature of our Government, so carefully guarded by our fathers in laying the foundation of the Republic. This freedom from all ecclesiastical entanglements is one of the chief glories of our Government and one of the chief elements of its success. We can not too carefully guard against all attempts at a retrogressive policy in this direction. If there is one lesson more plainly written than another on the institutions of the Old World it is the danger of a union of church and state, of civil and canon law, of theological speculations in the practical affairs of government. If the majority of women on the suffrage platform would vote thus wisely on five questions, they may show equal wisdom on others that may come up for future legislation.

On questions of land, labor, prohibition, and protection there would, no doubt, amongst us, be many differences of opinion, but I think we should all agree that that system of political economy that secures the greatest blessings to the greatest number must be the true one, and those laws which guard most sacredly the interests of the many rather than the few, we should vote for. When woman's voice is heard in Government our legislation will become more humane, and judgments in our courts be tempered with mercy Surely the mothers who rocked the cradle of this Republic may be safely trusted to sustain their sires and sons in all their best efforts to establish in the New World a government in which the sound principles of our Constitution and Declaration of Independence may be fully realized, in which there shall be no privileged classes, but equal rights for all. . . .

ANNA HOWARD SHAW,
"AUNT SUSAN," 1890

In this selection, Anna Howard Shaw described her friendship with Anthony and their common work for suffrage in the 1890s. Shaw was one of several younger women, including Rachel Foster Avery, Ida Husted Harper, Carrie Chapman Catt, and even Harriot Stanton Blatch, whom Anthony befriended and encouraged to become suffrage leaders in this period. Anthony's total dedication to "the Cause"—symbolized by the physical stamina she could muster at the age of seventy for the South Dakota campaign—had a powerful impact on Shaw's own commitment to the vote. After she met Anthony at the 1888 International Council, Shaw switched her allegiance from the WCTU to suffrage and eventually became president of the National American Woman Suffrage Association. Other suffragists disliked Anthony's insistence on maintaining personal control over all aspects of the movement's work, but they too recognized the absolute character of her identification with the cause of woman suffrage. "We *live* in this woman movement," her old friend, Clarina Nichols, wrote to Anthony, "because we see in it the divine development of humanity."*

Story of a Pioneer (New York: Harper and Brothers, Publishers, 1915), pp. 189–204
* Clarina Nichols to Susan B. Anthony, August 21, 1880, Susan B. Anthony Papers, Schlesinger Library

IN *The Life of Susan B. Anthony* it is mentioned that 1888 was a year of special recognition of our great leader's work, but that it was also the year in which many of her closest friends and strongest supporters were taken from her by death. A. Bronson Alcott was among these, and Louisa M. Alcott, as well as Dr. Lozier; and special stress is laid on Miss Anthony's sense of loss in the diminishing circle of her friends—a loss which new friends and workers came forward, eager to supply.

"Chief among these," adds the record, "was Anna Shaw, who, from the time of the International Council in '88, gave her truest allegiance to Miss Anthony."

It is true that from that year until Miss Anthony's death in 1906 we two were rarely separated; and I never read the paragraph I have just quoted without seeing, as in a vision, the figure of "Aunt Susan" as she slipped into my hotel room in Chicago late one night after an evening meeting of the International Council. I had gone to bed—indeed, I was almost asleep when she came, for the day had been as exhausting as it was interesting. But notwithstanding the lateness of the hour, "Aunt Susan," then nearing seventy, was still as fresh and as full of enthusiasm as a young girl. She had a great deal to say, she declared, and she proceeded to say it—sitting in a big easy-chair near the bed, with a rug around her knees, while I propped myself up with pillows and listened.

Hours passed and the dawn peered wanly through the windows, but still Miss Anthony talked of the Cause—always of the Cause—and of what we two must do for it. The previous evening she had been too busy to eat any dinner, and I greatly doubt whether she had eaten any luncheon at noon. She had been on her feet for hours at a time, and she had held numerous discussions with other women she wished to inspire to special effort. Yet, after it all, here she was laying out our campaigns for years ahead, foreseeing everything, forgetting nothing, and sweeping me with her in her flight toward our common goal until I, who am not easily carried off my feet, experienced an almost dizzy sense of exhilaration.

Suddenly she stopped, looked at the gas-jets paling in the morning light that filled the room, and for a fleeting instant seemed surprised. In the next she had dismissed from her mind the realization that we had talked all night. Why should we not talk all night? It was part of our work. She threw off the enveloping rug and rose.

"I must dress now," she said, briskly. "I've called a committee meeting before the morning session."

On her way to the door nature smote her with a rare reminder, but even then she did not realize that it was personal. "Perhaps," she remarked, tentatively, "you ought to have a cup of coffee."

That was "Aunt Susan." And in the eighteen years which followed I had daily illustrations of her superiority to purely human weaknesses. To her the hardships we underwent later, in our Western campaigns for woman suffrage, were as the airiest trifles. Like a true soldier, she could snatch a moment of sleep or a mouthful of food where she found it, and if either was not forthcoming she did not miss it. To me she was an unceasing inspiration—the torch that illuminated my life. We went through some difficult years together—years when we fought hard for each inch of headway we gained—but I found full compensation for every effort in the glory of working with her for the Cause that was first in both our hearts and in the happiness of being her friend. . . .

I wish to write of her bigness, her many-sidedness, her humor, her courage, her quickness, her sympathy, her understanding, her force, her supreme common-sense, her selflessness; in short, of the rare beauty of her nature as I learned to know it. . . .

[The] South-Dakota campaign was one of the most difficult we ever made. It extended over nine months; and it is impossible to describe the poverty which prevailed throughout the whole rural community of the State. There had been three consecutive years of drought. The sand was like powder, so deep that the wheels of the wagons in which we rode "across country" sank half-way to the hubs; and in the midst of this dry powder lay withered tangles that had once been grass. Every one had the forsaken, desperate look worn by the pioneer who has reached the limit of his endurance, and the great stretches of prairie roads showed innumerable canvas-covered wagons, drawn by starved horses, and followed by starved cows, on their way "Back East." Our talks with the despairing drivers of these wagons are among my most tragic memories. They had lost everything except what they had with them, and they were going East to leave "the woman" with her father and try to find work. Usually, with a look of disgust at his wife, the man would say: "I wanted to leave two years ago, but the woman kept saying, 'Hold on a little longer.'"

Both Miss Anthony and I gloried in the spirit of these pioneer women, and lost no opportunity to tell them so; for we realized what our nation owes to the patience and courage of such as they were. We often asked them what was the hardest thing to bear in their pioneer life, and we usually received the same reply:

"To sit in our little adobe or sod houses at night and listen to the wolves howl over the graves of our babies. For the howl of the wolf is like the cry of a child from the grave."

Many days, and in all kinds of weather, we rode forty and fifty miles in uncovered wagons. Many nights we shared a one-room cabin with all the members of the family. But the greatest hardship we suffered was the lack of water. There was very little good water in the state, and the purest water was so brackish that we could hardly drink it. The more we drank the thirstier we became, and when the water was made into tea it tasted worse than when it was clear. A bath was the rarest of luxuries. The only available fuel was buffalo manure, of which the odor permeated all our food. But despite these handicaps we were happy in our work, for we had some great meetings and many wonderful experiences.... I recall with special clearness one ride from Hill City to Custer City. It was only a matter of thirty miles, but it was thoroughly exhausting; and after our meeting that same night we had to drive forty miles farther over the mountains to get the early morning train from Buffalo Gap. The trail from Custer City to Buffalo Gap was the one the animals had originally made in their journeys over the pass, and the drive in that wild region, throughout a cold, piercing October night, was an unforgetable [sic] experience. Our host at Custer City lent Miss Anthony his big buffalo overcoat, and his wife lent hers to me. They also heated blocks of wood for our feet, and with these protections we started. A full moon hung in the sky. The trees were covered with hoar-frost, and the cold, still air seemed to sparkle in the brilliant light. Again Miss Anthony talked to me throughout the night—of the work, always of the work, and of what it would mean to the women who followed us; and again she fired my soul with the flame that burned so steadily in her own.

It was daylight when we reached the little station at Buffalo Gap where we were to take the train. . . . Miss Anthony sat down on the floor. I had a few raisins in my bag, and we divided them for breakfast. An hour passed, and another, and still the train did not come. Miss Anthony, her back braced against the wall, buried her face in her hands and dropped into a peaceful abyss of slumber, while I walked restlessly up and down the platform. The train arrived four hours late, and when eventually we had reached our destination we learned that the ministers of the town had persuaded the women to give up the suffrage meeting scheduled for that night, as it was Sunday.

This disappointment, following our all-day and all-night drive to keep our appointment, aroused Miss Anthony's fighting spirit. She sent me out to rent the theater for the evening, and to have some hand-bills printed and distributed, announcing that we would speak. At three o'clock she made the concession to her seventy years of lying down for an hour's rest. I was young and vigorous, so I trotted around town to get somebody to preside, somebody to introduce us, somebody to take up the collection, and somebody who would provide music—in short, to make all our preparations for the night meeting.

When evening came the crowd which had assembled was so great that men and women sat in the windows and on the stage, and stood in the flies. Night attractions were rare in that Dakota town, and here was something new. Nobody went to church, so the churches were forced to close. We had a glorious meeting. Both Miss Anthony and I were in excellent fighting trim. . . . The collection we took up paid all our expenses, the church singers sang for us, the great audience was interested, and the whole campaign was an inspiring success.

The meeting ended about half after ten o'clock, and I remember taking Miss Anthony to our hotel and escorting her to her room. I also remember that she followed me to the door and made some laughing remark as I left for my own room; but I recall nothing more until the next morning when she stood beside me telling me it was time for breakfast. She had found me lying on the cover of my bed, fully clothed even to my bonnet and shoes. I had fallen there, utterly exhausted, when I entered my room the night before; and I do not think I had even moved from that time until the moment—nine hours later—when I heard her voice and felt her hand on my shoulder.

STANTON, "ADDRESS TO THE FOUNDING CONVENTION OF THE NATIONAL AMERICAN WOMAN SUFFRAGE ASSOCIATION," FEBRUARY, 1890

Stanton's speech on the occasion of the merger of the National and American suffrage associations was far more controversial than her speech to the International Council, two years before, had been. In it, she began to challenge the newly achieved unity of the suffrage movement by exposing some of the political differences hidden beneath it. At one level, she was trying to influence suffragists' opinions on current political issues such as the separation of church and state, divorce legislation, and racial segregation. But even deeper, she was trying to shape the entire political perspective of the new suffrage organization. She continued to believe that the goal of the woman suffrage movement was not simply to win the vote for women but to build women into a force for radical political change. However, many of the new, younger leaders disagreed with her, and their approach soon came to dominate the National American Woman Suffrage Association.

Elizabeth Cady Stanton Papers, Library of Congress (I would like to thank Maurine Greenwald for providing me with a transcript of the manuscript of this speech.)

. . . THE chief barriers in the way to a more pronounced success in our movement have been: 1st, the apathy and indifference of society to all reforms. 2nd: Our lack of thorough and widespread organization. . . . [A]s to organization, for many years, we had no forces to organize. Each individual was a free lance to say or do whatsoever she listed. . . . [N]ow after twenty years of grand work in different lines, we have come to the conclusion that in Union there is strength, and added Power in thorough organization. In uniting all our forces today under one banner, with the hearty cooperation of every friend of the movement, victory might soon be ours. . . . Isolated effort is of little value in carrying any great measure. . . . With all our forces molded together and concentrated on one point, our influence on the near future will, I know, prove irresistible. . . .

In view of the many vital questions now up for consideration in which women are especially interested, it seems to me that the time has come for more aggressive measures, more self assertion on our part than was ever manifested before. . . .

For fifty years we have been plaintiffs at the bar of justice and three generations of statesmen, judges, and reformers have exhausted their able arguments and eloquent appeals in the courts and before the people. But as the Bench, the Bar and the Jury are all men, we are non-suited every time, and yet, some men tell us we must be patient and persuasive, that we must be womanly. My friends, what is man's idea of womanly? It is to have a manner that pleases him, quiet, deferential, submissive, that approaches him as a subject does a master. He wants no self-assertion on our part, no defiance, no vehement arraigning of him as a robber and a criminal. While the grand motto, "resistance to tyrants is obedience to God," has echoed and re-echoed around the globe electrifying the lovers of liberty in every latitude and making crowned heads tremble, while every right achieved by the oppressed has been wrung from tyrants by force, while the darkest page of human history is the outrages on women, shall men tell us today to be patient, persuasive, womanly? What do we know as yet as to what is womanly? The women we have seen thus far have been with rare exceptions the mere echoes of men. . . . Patience and persuasiveness are beautiful virtues in dealing with children and the feeble minded adults, but with those who have the gift of reason and understand the principles of justice, it is our duty to compel them to act up to the highest light that is in them and as promptly as possible. . . .

As women are taking an active part in pressing on the consideration of Congress many narrow sectarian measures, such as more rigid Sunday laws, to stop travel and distribution of the mail on that day, and intend to introduce the name of God into the constitution, this action on the part of some women is used as an argument for the disfranchisement of all. I hope this convention will declare that the Woman Suffrage Association is opposed to all Union of Church and State and pledges itself as far as possible, to maintain the secular nature of our government. As Sunday is the only day the laboring man can escape from the cities, to stop the street cars, omnibusses and rail roads would indeed be a lamentable exercise of arbitrary authority. No, no the duty of the state is to protect those who do the work of the world in the largest liberty and instead of shutting them up in their gloomy tenement houses on Sunday, we should open wide the parks, horticultural gardens, the museums, the libraries, the galleries of art, the music halls, where they can listen to the divine melodies of the great masters. All these are questions of legislation and what influence women will exert as voters is already being canvassed, hence the importance of this Association expressing its opinions on all questions in which woman's social, civil, religious, and political rights are involved.

Consider the thousands of women with babies in their arms year after year who have no change to the dull routine of their lives, except on Sunday when their husbands can go with them on some little excursion by land or sea, suddenly compelled to stay at home by passage of a rigid Sunday law, secured by the votes of those who can drive about at pleasure in their own carriages and go wherever they may desire. It is puerile to say "no matter how we use the ballot the right is ours," but if the presumption that we will use it wisely enters into the chance of our obtaining it, it is desirable for the public to know our opinions on practical questions of morals and politics.

We must demand a voice too in another field of labor, thus far bounded, fenced and titled by man alone, where according to his own statistics one may now gather more thorns and thistles than fruits and flowers. And this is the home. Many propositions are now floating about as to the laws regulating our family relations. . . . The message I should like to go out from this convention is that there should be no further legislation on the questions of marriage and divorce until woman has a voice in the state and national governments. Surely here is a relation in which above all others there should be equality; a relation in which woman really has a deeper interest than man and if the laws favor either party it should be the wife and mother. Marriage is a mere incident in a man's life. He has business interests and ambitions in other directions but as a general thing it is all of life to woman where all her interests and ambitions center. And if the conditions of her surroundings there are discordant and degrading she is indeed most unfortunate and needs the protection of the laws to set her free rather than hold her in bondage.

And yet it is proposed to have a national law restricting the right of divorce to a narrower basis. . . . Congress has already made an appropriation for a Report on the Question which shows that there are 10,000 divorces annually in the United States and other statisticians say, the majority asked for by women. If liberal divorce laws for wives are what Canada was for the slaves, a door of escape from bondage, we had better consult the women before we close the avenues to freedom. Where discontent is rocked in every cradle and complaints to heaven going up with every prayer, talk not of the sacredness of such relations, nor of the best interests of society requiring their permanent establishment. The best interests of society and the individual always lie in the same direction. Hence the state as well as the family is interested in building the home on solid foundation.

Some may say that none of these questions legitimately belong on this platform, but as they have been discussed on the women's rights platform from the beginning they probably always will be. Wherever and whatever any class of women suffer whether in the home, the church, the courts, in the world of work, in the statute books, a voice in their behalf should be heard in our conventions. We must manifest a broad catholic spirit for all shades of opinion in which we may differ and recognize the equal right of all parties, sects and races, tribes and colors. Colored women, Indian women, Mormon women and women from every quarter of the globe have been heard in these Washington conventions and I trust they always will be.

The enfranchisement of woman is not a question to be carried by political clap-trap, by strategem or art, but by the slow process of education, by constant agitation and in new directions, attacking in turn every stronghold of the enemy.... Let us ... stir up a whole group of new victims from time to time, by turning our guns on new strongholds. Agitation is the advance guard of education. When any principle or question is up for discussion, let us seize on it and show its connection, whether nearly or remotely, with woman's disfranchisement. There is such a thing as being too anxious lest someone "hurt the cause" by what he or she must say or do; or perhaps the very thing you fear is exactly what should be done. It is impossible for any one to tell what people are ready to hear....

Another question demanding consideration on our platform, is the race problem that was supposed to be settled a quarter of a century ago by the proclamation of emancipation.... How comes it ... that the race problem is again up for discussion in Congress and the civil rights bill in our hotels? Because every fundamental principle by which [the freedman] was emancipated and enfranchised was immediately denied in its application to women.... The denial of principle in the case of women at the North has reacted in the denial of the same principle in the case of the Freedman of the South, and now our statesmen are at their wits' end to know what to do with the Freedman and are actually proposing to colonize him. If the Russian system is to be adopted and all discontented citizens are to be sent to some Siberia, our turn will come next. Hence we had better make a stand on the Freedman and demand justice for him as well as ourselves. It is justice, and that alone that can end the impossible conflict between freedom and slavery going on in every nation on the globe. That is all the Nihilists, the socialists, the Communists ask, and that is all Ireland asks, and the Freedmen and women of this Republic ask no more.

DOCUMENT **19**

STANTON, "INTRODUCTION" AND COMMENTARIES ON GENESIS, CHAPTERS 1–4, *THE WOMAN'S BIBLE*; ANTHONY, RESPONSE TO THE NAWSA RESOLUTION DISAVOWING *THE WOMAN'S BIBLE*; STANTON, DRAFT OF "CRITICISM OF BIGOTRY OF WOMEN"

Stanton's lifelong interest in the relation of Christianity to the idea of women's inferiority grew stronger in the 1880s and 1890s, in reaction to the growing influence of organized religion, in the women's movement in particular and in American politics in general. *The Woman's Bible* was the most enduring product of the secularism that concerned her in her later years. It was also part of the general scholarly effort to interpret the Bible as an historical document, rather than as divine revelation. From her unique feminist perspective, Stanton argued that the historical impact of Christian ideas, particularly about sexuality and maternity, had been to degrade women. The body of the book was organized as a series of commentaries, deliberately informal and irreverent, on Biblical passages which mentioned or affected women. In these commentaries, Stanton criticized the Bible for its irrationalities and superstitions, but she also encouraged the development of a new, "rational" religion, deliberately designed "in

The Woman's Bible, Part One (New York: European Publishing Co., 1895), pp. 1–33.

harmony with science, common sense and the experience of mankind in natural laws." Soon after the publication of *The Woman's Bible*, the National American Woman Suffrage Association, horrified by the controversy the book raised, passed a resolution disavowing any connection with it. The objections of both Stanton and Anthony to this action, and to the conservative tendencies it revealed, are also included.

FROM the inauguration of the movement for woman's emancipation the Bible has been used to hold her in the "divinely ordained sphere," prescribed in the Old and New Testaments.

The canon and civil law; church and state; priests and legislators; all political parties and religious denominations have alike taught that woman was made after man, of man, and for man, an inferior being, subject to man. Creeds, codes, Scriptures and statutes, are all based on this idea. The fashions, forms, ceremonies and customs of society, church ordinances and discipline all grow out of this idea. . . .

The Bible teaches that woman brought sin and death into the world, that she precipitated the fall of the race, that she was arraigned before the judgment seat of Heaven, tried, condemned and sentenced. Marriage for her was to be a condition of bondage, maternity a period of suffering and anguish, and in silence and subjection, she was to play the role of a dependent on man's bounty for all her material wants, and for all the information she might desire on the vital questions of the hour, she was commanded to ask her husband at home. Here is the Bible position of woman briefly summed up.

Those who have the divine insight to translate, transpose and transfigure this mournful object of pity into an exalted, dignified personage, worthy our worship as the mother of the race, are to be congratulated as having a share of the occult mystic power of the eastern Mahatmas.

The plain English to the ordinary mind admits of no such liberal interpretation. The unvarnished texts speak for themselves. The canon law, church ordinances and Scriptures, are homogeneous, and all reflect the same spirit and sentiments.

These familiar texts are quoted by clergymen in their pulpits, by statesmen in the halls of legislation, by lawyers in the courts, and are echoed by the press of all civilized nations, and accepted by woman herself as "The Word of God." So perverted is the religious element in her nature, that with faith and works she is the chief support of the church and clergy; the very powers that make her emancipation impossible. When, in the early part of the Nineteenth Century, women began to protest against their civil and political degradation, they were referred to the Bible for an answer. When they protested against their unequal position in the church, they were referred to the Bible for an answer.

This led to a general and critical study of the Scriptures. Some, having made a fetish of these books and believing them to be the veritable "Word of God," with liberal translations, interpretations, allegories and symbols, glossed over the most objectionable features of the various books and clung to them as divinely inspired. Others, seeing the family resemblance between the Mosaic code, the canon law, and the old English common law, came to the conclusion that all alike emanated from the same source; wholly human in their origin and inspired by the natural love of domination in the historians. Others, bewildered with their doubts and fears, came to no conclusion. While their clergymen told them on the one hand, that they owed all the blessings and freedom they enjoyed to the Bible, on the other, they said it clearly marked out their circumscribed sphere of action: that the demands for political and civil rights were irreligious, dangerous to the stability of the home, the state and the church. Clerical appeals were circulated from time to time conjuring members of their churches to take no part in the anti-slavery or woman suffrage movements, as they were infidel in their tendencies, undermining the very foundations of society. No wonder the majority of women stood still, and with bowed heads, accepted the situation.

Listening to the varied opinions of women, I have long

thought it would be interesting and profitable to get them clearly stated in book form ... a large committee has been formed, and we hope to complete the work within a year.

Those who have undertaken the labor are desirous to have some Hebrew and Greek scholars, versed in Biblical criticism, to gild our pages with their learning. Several distinguished women have been urged to do so, but they are afraid that their high reputation and scholarly attainments might be compromised by taking part in an enterprise that for a time may prove very unpopular. Hence we may not be able to get help from that class.

Others fear that they might compromise their evangelical faith by affiliating with those of more liberal views, who do not regard the Bible as the "Word of God," but like any other book, to be judged by its merits. If the Bible teaches the equality of Woman, why does the church refuse to ordain women to preach the gospel, to fill the offices of deacons and elders, and to administer the Sacraments, or to admit them as delegates to the Synods, General Assemblies and Conferences of the different denominations? They have never yet invited a woman to join one of their Revising Committees, nor tried to mitigate the sentence pronounced on her by changing one count in the indictment served on her in Paradise.

The large number of letters received, highly appreciative of the undertaking, is very encouraging to those who have inaugurated the movement, and indicate a growing self-respect and self-assertion in the women of this generation. But we have the usual array of objectors to meet and answer. One correspondent conjures us to suspend the work, as it is "ridiculous" for "women to attempt the revision of the Scriptures." I wonder if any man wrote to the late revising committee of Divines to stop their work on the ground that it was ridiculous for men to revise the Bible. Why is it more ridiculous for women to protest against her present status in the Old and New Testament, in the ordinances and discipline of the church, than in the statutes and constitution of the state? Why is it more ridiculous to arraign ecclesiastics for their false teaching and acts of injustice to women, than members of Congress and the House of Com-

mons? Why is it more audacious to review Moses than Blackstone, the Jewish code of laws, than the English system of jurisprudence? Women have compelled their legislators in every
state in this Union to so modify their statutes for women that
the old common law is now almost a dead letter. Why not compel Bishops and Revising Committees to modify their creeds
and dogmas? Forty years ago it seemed as ridiculous to timid,
time-serving and retrograde folk for women to demand an ex-
purgated edition of the laws, as it now does to demand an ex-
purgated edition of the Liturgies and the Scriptures. Come,
come, my conservative friend, wipe the dew off your spectacles,
and see that the world is moving. Whatever your views may be
as to the importance of the proposed work, your political and
social degradation are but an outgrowth of your status in the
Bible. . . .

Others say it is not *politic* to rouse religious opposition. This
much-lauded policy is but another word for *cowardice.* How
can woman's position be changed from that of a subordinate to
an equal, without opposition, without the broadest discussion of
all the questions involved in her present degradation? For so
far-reaching and momentous a reform as her complete independence, an entire revolution in all existing institutions is inevita-
ble.

Let us remember that all reforms are interdependent, and
that whatever is done to establish one principle on a solid basis,
strengthens all. Reformers who are always compromising, have
not yet grasped the idea that truth is the only safe ground to
stand upon. The object of an individual life is not to carry one
fragmentary measure in human progress, but to utter the highest truth clearly seen in all directions, and thus to round out and
perfect a well balanced character. . . .

Again there are some who write us that our work is a useless
expenditure of force over a book that has lost its hold on the
human mind. Most intelligent women, they say, regard it simply as the history of a rude people in a barbarous age, and have
no more reverence for the Scriptures than any other work. So
long as tens of thousands of Bibles are printed every year, and
circulated over the whole habitable globe, and the masses in all

English-speaking nations revere it as the word of God, it is vain to belittle its influence. The sentimental feelings we all have for those things we were educated to believe sacred, do not readily yield to pure reason. . . .

The only points in which I differ from all ecclesiastical teaching is that I do not believe that any man ever saw or talked with God, I do not believe that God inspired the Mosaic code, or told the historians what they say he did about woman, for all the religions on the face of the earth degrade her, and so long as woman accepts the position that they assign her, her emancipation is impossible. Whatever the Bible may be made to do in Hebrew or Greek, in plain English it does not exalt and dignify woman . . .

There are some general principles in the holy books of all religions that teach love, charity, liberty, justice and equality for all the human family, there are many grand and beautiful passages, the golden rule has been echoed and re-echoed around the world. There are lofty examples of good and true men and women, all worthy our acceptance and imitation whose lustre cannot be dimmed by the false sentiments and vicious characters bound up in the same volume. The Bible cannot be accepted or rejected as a whole, its teachings are varied and its lessons differ widely from each other. In criticising the peccadilloes of Sarah, Rebecca and Rachel, we would not shadow the virtues of Deborah, Huldah and Vashti. In criticising the Mosaic code we would not question the wisdom of the golden rule and the fifth Commandment. . . .

The canon law, the Scriptures, the creeds and codes and church discipline of the leading religions bear the impress of fallible man, and not of our ideal great first cause, "the Spirit of all Good," that set the universe of matter and mind in motion, and by immutable law holds the land, the sea, the planets, revolving round the great centre of light and heat, each in its own elliptic, with millions of stars in harmony all singing together, the glory of creation forever and ever.

THE BOOK OF GENESIS.

CHAPTER I.

Genesis i: 26, 27, 28.

26 ¶ And God said, let us make man in our image, after our likeness: and let them have dominion over the fish of the sea, and over the fowl of the air, and over the cattle, and over all the earth, and over every creeping thing that creepeth upon the earth.

27 So God created man in his *own* image, in the image of God created he him; male and female created he them.

28 And God blessed them, and God said unto them, Be fruitful, and multiply, and replenish the earth, and subdue it; and have dominion over the fish of the sea, and over the fowl of the air, and over every living thing that moveth upon the earth.

HERE is the sacred historian's first account of the advent of woman; a simultaneous creation of both sexes, in the image of God. It is evident from the language that there was consultation in the Godhead, and that the masculine and feminine elements were equally represented. Scott in his commentaries says, "this consultation of the Gods is the origin of the doctrine of the trinity." But instead of three male personages, as generally represented, a Heavenly Father, Mother, and Son would seem more rational.

The first step in the elevation of woman to her true position, as an equal factor in human progress, is the cultivation of the religious sentiment in regard to her dignity and equality, the recognition by the rising generation of an ideal Heavenly Mother, to whom their prayers should be addressed, as well as to a Father.

If language has any meaning, we have in these texts a plain declaration of the existence of the feminine element in the Godhead, equal in power and glory with the masculine. The Heavenly Mother and Father! "God created man in his *own image, male and female.*" Thus Scripture, as well as science and philosophy, declares the eternity and equality of sex—the philosophical fact, without which there could have been no perpetuation of creation, no growth or development in the animal, vegetable, or mineral kingdoms, no awakening nor progressing in the world of thought. The masculine and feminine elements, exactly equal and balancing each other, are as essential to the maintenance of the equilibrium of the universe as positive and negative electricity, the centripetal and centrifugal forces, the laws of attraction which bind together all we know of this planet whereon we dwell and of the system in which we revolve.

In the great work of creation the crowning glory was realized, when man and woman were evolved on the sixth day, the masculine and feminine forces in the image of God, that must have existed eternally, in all forms of matter and mind. All the persons in the Godhead are represented in the Elohim the divine plurality taking counsel in regard to this last and highest form of life. Who were the members of this high council, and were they a duality or a trinity? Verse 27 declares the image of God male and female. How then is it possible to make woman an afterthought? We find in verses 5–16 the pronoun "he" used. Should it not in harmony with verse 26 be "they," a dual pronoun? We may attribute this to the same cause as the use of "his" in verse 11 instead of "it." The fruit tree yielding fruit after "his" kind instead of after "its" kind. The paucity of a language may give rise to many misunderstandings.

The above texts plainly show the simultaneous creation of man and woman, and their equal importance in the development of the race. All those theories based on the assumption that man was prior in the creation, have no foundation in Scripture.

As to woman's subjection, on which both the canon and the civil law delight to dwell, it is important to note that equal dominion is given to woman over every living thing, but not one word is said giving man dominion over woman.

Here is the first title deed to this green earth giving alike to the sons and daughters of God. No lesson of woman's subjection can be fairly drawn from the first chapter of the Old Testament.

CHAPTER II.

Genesis ii: 21–25.

21 And the Lord God caused a deep sleep to fall upon Adam, and he slept; and he took one of his ribs, and closed up the flesh thereof.

22 And the rib which the Lord God had taken from man, made he a woman, and brought her unto the man.

23 And Adam said, This *is* now bone of my bone, and flesh of my flesh: she shall be called Woman, because she was taken out of man.

24 Therefore shall a man leave his father and his mother, and shall cleave unto his wife; and they shall be one flesh.

25 And they were both naked, the man and his wife, and were not ashamed.

As the account of the creation in the first chapter is in harmony with science, common sense, and the experience of mankind in natural laws, the inquiry naturally arises, why should there be two contradictory accounts in the same book, of the same event? It is fair to infer that the second version, which is found in some form in the different religions of all nations, is a mere allegory, symbolizing some mysterious conception of a highly imaginative editor.

The first account dignifies woman as an important factor in the creation, equal in power and glory with man. The second makes her a mere afterthought. The world in good running order without her. The only reason for her advent being the solitude of man.

There is something sublime in bringing order out of chaos; light out of darkness; giving each planet its place in the solar system; oceans and lands their limits; wholly inconsistent with a petty surgical operation, to find material for the mother of the race. It is on this allegory that all the enemies of women rest their battering rams, to prove her inferiority. Accepting the view that man was prior in the creation, some Scriptural writers say that as the woman was of the man, therefore, her position should be one of subjection. Grant it, then as the historical fact is reversed in our day, and the man is now of the woman, shall his place be one of subjection?

The equal position declared in the first account must prove

more satisfactory to both sexes; created alike in the image of God—The Heavenly Mother and Father.

Thus, the Old Testament, "in the beginning," proclaims the simultaneous creation of man and woman, the eternity and equality of sex; and the New Testament echoes back through the centuries the individual sovereignty of woman growing out of this natural fact. Paul, in speaking of equality as the very soul and essence of Christianity, said, "There is neither Jew nor Greek, there is neither bond nor free, there is neither male nor female; for ye are all one in Christ Jesus." With this recognition of the feminine element in the Godhead in the Old Testament, and this declaration of the equality of the sexes in the New, we may well wonder at the contemptible status woman occupies in the Christian Church of to-day.

All the commentators and publicists writing on woman's position, go through an immense amount of fine-spun metaphysical speculations, to prove her subordination in harmony with the Creator's original design.

It is evident that some wily writer, seeing the perfect equality of man and woman in the first chapter, felt it important for the dignity and dominion of man to effect woman's subordination in some way. To do this a spirit of evil must be introduced, which at once proved itself stronger than the spirit of good, and man's supremacy was based on the downfall of all that had just been pronounced very good. This spirit of evil evidently existed before the supposed fall of man, hence woman was not the origin of sin as so often asserted.

CHAPTER III.

Genesis iii: 1–24.

1 Now the serpent was more subtle than any beast of the field which the Lord God had made. And he said unto the woman, Yea, hath God said, Ye shall not eat of every tree of the garden?

2 And the woman said unto the serpent, We may eat of the fruit of the trees of the garden:

3 But of the fruit of the tree which *is* in the midst of the garden, God hath said Ye shall not eat of it, neither shall ye touch it, lest ye die.

4 And the serpent said unto the woman, Ye shall not surely die:

5 For God doth know that in the day ye eat thereof then your eyes shall be opened, and

ye shall be as gods, knowing good and evil.

6 And when the woman saw that the tree *was* good for food, and that it *was* pleasant to the eyes, and a tree to be desired to make *one* wise, she took of the fruit thereof, and did eat and gave also unto her husband with her; and he did eat.

7 And the eyes of them both were opened, and they knew that they *were* naked; and they sewed fig leaves together, and made themselves aprons.

8 And they heard the voice of the Lord God walking in the garden in the cool of the day; and Adam and his wife hid themselves from the presence of the Lord God amongst the trees in the garden.

9 And the Lord God called unto Adam, and said unto him, Where *art* thou?

10 And he said, I heard thy voice in the garden, and I was afraid, because I *was* naked; and I hid myself.

11 And he said, Who told thee that thou *wast* naked? Hast thou eaten of the tree, whereof I commanded thee that thou shouldst not eat?

12 And the man said, The woman whom thou gavest *to be* with me, she gave me of the tree, and I did eat.

13 And the Lord God said unto the woman, What *is* this *that* thou hast done? And the woman said, The serpent beguiled me, and I did eat.

14 And the Lord God said unto the serpent, Because thou hast done this, thou *art* cursed above all cattle, and above every beast of the field; upon thy belly shalt thou go, and dust shalt thou eat all the days of thy life:

15 And I will put enmity between thee and the woman, and between thy seed and her seed; it shall bruise thy head and thou shalt bruise his heel.

16 Unto the woman he said, I will greatly multiply thy sorrow and thy conception; in sorrow thou shalt bring forth children: and thy desire *shall be* to thy husband, and he shall rule over thee.

17 And unto Adam he said, Because thou hast hearkened unto the voice of thy wife, and hast eaten of the tree, of which I commanded thee, saying, Thou shalt not eat of it; cursed *is* the ground for thy sake; in sorrow shalt thou eat *of* it all the days of thy life;

18 Thorns also and thistles shall it bring forth to thee; and thou shalt eat the herb of the field;

19 In the sweat of thy face shalt thou eat bread till thou return unto the ground; for out of it wast thou taken; for dust thou *art*, and unto dust shalt thou return.

20 And Adam called his wife's name Eve; because she was the mother of all living.

21 Unto Adam also and to his wife did the Lord God make coats of skins and clothed them.

22 ¶ And the Lord God

said, Behold the man is become as one of us, to know good and evil; and now, lest he put forth his hand, and take also of the tree of life, and eat, and live for ever;

23 Therefore the Lord God sent him forth from the garden of Eden, to till the ground from whence he was taken.

24 So he drove out the man: and he placed at the east of the garden of Eden cherubim, and a flaming sword which turned every way, to keep the way of the tree of life.

Adam Clarke, in his commentaries, asks the question, "is this an allegory?" He finds it beset with so many difficulties as an historical fact, that he inclines at first to regard it as a fable, a mere symbol, of some hidden truth. His mind seems more troubled about the serpent than any other personage in the drama. As snakes cannot walk upright, and have never been known to speak, he thinks this beguiling creature must have been an ourang-outang, or some species of ape. However, after expressing all his doubts, he rests in the assumption that it must be taken literally, and that with higher knowledge of the possibilities of all living things, many seeming improbabilities will be fully realized.

A learned professor in Yale College,* before a large class of students, expressed serious doubts as to the forbidden fruit being an apple, as none grew in that latitude. He said it must have been a quince. If the serpent and the apple are to be withdrawn thus recklessly from the tableaux, it is feared that with advancing civilization the whole drama may fall into discredit. Scientists tell us that "the missing link" between the ape and man, has recently been discovered, so that we can now trace back an unbroken line of ancestors to the dawn of creation.

As out of this allegory grows the doctrines of original sin, the fall of man, and woman the author of all our woes, and the curses on the serpent, the woman, and the man; the Darwinian theory of the gradual growth of the race from a lower to a higher type of animal life, is more hopeful and encouraging. However, as our chief interest is in woman's part in the drama, we are equally pleased with her attitude, whether as a myth in an allegory, or as the heroine of an historical occurrence.

---

* Daniel Cady Eaton.

In this prolonged interview, the unprejudiced reader must be impressed with the courage, the dignity, and the lofty ambition of the woman. The tempter evidently had a profound knowledge of human nature, and saw at a glance the high character of the person he met by chance in his walks in the garden. He did not try to tempt her from the path of duty by brilliant jewels, rich dresses, worldly luxuries or pleasures, but with the promise of knowledge, with the wisdom of the Gods. Like Socrates or Plato, his powers of conversation and asking puzzling questions, were no doubt marvellous, and he roused in the woman that intense thirst for knowledge, that the simple pleasures of picking flowers and talking with Adam did not satisfy. Compared with Adam she appears to great advantage through the entire drama.

The curse pronounced on woman is inserted in an unfriendly spirit to justify her degradation and subjection to man. With obedience to the laws of health, diet, dress, and exercise, the period of maternity should be one of added vigor in both body and mind, a perfectly natural operation should not be attended with suffering. By the observance of physical and psychical laws the supposed curse can be easily transformed into a blessing. Some churchmen speak of maternity as a disability, and then chant the Magnificat in all their cathedrals round the globe. Through all life's shifting scenes, the mother of the race has been the greatest factor in civilization.

We hear the opinion often expressed, that woman always has, and always will be in subjection. Neither assertion is true. She enjoyed unlimited individual freedom for many centuries, and the events of the present day all point to her speedy emancipation. Scientists now give 85,000 years for the growth of the race. They assign 60,000 to savagism, 20,000 to barbarism, and 5,000 to civilization. Recent historians tell us that for centuries woman reigned supreme. That period was called the Matriarchate. Then man seized the reins of government, and we are now under the Patriarchate. But we see on all sides new forces gathering, and woman is already abreast with man in art, science, literature, and government. The next dynasty, in which both will reign as equals, will be the Amphiarchate, which is close at hand.

Psychologists tell us of a sixth sense now in process of development, by which we can read each other's mind and communicate without speech. The Tempter might have had the sense, as he evidently read the minds of both the creature and the Creator, if we are to take this account as literally true, as Adam Clarke advises.

CHAPTER IV.

Genesis iv: 1–12, 19, 23.

1 And Adam knew Eve his wife; and she conceived, and bare Cain, and said, I have gotten a man from the Lord.

2 And she again bare his brother Abel. And Abel was a keeper of sheep, but Cain was a tiller of the ground.

3 And in process of time it came to pass, that Cain brought of the fruit of the ground an offering unto the Lord.

4 And Abel, he also brought of the firstlings of his flock and of the fat thereof. And the Lord had respect unto Abel and to his offering.

5 But unto Cain and to his offering he had not respect. And Cain was very wroth, and his countenance fell.

6 And the Lord said unto Cain, Why art thou wroth? and why is thy countenance fallen?

7 If thou doest well, shalt thou not be accepted: and if thou doest not well, sin lieth at the door: and unto thee *shall be* his desire, and thou shalt rule over him.

8 And Cain talked with Abel his brother: and it came to pass, when they were in the field, that Cain rose up against Abel his brother, and slew him.

9 ¶ And the Lord said unto Cain, where *is* Abel thy brother? And he said, I know not: *Am* I my brother's keeper?

10 And he said, What hast thou done? the voice of thy brother's blood crieth unto me from the ground.

11 And now *art* thou cursed from the earth which hath opened her mouth to receive thy brother's blood from thy hand.

12 When thou tillest the ground, it shall not henceforth yield unto thee her strength; a fugitive and a vagabond shalt thou be in the earth.

19 ¶ And Lamech took unto him two wives: the name of the one *was* Adah, and the name of the other Zillah.

23 And Lamech said unto his wives, Adah and Zillah, hear my voice; ye wives of Lamech, hearken unto my speech.

... The manner in which the writer of these chapters presents the women so in conflict with Chapters i and v, which immediately precede and follow, inclines the unprejudiced mind to relegate the ii, iii and iv chapters to the realm of fancy as no part of the real history of creation's dawn.

The curse pronounced on Cain is similar to that inflicted on Adam, both were to till the ground, which was to bring forth weeds abundantly. Hale's statistics of weeds show their rapid and widespread power of propagation. "A progeny," he says, "more than sufficient in a few years to stock every planet of the solar system." In the face of such discouraging facts, Hale coolly remarks. "Such provisions has the just God made to fulfil the curse which he promised on man."

It seems far more rational to believe that the curses on both woman and man were but figments of the human brain, and that by the observance of natural laws, both labor and maternity may prove great blessings.

With all the modern appliances of steam and electricity, and the new inventions in machinery, the cultivation of the soil is fast coming to be a recreation and amusement. The farmer now sits at ease on his plough, while his steed turns up the furrows at his will. With machinery the sons of Adam now sow and reap their harvests, keep the wheels of their great manufactories in motion, and with daily increasing speed carry on the commerce of the world. The time is at hand when the heavy burdens of the laborer will all be shifted on the shoulders of these tireless machines. And when the woman, too, learns and obeys the laws of life, these supposed curses will be but idle dreams of the past. The curse falls lightly even now on women who live in natural conditions, and with anaesthetics is essentially mitigated in all cases.

When these remedial agents were first discovered, some women refused to avail themselves of their blessings, and some orthodox physicians refused to administer them, lest they should interfere with the wise provisions of Providence in making maternity a curse.

Anthony, Response to NAWSA Resolution

The one distinct feature of our association has been the right of individual opinion for every member. We have been beset at each step with the cry that somebody was injuring the cause by the expression of sentiments which differed from those held by the majority. The religious persecution of the ages has been carried on under what was claimed to be the command of God. I distrust those people who know so well what God wants them to do, because I notice it always coincides with their own desires. All the way along the history of our movement there has been this same contest on account of religious theories. Forty years ago one of our noblest men said to me, "You would better never hold another convention than allow Ernestine L. Rose on your platform;" because that eloquent woman, who ever stood for justice and freedom, did not believe in the plenary inspiration of the Bible. Did we banish Mrs. Rose? No, indeed!

Every new generation of converts threshes over the same old straw. The point is whether you will sit in judgment on one who questions the divine inspiration of certain passages in the Bible derogatory to women. If Mrs. Stanton had written approvingly of these passages you would not have brought in this resolution for fear the cause might be injured among the *liberals* in religion. In other words, if she had written *your* views, you would not have considered a resolution necessary. To pass this one is to set back the hands on the dial of reform.

What you should say to outsiders is that a Christian has neither more nor less rights in our association than an atheist. When our platform becomes too narrow for people of all creeds and of no creeds, I myself can not stand upon it. Many things have been said and done by our *orthodox* friends which I have felt to be extremely harmful to our cause; but I should no more consent to a resolution denouncing them than I shall consent to this. Who is to draw the line? Who can tell now whether these commentaries may not prove a great help to woman's emancipation from old superstitions which have barred its way?

Ida Harper, *Life of Anthony,* Vol. 2, pp. 853–54

Lucretia Mott at first thought Mrs. Stanton had injured the cause of all woman's other rights by insisting upon the demand for suffrage, but she had sense enough not to bring in a resolution against it. In 1860 when Mrs. Stanton made a speech before the New York Legislature in favor of a bill making drunkenness a ground for divorce, there was a general cry among the friends that she had killed the woman's cause. I shall be pained beyond expression if the delegates here are so narrow and illiberal as to adopt this resolution. You would better not begin resolving against individual action or you will find no limit. This year it is Mrs. Stanton; next year it may be I or one of yourselves, who will be the victim.

If we do not inspire in women a broad and catholic spirit, they will fail, when enfranchised, to constitute that power for better government which we have always claimed for them. Ten women educated into the practice of liberal principles would be a stronger force than 10,000 organized on a platform of intolerance and bigotry. I pray you vote for religious liberty, without censorship or inquisition. This resolution adopted will be a vote of censure upon a woman who is without a peer in intellectual and statesmanlike ability; one who has stood for half a century the acknowledged leader of progressive thought and demand in regard to all matters pertaining to the absolute freedom of woman.

SUSAN B. ANTHONY

Stanton, Draft of "Criticism"

. . . Three different conventions of women have passed resolutions against "The Women's [*sic*] Bible" as if a Revising Committee of thirty women had not as good a right to express their opinion of what is taught in the Scriptures as a Committee of Bishops.

There is no persecution so bitter as that in the name of religion. I published a leaflet in favor of opening the Worlds Fair on

Stanton, unpublished manuscript draft, Elizabeth Cady Stanton Papers, Library of Congress

Sunday. Five hundred copies by chance fell into the hands of one of my devout friends, as sweet a little woman as I ever knew in other respects. She threw them all into the fire. Dear, said I, you have committed a state prison offence. However, I shall not incarcerate you, but if you had lived in the time of Calvin you would as readily [have] burned me and thought you did God service.

Much as I desire the suffrage, I would rather never vote, than to see the policy of our government at the mercy of the religious bigotry of such women. My heart's desire is to lift women out of all these dangerous and degrading superstitions and to this end will I labor my remaining days on earth.

Seeing the danger of a union in state and church in the old world, our fathers determined to lay the foundations of our republic in the equal rights of all citizens, without regard to sect or creed, Quaker, Baptist, Jew, Catholic, Protestant, Infidel, Agnostic all enjoying the same freedom. All encroachments on this principle should be firmly resisted.

ELIZABETH CADY STANTON

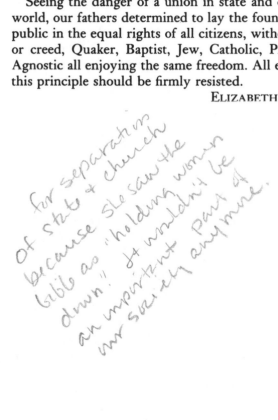

For separation of state & church because she saw the bible as "holding women down". It wouldn't be an important part of our society anymore.

DOCUMENT **20**

STANTON, "THE SOLITUDE OF SELF," JANUARY 18, 1892

Stanton delivered "The Solitude of Self" in 1892, at the convention at which she resigned the presidency of the suffrage movement. Anthony did not like the speech at first, but Stanton thought it "the best thing I have ever written" and it remains one of the most moving statements of feminism of any age.* Stanton's advanced age and her political isolation help to explain the speech's sad, wearied tone, but her ultimate message was a triumphant one, a powerful defense of the feminist philosophy by which she had lived her life and made most of her political decisions.

The essence of Stanton's feminism was the belief that, ultimately, life placed the same demands on women as on men, required the same resources of them, and therefore, in justice, should provide them with the same individual rights. In this speech, however, her emphasis was shifting from individualism as a political philosophy to individualism as a psychological theory, a description of the inner experience common to men and women. As such, Stanton anticipated the existentialist philosophy associated with the rebirth of feminism in our own time, and modern feminism's concern with the "personal" elements of women's experience.

The Woman's Column, January, 1892, pp. 2–3
* *Stanton Letters,* p. 280.

THE point I wish plainly to bring before you on this occasion is the individuality of each human soul; our Protestant idea, the right of individual conscience and judgement; our republican idea, individual citizenship. In discussing the rights of woman, we are to consider, first, what belongs to her as an individual, in a world of her own, the arbiter of her own destiny, an imaginary Robinson Crusoe, with her woman, Friday, on a solitary island. Her rights under such circumstances are to use all her faculties for her own safety and happiness.

Secondly, if we consider her as a citizen, as a member of a great nation, she must have the same rights as all others members, according to the fundamental principles of our Government.

Thirdly, viewed as a woman, an equal factor in civilization, her rights and duties are still the same—individual happiness and development.

Fourthly, it is only the incidental relations of life, such as mother, wife, sister, daughter, which may involve some special duties and training. . . .

The strongest reason for giving woman all the opportunities for higher education, for the full development of her faculties, her forces of mind and body; for giving her the most enlarged freedom of thought and action; a complete emancipation from all forms of bondage, of custom, dependence, superstition; from all the crippling influences of fear—is the solitude and personal responsibility of her own individual life. The strongest reason why we ask for woman a voice in the government under which she lives; in the religion she is asked to believe; equality in social life, where she is the chief factor; a place in the trades and professions, where she may earn her bread, is because of her birthright to self-sovereignty; because, as an individual, she must rely on herself. No matter how much women prefer to lean, to be protected and supported, nor how much men desire to have them do so, they must make the voyage of life alone, and for safety in an emergency, they must know something of the laws of navigation. To guide our own craft, we must be captain, pilot, engineer; with chart and compass to stand at the wheel; to watch the winds and waves, and know when to take in the sail, and to read the signs in the firmament over all. It matters not whether the solitary voyager is man or woman; nature, having endowed them equally, leaves them to their own skill and judgment in the hour of danger, and, if not equal to the occasion, alike they perish.

To appreciate the importance of fitting every human soul for independent action, think for a moment of the immeasurable solitude of self. We come into the world alone, unlike all who have gone before us, we leave it alone, under circumstances peculiar to ourselves. No mortal ever has been, no mortal ever will be like the soul just launched on the sea of life. There can never again be just such a combination of prenatal influences; never again just such environments as make up the infancy, youth and manhood of this one. Nature never repeats herself, and the possibilities of one human soul will never be found in another. No one has ever found two blades of ribbon grass alike, and no one will ever find two human beings alike. Seeing, then, what must be the infinite diversity in human character, we can in a measure appreciate the loss to a nation when any large class of the people is uneducated and unrepresented in the government.

We ask for the complete development of every individual, first, for his own benefit and happiness. In fitting out an army, we give each soldier his own knapsack, arms, powder, his blanket, cup, knife, fork and spoon. We provide alike for all their individual necessities; then each man bears his own burden.

Again, we ask complete individual development for the general good; for the consensus of the competent on the whole round of human interests, on all questions of national life; and here each man must bear his share of the general burden. It is sad to see how soon friendless children are left to bear their own burdens, before they can analyze their feelings; before they can even tell their joys and sorrows, they are thrown on their own resources. The great lesson that nature seems to teach us at all ages is self-dependence, self-protection, self-support. . . .

In youth our most bitter disappointments, our brightest hopes and ambitions, are known only to ourselves. Even our friendship and love we never fully share with another; there is something of every passion, in every situation, we conceal. Even so in our triumphs and our defeats. . . .

We ask no sympathy from others in the anxiety and agony of a broken friendship or shattered love. When death sunders our nearest ties, alone we sit in the shadow of our affliction. Alike amid the greatest triumphs and darkest tragedies of life, we walk alone. On the divine heights of human attainment, eulogized and worshipped as a hero or saint, we stand alone. In ignorance, poverty and vice, as a pauper or criminal, alone we starve or steal; alone we suffer the sneers and rebuffs of our fellows; alone we are hunted and hounded through dark courts and alleys, in by-ways and high-ways; alone we stand in the judgment seat; alone in the prison cell we lament our crimes and misfortunes; alone we expiate them on the gallows. In hours like these we realize the awful solitude of individual life, its pains, its penalties, its responsibilities; hours in which the youngest and most helpless are thrown on their own resources for guidance and consolation. Seeing, then, that life must ever be a march and a battle, that each soldier must be equipped for his own protection, it is the height of cruelty to rob the individual of a single natural right.

To throw obstacles in the way of a complete education is like putting out the eyes; to deny the rights of property is like cutting off the hands. To refuse political equality is to rob the ostracized of all self-respect; of credit in the market place; of recompense in the world of work, of a voice in choosing those who make and administer the law, a choice in the jury before whom they are tried, and in the judge who decides their punishment. [Think of] . . . woman's position! Robbed of her natural rights, handicapped by law and custom at every turn, yet compelled to fight her own battles, and in the emergencies of life to fall back on herself for protection. . . .

The young wife and mother, at the head of some establishment, with a kind husband to shield her from the adverse winds of life, with wealth, fortune and position, has a certain harbor of

modern lament

safety, secure against the ordinary ills of life. But to manage a household, have a desirable influence in society, keep her friends and the affections of her husband, train her children and servants well, she must have rare common sense, wisdom, diplomacy, and a knowledge of human nature. To do all this, she needs the cardinal virtues and the strong points of character that the most successful statesman possesses. An uneducated woman trained to dependence, with no resources in herself, must make a failure of any position in life. But society says women do not need a knowledge of the world, the liberal training that experience in public life must give, all the advantages of collegiate education; but when for the lack of all this, the woman's happiness is wrecked, alone she bears her humiliation; and the solitude of the weak and the ignorant is indeed pitiable. In the wild chase for the prizes of life, they are ground to powder.

empty-nest

In age, when the pleasures of youth are passed, children grown up, married and gone, the hurry and bustle of life in a measure over, when the hands are weary of active service, when the old arm chair and the fireside are the chosen resorts, then men and women alike must fall back on their own resources. If they cannot find companionship in books, if they have no interest in the vital questions of the hour, no interest in watching the consummation of reforms with which they might have been identified, they soon pass into their dotage. The more fully the faculties of the mind are developed and kept in use, the longer the period of vigor and active interest in all around us continues. If, from a life-long participation in public affairs, a woman feels responsible for the laws regulating our system of education, the discipline of our jails and prisons, the sanitary condition of our private homes, public buildings and thoroughfares, an interest in commerce, finance, our foreign relations, in any or all these questions, her solitude will at least be respectable, and she will not be driven to gossip or scandal for entertainment.

gossip temptation

The chief reason for opening to every soul the doors to the whole round of human duties and pleasures is the individual development thus attained, the resources thus provided under all circumstances to mitigate the solitude that at times must come to everyone.

... Inasmuch, then, as woman shares equally the joys and sorrows of time and eternity, is it not the height of presumption in man to propose to represent her at the ballot box and the throne of grace, to do her voting in the state, her praying in the church, and to assume the position of high priest at the family altar?

Nothing strengthens the judgment and quickens the conscience like individual responsibility. Nothing adds such dignity to character as the recognition of one's self-sovereignty; the right to an equal place, everywhere conceded—a place earned by personal merit, not an artificial attainment by inheritance, wealth, family and position. Conceding, then, that the responsibilities of life rest equally on man and woman, that their destiny is the same, they need the same preparation for time and eternity. The talk of sheltering woman from the fierce storms of life is the sheerest mockery, for they beat on her from every point of the compass, just as they do on man, and with more fatal results, for he has been trained to protect himself, to resist, and to conquer. Such are the facts in human experience, the responsibilities of individual sovereignty. Rich and poor, intelligent and ignorant, wise and foolish, virtuous and vicious, man and woman; it is ever the same, each soul must depend wholly on itself.

Whatever the theories may be of woman's dependence on man, in the supreme moments of her life, he cannot bear her burdens. Alone she goes to the gates of death to give life to every man that is born into the world; no one can share her fears, no one can mitigate her pangs; and if her sorrow is greater than she can bear, alone she passes beyond the gates into the vast unknown.

From the mountain-tops of Judea long ago, a heavenly voice bade his disciples, "Bear ye one another's burdens"; but humanity has not yet risen to that point of self-sacrifice; and if ever so willing, how few the burdens are that one soul can bear for another! ...

Jesus

So it ever must be in the conflicting scenes of life, in the long, weary march, each one walks alone. We may have many friends, love, kindness, sympathy and charity, to smooth our pathway in everyday life, but in the tragedies and triumphs of human experience, each mortal stands alone.

But when all artificial trammels are removed, and women are recognized as individuals, responsible for their own environments, thoroughly educated for all positions in life they may be called to fill; with all the resources in themselves that liberal thought and broad culture can give; guided by their own conscience and judgment, trained to self-protection, by a healthy development of the muscular system, and skill in the use of weapons and defence; and stimulated to self-support by a knowledge of the business world and the pleasure that pecuniary independence must ever give; when women are trained in this way, they will in a measure be fitted for those hours of solitude that come alike to all, whether prepared or otherwise. As in our extremity we must depend on ourselves, the dictates of wisdom point to complete individual development.

In talking of education, how shallow the argument that each class must be educated for the special work it proposes to do, and that all those faculties not needed in this special work must lie dormant and utterly wither for want of use, when, perhaps, these will be the very faculties needed in life's greatest emergencies! Some say, "Where is the use of drilling girls in the languages, the sciences, in law, medicine, theology. As wives, mothers, housekeepers, cooks, they need a different curriculum from boys who are to fill all positions. The chief cooks in our great hotels and ocean steamers are men. In our large cities, men run the bakeries; they make our bread, cake and pies. They manage the laundries; they are now considered our best milliners and dressmakers. Because some men fill these departments of usefulness, shall we regulate the curriculum in Harvard and Yale to their present necessities? If not, why this talk in our best colleges of a curriculum for girls who are crowding into the trades and professions, teachers in all our public schools, rapidly filling many lucrative and honorable positions in life?"

... Women are already the equals of men in the whole realm of thought, in art, science, literature and government.... The poetry and novels of the century are theirs, and they have touched the keynote of reform, in religion, politics and social life. They fill the editor's and professor's chair, plead at the bar of justice, walk the wards of the hospital, speak from the pulpit and the platform. Such is the type of womanhood that an enlightened public sentiment welcomes to-day, and such the triumph of the facts of life over the false theories of the past.

Is it, then, consistent to hold the developed woman of this day within the same narrow political limits as the dame with the spinning wheel and knitting needle occupied in the past? No, no! Machinery has taken the labors of woman as well as man on its tireless shoulders; the loom and the spinning wheel are but dreams of the past; the pen, the brush, the easel, the chisel, have taken their places, while the hopes and ambitions of women are essentially changed.

We see reason sufficient in the outer conditions of human beings for individual liberty and development, but when we consider the self-dependence of every human soul, we see the need of courage, judgment and the exercise of every faculty of mind and body, strengthened and developed by use, in woman as well as man.

Whatever may be said of man's protecting power in ordinary conditions, amid all the terrible disasters by land and sea, in the supreme moments of danger, alone woman must ever meet the horrors of the situation. The Angel of Death even makes no royal pathway for her. Man's love and sympathy enter only into the sunshine of our lives. In that solemn solitude of self, that links us with the immeasurable and the eternal, each soul lives alone forever. A recent writer says: "I remember once, in crossing the Atlantic, to have gone upon the deck of the ship at midnight, when a dense black cloud enveloped the sky, and the great deep was roaring madly under the lashes of demoniac winds. My feeling was not of danger or fear (which is a base surrender of the immortal soul) but of utter desolation and loneliness; a little speck of life shut in by a tremendous darkness. . . ."

And yet, there is a solitude which each and every one of us has always carried with him, more inaccessible than the ice-cold mountains, more profound than the midnight sea; the solitude of self. Our inner being which we call ourself, no eye nor touch of man or angel has ever pierced. It is more hidden than the caves of the gnome; the sacred adytum of the oracle; the hidden chamber of Eleusinian mystery, for to it only omniscience is permitted to enter.

Such is individual life. Who, I ask you, can take, dare take on himself the rights, the duties, the responsibilities of another human soul?

ANNA HOWARD SHAW, "THE PASSING OF AUNT SUSAN"; HELEN GARDENER, "ELIZABETH CADY STANTON"

Stanton died in 1902, at the age of eighty-seven, Anthony in 1906, when she was eighty-six. Their eulogies suggest several important comparisons between the political leadership each woman provided. The tribute to Anthony was written by Anna Howard Shaw, the first woman ordained as a Methodist minister and a representative of Christian feminism. Stanton's obituary was written by an atheist, published in a secularist magazine, and stressed the challenges Stanton had mounted against religious authority. Shaw's account of Anthony shows us a woman totally identified with the organized women's movement, simultaneously selfless and arrogantly ordering others about. Gardener's portrait of Stanton is that of a political independent and thoroughgoing radical, an individualist who was often the only one "great enough to be honest with her own soul."

Above all, it is the last minutes of the lives of Stanton and Anthony that provide us with a striking contrast and perfect complement: Anthony, the organizer, murmuring the names of "an endless, shadowy review" of women, famous and unknown; Stanton, the philosopher, composing her last address.

Story of a Pioneer (New York: Harper and Brothers, Publishers, 1915), pp. 221–35; *Free Thought Magazine*, January, 1903, pp. 6–9

In 1906, when the date of the annual convention of the National American Woman Suffrage Association in Baltimore was drawing near, she became convinced that it would be her last convention. She was right. She showed a passionate eagerness to make it one of the greatest conventions ever held in the history of the movement; and we, who loved her and saw that the flame of her life was burning low, also bent all our energies to the task of realizing her hopes. In November preceding the convention she visited me and her niece, Miss Lucy Anthony, in our home in Mount Airy, Philadelphia, and it was clear that her anxiety over the convention was weighing heavily upon her. She visibly lost strength from day to day. One morning she said abruptly, "Anna, let's go and call on President M. Carey Thomas, of Bryn Mawr."

I wrote a note to Miss Thomas, telling her of Miss Anthony's desire to see her, and received an immediate reply inviting us to luncheon the following day. We found Miss Thomas deep in the work connected with her new college buildings, over which she showed us with much pride. . . .

"We want your co-operation, and that of Miss Garrett," began Miss Anthony, promptly, "to make our Baltimore Convention a success. We want you to persuade the Arundel Club of Baltimore, the most fashionable club in the city, to give a reception to the delegates; and we want you to arrange a college night on the programme—a great college night, with the best college speakers ever brought together."

These were large commissions for two extremely busy women, but both Miss Thomas and Miss Garrett—realizing Miss Anthony's intense earnestness—promised to think over the suggestions and see what they could do. The next morning we received a telegram from them stating that Miss Thomas would arrange the college evening, and that Miss Garrett would reopen her Baltimore home, which she had closed, during the convention. She also invited Miss Anthony and me to be her guests there, and added that she would try to arrange the reception by the Arundel Club.

"Aunt Susan" was overjoyed. I have never seen her happier than she was over the receipt of that telegram. She knew that whatever Miss Thomas and Miss Garrett undertook would be accomplished, and she rightly regarded the success of the convention as already assured. . . .

From beginning to end the convention was probably the most notable yet held in our history. Julia Ward Howe and her daughter, Florence Howe Hall, were also guests of Miss Garrett, who, moreover, entertained all the speakers of "College Night." Miss Anthony, now eighty-six, arrived in Baltimore quite ill, and Mrs. Howe, who was ninety, was taken ill soon after she reached there. The two great women made a dramatic exchange on the programme, for on the first night, when Miss Anthony was unable to speak, Mrs. Howe took her place, and on the second night, when Mrs. Howe had succumbed, Miss Anthony had recovered sufficiently to appear for her. . . .

On the 15th of February we left Baltimore for Washington, where Miss Anthony was to celebrate her eighty-sixth birthday. For many years the National American Woman Suffrage Association had celebrated our birthdays together, as hers came on the 15th of the month and mine on the 14th. . . . "Aunt Susan" should not have attempted the Washington celebration, for she was still ill and exhausted by the strain of the convention. But notwithstanding her sufferings and the warnings of her physicians, she insisted on being present; so Miss Garrett sent the trained nurse to Washington with her, and we all tried to make the journey the least possible strain on the patient's vitality. . . .

The birthday celebration that followed our executive meeting was an impressive one. It was held in the Church of Our Father, whose pastor, the Rev. John Van Schaick, had always been exceedingly kind to Miss Anthony. Many prominent men spoke. President Roosevelt and other statesmen sent most friendly letters, and William H. Taft had promised to be present. He did not come, nor did he, then or later, send any excuse for not coming—an omission that greatly disappointed Miss Anthony, who had always admired him. I presided at the meeting, and though we all did our best to make it gay, a strange hush hung over the assemblage—a solemn stillness, such as one feels in the presence of death. We became more and more conscious that Miss Anthony was suffering, and we hastened the exercises all we could. When I read President Roosevelt's long tribute to her, Miss Anthony rose to comment on it.

"One word from President Roosevelt in his message to Congress," she said, a little wearily, "would be worth a thousand eulogies of Susan B. Anthony. When will men learn that what we ask is not praise, but justice?"

At the close of the meeting, realizing how weak she was, I begged her to let me speak for her. But she again rose, rested her hand on my shoulder, and, standing by my side, uttered the last words she ever spoke in public, pleading with women to consecrate themselves to the Cause, assuring them that no power could prevent its ultimate success, but reminding them also that the time of its coming would depend wholly on their work and their loyalty. She ended with three words—very fitting words from her lips, expressing as they did the spirit of her life-work—*"Failure is impossible."*

The next morning she was taken to her home in Rochester, and one month from that day we conducted her funeral services. . . . During the first three weeks of her last illness, . . . I did what she wished me to do—I continued our work, trying to do hers as well as my own. But all the time my heart was in her sick-room, and at last the day came when I could no longer remain away from her. I had awakened in the morning with a strong conviction that she needed me, and at the breakfast-table I announced to her niece, Miss Lucy Anthony, the friend who for years has shared my home, that I was going at once to "Aunt Susan." . . .

When I reached my friend's bedside one glance at her face showed me the end was near; and from that time until it came, almost a week later, I remained with her; while again, as always, she talked of the Cause, and of the life-work she must now lay down. The first thing she spoke of was her will, which she had made several years before, and in which she had left the small property she possessed to her sister Mary, her niece Lucy, and myself, with instructions as to the use we three were to make of it. Now she told me we were to pay no attention to these instructions, but to give every dollar of her money to the $60,000 fund Miss Thomas and Miss Garrett were trying to raise. She was vitally interested in this fund, as its success meant that for five years the active officers of the National American Woman Suffrage Association, including myself as president, would for the first time receive salaries for our work. When she had given her instructions on this point she still seemed depressed.

"I wish I could live on," she said, wistfully. "But I cannot. My spirit is eager and my heart is as young as it ever was, but my poor old body is worn out. Before I go I want you to give me a promise: Promise me that you will keep the presidency of the association as long as you are well enough to do the work."

"But how can I promise that?" I asked. "I can keep it only as long as others wish me to keep it."

"Promise to make them wish you to keep it," she urged. "Just as I wish you to keep it."

I would have promised her anything then. So, though I knew that to hold the presidency would tie me to a position that brought in no living income, and though for several years past I had already drawn alarmingly upon my small financial reserve, I promised her that I would hold the office as long as the majority of the women in the association wished me to do so. "But," I added, "if the time comes when I believe that some one else can do better work in the presidency than I, then let me feel at liberty to resign it."

This did not satisfy her.

"No, no," she objected. "You cannot be the judge of that. Promise me you will remain until the friends you most trust tell you it is time to withdraw, or make you understand that it is time. Promise me that."

I made the promise. She seemed content, and again began to talk of the future.

"You will not have an easy path," she warned me. . . . "No matter what is done or is not done, how you are criticized or misunderstood, or what efforts are made to block your path, remember that the only fear you need have is the fear of not standing by the thing you believe to be right. Take your stand and hold it; then let come what will, and receive blows like a good soldier."

During the last forty-eight hours of her life she was unwilling that I should leave her side. So day and night I knelt by her bed, holding her hand and watching the flame of her wonderful spirit grow dim. At times, even then, it blazed up with startling suddenness. On the last afternoon of her life, when she had lain quiet for hours, she suddenly began to utter the names of the women who had worked with her, as if in a final roll call. Many of them had preceded her into the next world; others were still splendidly active in the work she was laying down. But young or old, living or dead, they all seemed to file past her dying eyes that day in an endless, shadowy review, and as they went by she spoke to each of them.

Not all the names she mentioned were known in suffrage ranks; some of these women lived only in the heart of Susan B. Anthony, and now, for the last time, she was thanking them for what they had done. Here was one who, at a moment of special need, had given her small savings; here was another who had won valuable recruits to the Cause; this one had written a strong editorial; that one had made a stirring speech. In these final hours it seemed that not a single sacrifice or service, however small, had been forgotten by the dying leader. Last of all, she spoke to the women who had been on her board and had stood by her loyally so long—Rachel Foster Avery, Alice Stone Blackwell, Carrie Chapman Catt, Mrs. Upton, Laura Clay, and others. Then, after lying in silence for a long time with her cheek on my hand, she murmured: "They are still passing before me—face after face, hundreds and hundreds of them, representing all the efforts of fifty years. I know how hard they have worked. I know the sacrifices they have made. But it has all been worth while!"

Just before she lapsed into unconsciousness she seemed restless and anxious to say something, searching my face with her dimming eyes.

"Do you want me to repeat my promise?" I asked, for she had

already made me do so several times. She made a sign of assent, and I gave her the assurance she desired. As I did so she raised my hand to her lips and kissed it—her last conscious action. For more than thirty hours after that I knelt by her side, but though she clung to my hand until her own hand grew cold, she did not speak again.

She had told me over and over how much our long friendship and association had meant to her, and the comfort I had given her. But whatever I may have been to her, it was as nothing compared with what she was to me. Kneeling close to her as she passed away, I knew that I would have given her a dozen lives had I had them, and endured a thousand times more hardship than we had borne together, for the inspiration of her companionship and the joy of her affection. They were the greatest blessings I have had in all my life, and I cherish as my dearest treasure the volume of her *History of Woman Suffrage* on the fly-leaf of which she had written this inscription:

> Reverend Anna Howard Shaw:
>   This huge volume IV I present to you with the love that a mother beareth, and I hope you will find in it the facts about women, for you will find them nowhere else. Your part will be to see that the four volumes are duly placed in the libraries of the country, where every student of history may have access to them.
>
> With unbounded love and faith,
SUSAN B. ANTHONY.

That final line is still my greatest comfort. When I am misrepresented or misunderstood, when I am accused of personal ambition or of working for personal ends, I turn to it and to similar lines penned by the same hand, and tell myself that I should not allow anything to interfere with the serenity of my spirit or to disturb me in my work. At the end of eighteen years of the most intimate companionship, the leader of our Cause, the greatest woman I have ever known, still felt for me "unbounded love and faith." Having had that, I have had enough.

One of the most versatile of women she was, and yet, for so many years her tongue and pen led the contest in this and other

countries for what is commonly called the rights of woman—
that is, for woman's right to stand as a unit among other units of
the race—so it happens that her name naturally is fixed in the
general public mind as belonging to that step of progress alone.

Indeed, in one of the most intelligently appreciative editorials
I have yet seen on her life and death, which editorial appeared
in a leading New York daily paper, she was spoken of as "a
woman with one idea—suffrage—to which she had held, steadfastly, for fifty years."

This might be said of many of her associates, perhaps, either
in praise or criticism; but a woman of one idea was precisely
what Mrs. Stanton was not. Hers was a wonderfully well-
rounded mentality, poised and strong on every side. Fearless
and truth-loving, sincere and frank. But she did not allow her
frankness to degenerate into rudeness. Her truth-loving never
led her to disregard the feelings and rights of those who did not
agree with her. She never mistook a loud voice and a sharp re-
tort for argument, or for proof of the justice of her position.

She wished her body to be cremated. This, also, was because
of her firm conviction of the right and value to the living, of this
method of disposing of the dead.

She hugged to her breast no superstitions that prevented her
from thinking first and always of the highest good to the living—to those who come after. Many of her constituents in the
suffrage work deeply deplored her activity in free religious
lines; but she calmly replied that woman would never be fit for
freedom, nor understand its benefits and bearing until she
ceased to hold to her bosom the primary cause of her degradation—her religious superstitions, which bind her to the degraded status assigned her as "the will of God" in all accepted
"revelations." . . .

So, for the past few years, much of Mrs. Stanton's time and
literary energy have been spent in an effort to bring women up
to this vantage ground—in a contest against religious superstitions, rather than against purely political ones, which she perceived had their basis and origin in the religious ones. Like
Wendell Phillips, in the anti-slavery work, she believed in strik-

ing at the root, rather than in breaking of the branches of a fundamental wrong in the hope to eradicate it. She was deeply blamed by some of her old associates for putting out what she called "The Woman's Bible." That is to say, she gathered together all of the passages in the Bible which related especially to woman, and interpreted them (as man had done with all of them relating to himself—and to woman, also) in the light of modern thought.

For eighteen years past it has been my good fortune to be a close friend of this wonderful woman. I have hundreds of letters from her on the work of this "Woman's Bible," and on other topics, and I believe I may claim to know her aims and intent in it as well as any other person. In fact, I was one of the original "revision committee," and while the usual objection made to it by her critics is that it is too radical, my own objection was, always, that it was not radical enough! But to neither criticism did she give heed. She had her own ideal and plan and she went steadily about it without fear and without bigotry.

In 1887 she wrote me from England thus: "Think of it, she (referring to a fine suffrage leader) says she wishes to break down the material slavery of woman. If she wanted to get the Turkish women out of the harem, would she begin with arguments on republican government? No, indeed; she would know that they are held in sexual slavery by the power of their religion—and so are we. If women were emancipated from their religious superstitions they would understand their interests in the things of this life more readily. But believing that all things here are regulated by the finger of God, the Bible written by him, expressing his will, how can you rouse them to a desire for or belief in their social and political freedom until you first show them that all these things are the outgrowth of man's thought and selfishness, largely based upon his own superstitions and ignorance of Nature's laws, and resulting in woman's degradation and subjection? Do write whenever you have time. We enjoy your good, wholesome common sense. You, at least, never aim at one thing and try thereby to hit another."

Gladstone was called "the grand old man" because it was believed by many of his constituents that he had the faculty of always seeing and dealing with any new subject or difficulty wisely and ably.

I always called Elizabeth Cady Stanton "My Mother Superior," but she may well be known as "the grand old woman," for upon almost every social and political question of her time, her voice and pen expressed her clear and lucid thought in luminous language, and never once did she fail to face toward the light; never once did her steady eye look away from Justice, Freedom and Fair-dealing for all.

She asked no privileges and opposed those who did.

What she sought for herself, she sought, also, for others. She did not believe that mistakes, however hoary, were sacred. She believed in progress—in rectifying the blunders of the past. The last bubble punctured by her keen pen was done, as I say, only three days before she died. It was in the interest of a clean, wholesome, happy home life—in the interest of honest, loving parenthood, in the interest of a child-life spent in an atmosphere of harmony and freed from one of pretense and domestic warfare—a plea, in short, for the right of children to be born of love and reared in its pure light. It was the last protest of this clear, fearless brain against the sophistries of those who hold that it is for the dignity and honor of woman and home that a mistake should be made perpetual—that the "Almighty" has joined together two who hate each other and on this theory they must continue to live out the farce to the bitter end. Her last printed utterance was an able protest against this absurdity, and was an honor to both head and heart of one who, seeing clearly, is not afraid to express her thought even though she be (as she was in this case) the only champion whose bugle note did not quaver behind the mists and fogs of past ideas and lose its values in the defective acoustics of rock-bound superstitions.

Harriot Stanton Blatch, worthy daughter of this splendid mother, writes me of her last hours: "None of us knew mother was so near her end 'til Sunday really (the day she died). She had been suffering from shortness of breath lately, from time to time, and from that cause felt under the mark. On Saturday she said to the doctor, very emphatically, 'Now, if you can't cure this difficulty of breathing, and if I am not to feel brighter and more like work again, I want you to give me something to send me pack-horse speed to heaven.' " And I can just see the twinkle in her eye when she said it.

Her daughter continues: "Two hours before her death (on Sunday) she said she wished to stand up. She was sitting in her arm chair in the drawing-room, not dressed, but in her dressing-gown, and with her hair all arranged as usual." In those beautiful white puffs, like a halo around her massive head—how well we all know and love them! "She had told her maid earlier in the day to dress her hair, and when it was finished she said: 'Now, I'll be dressed.' But I dissuaded her, seeing she was weary. The trained nurse (who had only been summoned an hour earlier), and the doctor, when she asked to stand, helped her to rise and stood on either side of her. I placed a table for her to rest her hands on. She drew herself up very erect (the doctor said the muscular strength was extraordinary) and there she stood for seven or eight minutes, steadily looking out, proudly before her. I think she was mentally making an address. When we urged her to sit down she fell asleep. Two hours later, the doctor thinking her position constrained in her chair, we lifted her to her bed, and she slipped away peacefully in a few minutes." And so passed from our sight and touch that splendid-all-embracing personality. Could any death be more ideally beautiful—more what she would have wished? I can see her now, standing there in her last hours, with that delicate halo of soft, white curls around her death-touched face, pleading once again the cause of the mothers of the race, before an imaginary audience of sons and fathers of those who have lost in her their most eloquent, far-reaching voice.

For in her the world has lost its greatest woman, its noblest mother, its clearest thinker. She embraced in her motherhood all who were under the ban of oppression; she thought for the thoughtless of whatever sex; she was great enough to be honest with her own soul, and to walk in the light of the sun, hand in hand with the naked Truth! And in this she stood almost alone.

Other women there are and were, who walked side by side with her on certain planes, it is true. But none kept perfect step. Not one matched her in all-around ability, in versatility, in the capacity to be supremely clear and strong in every field of thought, in every line of progress.

PART FOUR
Supplementary Documents

PHRENOLOGICAL REPORTS, 1853

In the 1850s phrenology was all the rage, especially among reformers and radicals. The phrenologist "read" an individual's mental traits, such as combativeness, affectiveness, firmness, and so on, by feeling a precise location on the brain through the outside of the skull; the size of the "organ" which contained that trait indicated whether it was too strong, too weak, or moderately developed. As a system of reading character, phrenology linked the lure of self-knowledge with the promise of self-improvement: once the phrenologist had made a scientific assessment, the shape of one's character could be improved, the bumps raised or depressed, by deliberate effort. In retrospect phrenology seems one of the more notable "cranks" of the period, but at the time, in an age in which the majority still looked outward to God for guidance, it constituted one of the only psychological alternatives, a way to find personal truth from within.[1]

Elizabeth Stanton appreciated phrenology for its hopefulness and apparent rationality; there were no sins in this faith, only undeveloped organs. The fact that phrenology was controversial only added to its appeal. Phrenology was one of "the isms by which I differ from the common herd I am happy to say, but which give soul and zest to my life," she boasted in a letter to her father. She had her "bumps and hollows" read in 1853 by one of America's foremost phrenologists, Lorenzo Fowler, and sent the results to her father. "Do give me your honest opinion about it and let mother see it too," she wrote. "Tell me what you really think, even if you do have to come down from your high horse a little."[2]

Susan B. Anthony had her phrenological character read that same year. She was in New York City for a grand women's temperance meeting presided over by Lorenzo Fowler's wife, the women's rights advocate and pioneering woman physician Lydia Folger Fowler. Anthony's reading was done by Nelson Sizer; although the original has disappeared, she so appreciated his assessment that thirty years later she had a version of it included in her official biography.

As a cultural practice, American phrenology was linked to various advanced beliefs of the period, including health and dress reform and women's rights.[3] Nonetheless, like the rest of society, practitioners of phrenology believed that character was fundamentally linked to sex and that traits which graced a woman—for instance, benevolence—were somewhat different from those appropriate to men—such as combativeness. By the time Stanton and Anthony had their readings, they were both becoming known as "strong-minded women," and their phrenological reports reflect this. Although the phrenologically ideal woman possessed the "negative and passive qualities," Anthony's "intellect [was found to be] active and [her] mind more naturally [ran] in the channel of intellect than of feeling."[4] Similarly, Stanton's reading observes that she had "more individuality and positiveness than females generally."

1. See Madeline B. Stern, *Heads and Headlines: The Phrenological Fowlers* (Norman: University of Oklahoma Press, 1971).

2. Elizabeth Cady Stanton to Daniel Cady, January 12, 1853, *Elizabeth Cady Stanton as Revealed in Her Letters, Diary and Reminiscences*, ed. Theodore Stanton and Harriot Stanton Blatch (New York: Harper & Brothers, 1922), pp. 46–47.

3. The center of American phrenology, the New York–based firm of Fowler and Wells, was also a publishing house, which issued the first two volumes of *The History of Woman Suffrage*, edited by Stanton, Anthony, and Matilda Gage in the early 1880s (Stern, *Heads and Headlines*, p. 229).

4. The reference to "negative and passive qualities" comes from Lorenzo Fowler's own writings, as quoted in Stern, *Heads and Headlines*, p. 166.

Phrenological Character of Mrs. Elizabeth C. Stanton, Given at Seneca Falls by Lorenzo Fowler, January 10, 1853

"SELF-KNOWLEDGE IS THE KEY TO SELF-IMPROVEMENT"

Mrs. Elizabeth Stanton

You have a predominance of the vital and mental temperaments with a full degree of the motive but the last is not so sustaining in its influence, the vital having the ascendancy and not being abused.

So your life principle is ample and health perfect; few persons have a better organization for longevity.

You derive the tone of your mind and constitution from your mother hence partake of the nature of the Livingston family rather than that of your father. You have a plump round form fair complexion and animated expression.

Your brain is above the common size, large at the base, occipital and frontal regions. Some faculties are quite large, while others are inferior in strength and influence.

All the social faculties are large with large Combativeness, Destructiveness, Alimentiveness, Firmness, Benev[olent] Construc[tiveness]; and several of the intellectual organs. You are characterized for the following traits.

First, are warm hearted, capable of enjoying the society of your friends much, are greatly attached to your kin, and find it especially difficult to give up those whom you have once loved, enjoy the society of the gentlemen, are not cold hearted toward them and under favorable circumstances are ready to respond to the expressions of sympathy and affection from them, are better adapted to the business and subjects of conversation peculiar to men than those of woman, are capable of enjoying the connubial relation in a high degree, are very fond of children, well qualified to sympathize with them in their helplessness. Attachment to

Published by permission of the Elizabeth Cady Stanton Collection, Mabel Smith Douglass Library, Rutgers, the State University of New Jersey. An edited version of this reading first appeared in Elisabeth Griffith, *In Her Own Right: The Life of Elizabeth Cady Stanton* (New York: Oxford University Press, 1984), pp. 230–32; my transcription differs somewhat.

place is also strong. You are fond of home and its associations, still would enjoy traveling by way of gratifying the other faculties.

You lack continuity of mind and close application to one thing, find it difficult to attend to details either in business or in thought, prefer to have your mind occupied with things that are extensive and comprehensive in their nature. Your thoughts and feelings are more intense and vivid than prolonged and connected. Love of life is strong. You have great desire to live and enjoy the pleasures of life. Your large Combat[iveness] and Destruc-[tiveness] joined with your vital temperament give an unusual degree of force, energy and executiveness of mind. You never stop at trifles, are much more inclined to labor where there are severe difficulties to overcome than to walk in the smoother paths of life, are full of resolution and have a daring spirit and when provoked are capable of being decidedly indignant. Your feelings are not of the tame, quiet class. You are capable of being very sarcastic, vigorous in your style of conversation or writing and at times are not sufficiently gentle and easy in your manners. Appetite is strong and digestion good, none better.

You desire for gain is comparatively good, but owing to the combination of your faculties you are not naturally qualified to attend to the details of business or to make it a special matter of effort to economize, but you prefer to live as you go along and have what you like.

Secret[iveness] and Caut[iousness] are rather wanting, hence with so much propelling and executive power are liable to act from the impulse of the moment and exhibit a boldness and energy of character, that the occasion does not warrant. You are afraid of nothing, are not restrained from acting or speaking through fear of consequences. You show your character just as it is, hence have more individuality and positiveness than females generally. You are no hypocrite, tho' you may not always express in words the depths of your feelings. You detest nothing so much as underhanded means and do not as many do take advantage of circumstances to show off and would be as likely to exhibit those captivating qualities of love or make that display in the manifes-tation of agreeable qualities necessary to attract attention. Appro-bativeness is rather prominent but its function joined with self-

Esteem in your case is rather to give sense of character, independence of thought and moral courage than love of Show and display, or desire for attention and flattery. You are not naturally dignified, have not the feeling of Self-love, are not devoted to yourself, care more to exert a moral and intellectual influence on society than to put yourself forward as an object of attraction.

Your energy of character might so manifest itself that you would get the credit of being proud and haughty but in reality you are not so, indeed are at times wanting in true pride and self-love. You have remarkable Firmness and perseverance when you have once laid out your plans and taken your position. You are not to be driven from your purposes or prevented from consummating your designs. Your moral brain is unevenly developed. Conscien[tiousness] as connected with Firmness is fully developed and its Manifestations are particularly seen with reference to the higher Law.

It should have a distinct influence in your character, while that portion joining Cautiousness is defective. Hence your regard for human law and the consequences of conduct is less active which may sometimes manifest itself in want of circumspection as seen by others. No law is law to you unless sanctioned by the intellect and in harmony with moral obligation.

Hope is full and has a sustaining influence on your mind, tho' you are not particularly elated by enthusiasm and extravagant expectations of success, still are not easily discouraged and have a disposition to regard things in a favorable more than a discouraging light. Veneration and Marvelousness are also average and their influence would be comparatively small and guided mostly by other faculties.

Veneration as manifested toward intellect and superior merit has a fair influence over your character and conduct, but as giving deference for mere opinions forms and customs as such is not distinct. Whatever others value as superior is no criterion to you. Faith is weak when compared with your reason. You are governed by what you can understand and comprehend, more than by faith. Benevolence is large, you are naturally kind, humane, generous in your feelings, anxious for the good of society, delight in rendering service and promoting the happiness of others. This is the strongest and most influential impulse in your moral nature. Your mechanical capacity is good, particularly in contriving ways and means to secure ends, also your sense of the beautiful, poetical and love of the sublime in nature and oratory.

You have uncommon power to insulate and conform to circumstances, to adapt yourself to changes of society or to different kinds of labor, are particularly fond of fun, disposed to joke, can appreciate wit, are however more sarcastic, personal, pointed and truthful in your remarks than funny and mirthful.

Your intellectual faculties are, as a whole, fully developed, and the strength of your intellect lies chiefly in your disposition to reason, inquire into causes in comprehending principles and becoming acquainted with the relations of things and your faculty to originate thoughts and follow your own ideas.

You are not noted for your power to apply thoughts and make it tangible and practical. Larger Comparison would give more power of analysis and ability to apply principles to every day life. You would then more readily see the affinities between principles and the wants of mankind. You have a good degree of suavity of manner and youthfulness of mind and prefer younger society rather than older.

But the organ of Intuition is not paticularly large, still owing to the strength and vigor of your intellect you may readily see the motives of others but this state of mind is not the result of Intuition. Language is fully developed but you are more energetic and forcible than copious, can write better than speak, are decidedly fond of music, appreciate good tones, have good memory of time and events, excellent memory of places, are naturally systematic, fond of order, quite inclined to arrange and systematize your thoughts, are very much annoyed at a want of system and method in business. Capacity in figures is good, you might excel in Mathematics and the Study of the Languages, have a good mechanical eye, are a good judge of proportions, forms and outlines but are not as ready in seeing adaptations of things, are more given to thought and investigation than to observation. Reported Phonographically by E. D. Stark.

Phrenological Examination of Susan B. Anthony, February 1853

You have a finely organized constitution and a good degree of compactness and power. There is such a balance between the brain and the body that you are enabled to sustain mental effort with less exhaustion than most persons. You have an intensity of emotion and thought which makes your mind terse, sharp, spicy and clear. You always work with a will, a purpose and a straight-forwardness of mental action. You seldom accomplish ends by indirect means or circuitous routes, but unfurl your banner, take your position and give fair warning of the course you intend to pursue. You are not naturally fond of combat, but when once fairly enlisted in a cause that has the sanction of your conscience and intellect, your firmness and ambition are such, combined with thoroughness and efficiency of disposition, that all you are in energy and talent is enlisted and concentrated in the one end in view.

You are watchful but not timid, careful to have everything right and safe before you embark; but when times of difficulty and danger arrive, you meet them with coolness and intrepidity. You have more of the spirit of acquisition than of economy; you would rather make new things than patch the old. Your continuity is not large enough. You find it at times difficult to bring the whole strength of your mind to bear upon a subject and hold it there patiently in writing or speaking. You are apt to seize upon fugitive thoughts and wander, unless it be a subject on which you have so drilled your intellect as to become master of it.

You have a full development of the social group. I judge that in the main you have your father's character and talents and your mother's temperament. You have the spirit of her nature, but the framework in the main is like the father. You have large benevo-lence, not only in the direction of sympathy but of gratitude. You have frankness of character, even to sharpness, and you are obliged to bridle your tongue lest you speak more than is meet. You have mechanical ingenuity, the planning talent, and the

---

This edited version is taken from Ida Husted Harper, *The Life and Work of Susan B. Anthony*, Vol. I (Indianapolis: Bowen-Merrill Co., 1899), pp. 85–86.

minds of others are apt to be used as instruments to accomplish your objects. For instance, if you were a lawyer, you would arrange the testimony and the mode of argument in such a way that the best final result would be achieved. You judge correctly of the fitness and propriety, as well as of the power, of the means you have to be employed. You would plan a thing better than you could use the tools to make it. Your reasoning organs are gaining upon your perceptions. At fifteen your mind was devoted to facts and phenomena; of late years you have been thinking of principles and ideas. You are a keen critic, especially if you can put wit as a cracker on your whip; you can make people feel little and mean if they are so, and when you are vexed can say very sharp things.

You are a good judge of character. You have a full development of language devoted rather to accuracy and definiteness of meaning than volubility; and yet I doubt not you talk fast when excited—that belongs to your temperament. Your intellect is active and your mind more naturally runs in the channel of intellect than of feeling. It seeks an intellectual development rather than to be developed through the affections merely. You have fair veneration and spirituality but are nothing remarkable in these respects. Your chief religious elements are conscience and benevolence; these are your working religious organs, and a religion that does not gratify them is to you "as sounding brass and a tinkling cymbal."

STANTON AND ANTHONY, LETTERS,
JULY 24, 1895–OCTOBER 26, 1902

THE FOLLOWING SET of letters between Elizabeth Stanton and
Susan B. Anthony represents the final years of their half-century–long correspondence. In the 1850s, when they first began
writing to each other (see document 4 above), Stanton's letters
predominated. Here Anthony's voice is by far the stronger.
There are several reasons for this. Stanton, now in her eighties
and frail, had retired to home life with her children and grand-
children. By contrast, Anthony continued to live in and through
the woman suffrage movement and to be happiest when she was
traveling for the movement, organizing conventions, and writing
to her "coadjutors." Anthony's many letters are full of information on the political possibilities she was still pursuing, along
with futile efforts to get Stanton to join her. Stanton insisted that
they had "earned the right to sit in [their] rocking-chairs and
think and write," but she knew "that that would be purgatory for
Susan."[1]

Stanton and Anthony also saw very different things as they
looked back over their half century of common labor for women's
emancipation. Anthony's last years were filled with the approval
and appreciation of other women that she had been denied in her
early years and this made her hopeful about the future, despite
the fact that actual victories for woman suffrage were few and far
between. Stanton, on the other hand, ended her political career
on a profoundly pessimistic note. She disliked the conventional
air that was settling over the woman suffrage movement, and
looked back nostalgically to the time when suffragists had staked

out new frontiers for their sex. While Anthony wrote frequently to Stanton to beg her old friend to "Jimmy-Grind" out some speech or article, Stanton shared her discontent with other confidantes, especially the Nebraskan radical Clara Colby and her own daughter, Harriot Stanton Blatch. Anthony had acolytes as well, younger leaders of the National American Woman Suffrage Association such as Rachel Foster Avery, Carrie Chapman Catt, and Anna Howard Shaw.

These were the years when both women were preparing the official versions of their lives for publication—Stanton in her autobiography and Anthony in the biography that Ida Husted Harper wrote under her supervision—and in doing so were reviewing the written evidence of a half century's work. Anthony, who regarded her public and private life as one, compiled her newspaper clippings, letters, and other ephemera into scrapbooks to document the history of which she was so proud to have been a part.[2] Stanton, by contrast, insisted on a distinction between her private side and her public role. "My chief occupation has been looking over my papers," she wrote in her diary while she was preparing her reminiscences for publication, "destroying many and putting the rest in order."[3]

Despite these considerable differences, the bond between the two old friends was deep and enduring through their final years. These letters—especially those from Anthony to the woman she had always regarded as the lodestone of political integrity—express a moving tension between political differences and personal attachment. Harriot Stanton Blatch praised this aspect of the relationship between Anthony and her mother. "The fruit of friendship between [them] has grown through half a hundred years, . . ." she explained in 1900 (see letter of Feb. 15, 1900, below). "But you have not been weak echoes of each other; nay, often for the good of each you were thorns in the side." Like so many other aspects of their leadership of the woman suffrage movement, even their love for each other was strong-minded. "Oh how I do wish you were where I could run in to chat over [things]," wrote Anthony to Stanton in 1895 (see letter of July 24, 1895, below), "but we are always so far apart." In light of the complex nature of their bond in these final years, this remark has special poignancy.

In the first two of these letters, Anthony refers to the divergent agendas that she and Stanton were pursuing. While Stanton was publishing the first volume of her controversial *Woman's Bible* (document 19), Anthony had her sights set on more "secular, . . . political fellows," the 1896 California referendum on woman suffrage. The California contest was one of several important state referenda on woman suffrage made possible by the rise of Populism in the west in the 1890s. In California the energetic opposition of the liquor industry became for the first time a factor with which suffragists had to reckon. However, whereas in other states (notably Kansas in 1894) woman suffrage had fallen victim to interparty conflict, in California all parties appeared to support the issue. Anthony was hopeful of victory and, at the age of seventy-five, made two long visits to the state.

Despite her impatience with Stanton's preoccupation with "that Bible Committee," Anthony was also busy devising ways to do her old friend public honor. She refers here to plans for an eightieth birthday celebration to be sponsored in November 1895 by the National Council of Women.

Rochester N.Y.
July 24 1895

Well! Well! My Dear[4]

It is really good to see your pen-tracks once more. *No*, I don't want my name on that Bible Committee. You fight that battle and leave me to fight the secular, the political fellows. I haven't seen a half dozen of the Tribunes or Journals since I went to California so haven't read yours or any one's comments.

I know your [*sic*] doing good because you are making Rome

howl. So go ahead, but do at least have the members of your Committee [made up] of those who have even read the Bible once through consecutively in their lives. I simply don't want the enemy to be diverted from *my* practical ballot fight, to that of scoring me for belief one way or the other about the bible. The religious *part* has *never been mine*, you know, and I won't take it up, so long as the men who hold me in durance vile won't care a dime what the Bible says. All they care for is what the *saloon* says. So go ahead, in your own way, and let me stick to my own. . . .

Rachel [Foster Avery], Mrs. Chapman Catt & Mrs. [Harriet Taylor] Upton are to be [here] Saturday night to enlightmen[t] of things in general. Program for your Celebration for one thing. Rachel & the Council President Mrs. [Mary Lowe] Dickinson have had the matter in hand. If you think of any points you'd like to have made, please write them to me instanter. I do [hope] we can make your 8oth birthday tell tremendously the world over. So do put your thoughts to it & write me at once.

It is dark so must stop. Take the 10:37 train to night for Lakeside assembly Ohio to speak. Shall be back Saturday night.

Oh how I do wish you were where I could run in to chat over, but we are always so far apart.

Lovingly yours
Susan B. Anthony

[*in Stanton's hand, probably to Clara Colby:*] I get my share of criticism too. You need not return. Read & burn.

San Francisco
Sept. 8 1896

My Dear Mrs. Stanton[5]

. . . I enclose a letter from a dear soul who has cherished your lovely curls & loving words all these years, as belonging to me. It is too funny the way people[']s memories do carry you & me one for the other & both as one. Well so [will?] it be.

I was at Ukiah last Sataurday, spoke at the opening of the Mendocino County Democratic campaign to a big crowd fully *one half* women. I never saw women turn out en masse before at political meetings. They go just the same when no woman is announced to speak, they say. . . .

Our scheme is getting well into operation, that is, we are being invited to speak in the regular meetings of each & all of the political parties. I have spoken at the opening of the Democratic, Republican & Populist Campaigns in this city & Oakland & in several of the Counties already & so has Miss Shaw. And we hold a rally in the finest audience chamber in this city, Metropolitan Temple, on Thursday night to introduce Mrs. *Catts*—[as] they print it here—on the 10th, after which the invitations will come for her also. We are proving that *all parties* are *glad* to get us *non-* or *all partisan* speakers. And if we carry the state we shall prove that by thus advocating the cause before the voters of all parties is the way to convert the men of a state. I have no meeting to day or evening. Have staid home from Mrs. Catt's parlor meeting so as to write & this is the 15th not short scratch. And I am awfully tired of it. You see I give my secretary to the State Committee, free gratis & then do my own work myself just as I used to when I didn't scratch my last dollar to pay a secretary.

I am now writing around to many rich women at the east begging them to help California. They cannot raise the money to pay expenses. I have never seen harder times anywhere. . . .

I do hope my next [letter] will be more decent but really it is this or nothing. Oh, how I do think of you & wish I had you here to help on the work. Can't you write on some point & send it on. I can get all and more published than I can get.

Lovingly yours
Susan B. Anthony

At the November 1896 election, California Republicans reneged on their pledges, and the woman suffrage measure was defeated by fewer than 28,000 votes. The next piece of correspondence, a fragment of a letter written a few months later, reveals Anthony turning away from such political defeats to concentrate on perfecting "the Association" [NAWSA], the legacy she was determined to leave to "the cause." The task she worries will not be "well done" was the annual memorial session at the upcoming NAWSA convention, at which the contributions of suffragist activists who had "passed on" that year were officially honored. Stanton had turned this responsibility over to her protégée, the suffragist journalist Clara Colby, founder and editor of the *Woman's Tribune*. Anthony's impatience with Colby's "whims and prejudices" gives a good sense of the depth of her commitment to maintaining organizational unity at the cost of engagement with and debate over the compelling issues of the day.

[Rochester, N.Y.
January 8, 1897]⁶

[Fragment, Anthony to Stanton]

N.B. Just to think of the work that will not be well done, the right word on Mary Grew, Mrs. Cooper & lots of others. The work is placed in Mrs. Colby's hands. So it was last year after you refused but in her usual hurry she didn't get time to do it well, as she is capable!!

Mrs. Colby writes she will start for Des Moines the 21st. She has sent me a *big batch* of new rules for the Association. I do wish she had the faculty of chiming in with the other young girls, and so become a helper and not a mere criticiser!!

If she could be a *free editor* for a *National suffrage* paper, one that would really be an organ of our Society, it would be splendid. But she won't abate one jot or tittle of her own personality on Ghandi [*sic*] or Coxey. And no Association [supports] her position and words on them & sundry other things.

Both the W[oman's] T[ribune] and the W[oman's] J[ournal] are wholly & merely *personal papers*, giving their own special freaks the prominence, never studying & publishing only what will build up the Association. The time is fast [going] when the mass of the suffrage women will be compromised by any one person's pecularities!! We number over 10,000 women & each one has opinions & rights &c. And we can only hold them together to

work for the ballot by letting alone their whims & prejudices on
other subjects!!

Well I wish you hadn't thrown up the office you filled so well,
the one that no other woman can fill so well.

Lovingly SBA

The next set of letters illuminates Stanton's and Anthony's continuing disagreement over the scope of the
suffrage movement. Anthony pleads with Stanton to
make her "final and most complete utterances on the
question of the enfranchisement of women" at the 1898
and 1900 conventions of NAWSA. Although Stanton
refused to attend these meetings, she did send formal
letters to Anthony to be read to the assembled suffrage
hosts. But whereas Anthony was concerned lest the
platform of the suffrage movement become too "broad,"
Stanton's fears were that it had been made too "narrow."
Anthony wrote to Stanton to "[round] out your half-
century's magnificent utterances for woman's Emancipation"; by concentrating on suffage, Stanton wanted to
"consider the next step in progress." Each woman's
injuctions for the future also involved an evaluation of
the past, of the changes in women's lives over the preceding half century, and of their own roles in bringing them
about. Anthony's optimistic assessment was that emancipation had largely been won—with the lone exception
of enfranchisement, its crowning jewel. Stanton was
more pessimistic; the conservative character of organized
suffragism seemed a far cry from her original hope that
the women's rights movement would liberalize and em-
bolden her sex.

Most basically, Anthony wanted Stanton to concentrate on the necessity of securing the vote and relegate
her other interests to the sidelines. But Stanton was
coming to regard suffrage as a formal but insubstantial
right. As she wrote elsewhere, "Logically our enfranchisement should have occurred in 1776 or at least in
Reconstruction days. . . . Our movement is belated and
like all things too long postponed now gets on every-

body's nerves."[7] Eventually, she came to believe as strongly in limiting the vote by "education" as extending it by gender. Despite this, she insisted to Anthony that her own highest priority was not suffrage, but the replacement of the "present competitive system" with "cooperation," both in economics and in daily life. She regarded socialism as "the natural outgrowth" of the democratic principle that had always animated her politics, "equal rights for all."

Anthony herself longed to do battle against the revival of anti-Black prejudice in the 1890s, a development accelerated by the United States' entry into its first imperial war. She was enraged to see the suffragist call for equal citizenship for women and men perverted by a group that excluded nonwhites. But like Stanton's socialism, Anthony's antiracism was complex and riddled with contradiction. More than a decade before, she had objected vehemently to Stanton's desire to welcome Frederick Douglass's marriage to a white woman.[8] Even when it came to the very issue that animates her letter of December 2, 1898 (below), the discrimination suffered by women of color on public transportation, she was unwilling to press her convictions on other suffragists, lest she split the movement; at the 1899 convention in Grand Rapids, Michigan, she made no objections when NAWSA voted against registering a protest on this issue.[9]

Rochester, N.Y.
Sept. 7, 1897

My Dear Mrs. Stanton[10]

I have rejoiced all day long that the sun has lessened its scorchings. It was so fearfully hot yesterday when I reached home, that I felt like telegraphing [you] not to start for New York this morning, but my first thought this A.M. was how much cooler & how much nicer for Mrs. Stanton. And so all day as I have plodded in my old papers I have rejoiced for you and when at 6:30 sister Mary & I sat down to supper, I said well, Mrs.

Stanton is in her flat by this time & I am very glad the weather is so cool & nice!!

Well, I am glad I went to Geneva and that we have had another chat over everything & everybody, not excluding Educated Suffrage. And now while I plod on until my job is done, I do hope you will give your thought to saying your best word [for] the first session of the 50th Anniversary on the

The first organized demand of Woman for liberty, Seneca Falls, July 19 1848!!

In the state, the church, the home!!

I feel sure you will be *inspired* for this occasion, this rounding out of your half-century's magnificent utterances for woman's Emancipation—perfect equality of rights in the state, the church, the home! And I hope, too, that darling Harriot will be inspired to come over & help make the occasion glorious.

Lovingly Yours—& Margaret & Rob also
Susan B. Anthony

[P.S.] It is such a comfort to feel that you haven't been broiling all day, & that you are now at home, cool and comfortable!!

Rochester, N.Y.
Dec. 1. 1897

My dear Mrs. Stanton:[11]

I am just home. . . . I was gone sixteen nights, and spent six of them in sleeping cars, and now I am home again, alive and hard at work, and bound not to be tempted away again until you and I start for Washington the very first of February.

I want you to plan to go with me then without fail, and just settle down there for the whole three weeks—or four if you can—for I think we shall both want to stay at least one week after the celebration. We have always been obliged to rush home or off at lecturing work the moment a convention was over, and this time we want to take things deliberately, both before and after the meeting. . . . Of course, you will not make any calls in person, but you will send your cards by any of us that do go out to make the calls, and that will bring the wives of the Senators, M.C.'s and Judges out in return calls. . . .

I hope you are concentrating your every thought on the addresses which you wish to make to go down to history as your final and most complete utterances on the question of the enfranchisement of women. I wish it were possible for me to be in two places and to do two things at once. If it were, I should certainly be with you and keep you stirred up to do this one thing of getting your best thoughts arranged in your best sentences for this great celebration of the great principle you declared fifty years ago, and the great work that all women together have done during the last half-century to bring about its realization. I tell you, my dear, the summing up of the momentous achievements of women in the past fifty years is a big job, and one that you alone are equal to, so don't let anybody or anything divert you from getting your papers written, one for the Judiciary Committee of the House, another for the Suffrage Committee of the Senate, another for the opening of the Jubilee Celebration, and yet another for its closing session. Then, of course, there will be times when, if your spirit moves you, you can speak in accordance with its promptings. It will be an awful pity almost a crime—if you should fail to make these last words before Congress and before the people, both in your audiences and in that greater audience which the press reports will give you, combine the very best thoughts you have ever had and the very best words you have ever uttered on this whole question. If possible, you should overtop and surpass anything and everything you have ever written or spoken before.

Now my dear, this is positively the last time I am ever going to put you on the rack and torture you to make the speech or the speeches of your life. So let "Jimmy Grind" of yore and all will be well.

Lovingly your
Susan B. Anthony

A few days before Stanton wrote the following address and Anthony delivered it to the Fiftieth Anniversary Woman Suffrage Convention in Rochester, New York, Congress authorized the president to go to war with Spain in defense of Cuba.

The War a Minor Question[12]

Mrs. Stanton was invited by Miss Anthony to send to the Woman Suffrage Conference, held recently in Rochester, N.Y., a letter on "Woman and War." She replied as follows:

New York,
April 27 1898

My Dear Miss Anthony:

You ask me to send a letter as to woman's position in regard to the war. Many with whom I talk feel aggrieved that they have no voice in declaring war with Spain, or in protesting against it. The vast majority of men are in the same position. Why care for a voice in an event that may happen once in a lifetime, more than in those of far greater importance continually before us? Why groan over the horrors of war, when the tragedies of peace are forever before us? Our boys in blue, well fed and clothed in camp and hospital, are better off than our boys in rags, overworked in mines, in factories, in prison houses, and in bare, dingy dwellings called homes where the family meet at scanty meals after working ten hours, to talk over their hopeless situation in the despair of poverty.

A friend of mine visited the bleaching department in one of our New England factories, where naked boys, oiled from head to foot, are used to tramp pieces of shirting in a large vat. The chemicals necessary for bleaching are so strong as to eat the skin unless well oiled. In time they affect the eyes and lungs. There these boys, in relays, tramp, tramp all day, but not to music nor inspired with the love of country. In England they have machinery for such work; but in the land of the Puritans, boys are cheaper than machinery.

On the platform of one idea mothers cannot discuss these wrongs. We may talk of the cruelties in Cuba now on any platform, but not of the outrages of rich manufacturers in the State of Massachusetts.

Under the present competitive system existence is continual war, the law is each one for himself, starvation and death for the hindmost! My message to-day to our coadjutors is that we have a

higher duty than the demand for suffrage; we must now, at the
end of fifty years of faithful service, broaden our platform and
consider the next step in progress, to which the signs of the times
clearly point—namely, cooperation, a new principle in industrial
economics. We see that the right of suffrage avails nothing for the
masses, in competition with the wealthy classes and, worse still,
with each other. Women all over the country are working earnestly in many fragmentary reforms, each believing that her own,
if achieved, would usher in a new day of peace and plenty. With
woman suffrage, temperance, social purity, rigid Sunday laws,
and physical culture, could any or all be successful, we should
see no change in the condition of the masses. We need all these
reforms and many more to make existence endurable. What is
life to-day to the prisoner in his lonely cell? to the feeble hands
that keep time with machinery in all our marts of trade? to those
that have no abiding-place, no title to one foot of land on this
green earth? Such are the fruits of competition. Our next experiment is to be made on the broad principle of cooperation. At the
end of fifty years, whose achievement we celebrate here to-day,
let us reason together as to the wisdom of laying some new planks
in our platform.

The cooperative idea will remodel codes and constitutions,
creeds and catechisms, social customs and conventionalisms, the
curriculum of schools and colleges; it will give a new sense of
Justice, Liberty and Equality in all the relations of life. Those
who have eyes to see recognize the fact that the period for all
these fragmentary reforms is ended. Agitation of the broader
question of philosophical socialism is now in order. This next
step in progress has long been foreshadowed by our seers and
prophets, from Mazzini and Fourier to Thomas Paine and Henry
George; and is now being agitated by able thinkers and writers
in all civilized countries.

"The few have no right to the luxuries of life, while the many
are denied its necessities." This motto is the natural outgrowth of
the one so familiar on our platform and our official paper—
"Equal rights for all." It is impossible to have "equal rights for
all" under our present competitive system. "All men are born
free, with an equal right to life, liberty and happiness." The

natural outgrowth of this sentiment is the vital principle of the Christian religion—"Love thy neighbor as thyself." In broad, liberal principles the Suffrage Association should be the leader of thought for women, and not narrow its platform from year to year to one idea, rejecting all relative ideas as side issues.

"Progress is the victory of a new thought over old superstitions."

Elizabeth Cady Stanton

Rochester, N.Y.
Dec. 2 1898

My Dear Mrs. Stanton[13]

. . . Every day's papers bring something that I want my "*Jimmy Grind*" to put into her hopper for criticism, not in a specially W.S. paper, but in the very great Daily that brings to me the false thing. In to day's it is the organization of "The National Society of the Spanish American War," its object to foster ["]True Patriotism and honor Heroes of the War." In its second paragraph it says, "Membership in the Society is open to all patriotic *white* Americans. Applications must be approved by the Executive Council—Men & Women (that is white men & women) share equally in the honors & duties of citizenship." Now this seems to me the false religion of this day. The old slaveocrats are bound to push out every man & woman of color from the *enjoyment of civil rights*.

Did you see that South Carolina has asked if not demanded that the Pullmans shall put *negro sleepers* on Southern Rail Roads. Up to this Frederick Douglass, Booker Washington & other cultivated Negroes could escape the *Jim Crow Cars* in the South by purchasing a through sleeping car ticket from Chicago, Boston, New York &c to New Orleans or Tampa. *All* of the poorer colored people are compelled to travel in the *Negro cars* which [are] little better than pig-pens. On every hand *American civilization*, which we are introducing into Isles of the Atlantic & Pacific is putting its heel on the head of the Negro race. Now this barbarism does not grow out of ancient Jewish Bibles, but out of our own sordid meanness!! And the like of you ought to stop hitting poor old St. Paul, and give your heaviest raps on the head of every nabob—man & woman—who does injustice to a human being for the *crime!* of color or sex!!

Nobody does right or wrong because Saint Paul [told] them to but because of their own *black "true inwardness."* The trouble is in *ourselves to day* not in men or books of thousands of years ago.

I do wish you could centre your big brain on the crimes we ourselves as a people are responsible for. To charge our offenses to false books or false interpretations is but a way of seeking a *"refuge of lies."* *We know* it hurts when we are pricked to the quick, & we know just as well when we prick another to the quick that it hurts them. We don't [need] any St. Paul to tell us it doesn't. Now dearie, do let *"Jimmy Grind"* out against the Colorphobia & Sexphobia [of] men & women of to day.

Lovingly yours
Susan B. Anthony

There is no record that the following letter from Stanton to Anthony was ever read to the 1900 NAWSA convention. The 1900 convention was taken up with a celebration of Anthony's retirement and Carrie Chapman Catt's succession to the association's presidency. In this letter to Anthony copied into her diary, Stanton warns of rising opposition to women in the labor force, especially to wage-earning wives, whose numbers and importance were steadily increasing. This was a concern that Anthony shared, as indicated in her last letter to Stanton, in October 1902.

From Elizabeth Stanton's Diary, December 3, 1899[14]

Susan writes asking me to put on paper what I think ought to be done by our national association at its next annual meeting. So I have replied as follows:

1. A resolution should be passed in favor of establishing a new

government in Hawaii. It is a disgrace to the civilization of the nineteenth century to make that island a male oligarchy.

2. We should protest in clarion tones against the proposal by railroad kings to turn women out of all the positions which they hold in the North Western Railroad, especially as it is generally admitted that they have given faithful service.

3. We should discuss and pass a resolution against the proposition of the Knights of Labor to remove women from all factories and industries which take them from home. If these gentlemen propose to provide every woman with a strong right arm on which she may lean until she reaches the other side of Jordan; a robust generous man pledged to feed, clothe and shelter the woman and her children to the end of life; a husband or a brother sure not to die or default on the way—why then this proposal might be worthy of woman's consideration. But as long as she is often forced to be the breadwinner for herself, husband and children, it would be suicidal for her to retire to the privacy of home and with folded hands wait for the salvation of the Lord. There is an immense amount of sentimental nonsense talked about the isolated home. This is evident when we see what it really means for the mass of the human family. For Deacon Jones, a millionaire surrounded with every luxury, no material change may be desirable. But for a poor farmer with wife and child in the solitude of a prairie home, a co-operative household with society would be inestimable blessing. Woman's work can never be properly organized in the isolated home. One woman cannot fill all the duties required as housekeeper, cook, laundress, nurse, and educator of her children. Therefore we should oppose all sly moves to chain woman in the home.

4. To my mind, our Association cannot be too broad. Suffrage involves every basic principle of republican government, all our social, civil, religious, educational, and political rights. It is therefore germane to our platform to discuss every invidious distinction of sex in the college, home, trades, and professions, in literature, sacred and profane, in the canon as well as in the civil law. At the inauguration of our movement, we numbered in our Declaration of Rights eighteen grievances covering the whole range of human experience. On none of these did we talk with

bated breath. Note the radical claims we made, and think how the world responded. Colleges were built for women, and many of the older male colleges opened their doors to our sex. Laws were modified in our favor. The professions were thrown open to us. In short, in response to our radicalism, the bulwarks of the enemy fell as never since. At that time you gave on many occasions a radical lecture on social purity. I was responsible for an equally advanced one on marriage and divorce. Lucretia Mott was not less outspoken on theological questions. But at present our association has so narrowed its platform for reasons of policy and propriety that our conventions have ceased to point the way.

5. Our national convention should always be held in Washington, where we could examine intelligently the bills before Congress which nearly or remotely affect the women of the nation. We should have a sort of Woman's Congress, if we can afford it, which should sit at the federal capital for a longer or shorter period every year.

In these last few letters, Stanton and Anthony accept the inevitability that, as the latter put it, "we [will] be compelled to leave the finish of the battle to another generation of women." "To younger hands resign the reins," wrote Stanton in a lighter vein, "with all the honors, and the gains." She was particularly anxious that her own daughter, Harriot Stanton Blatch, be assured of an authoritative position alongside Carrie Chapman Catt, the most talented of Anthony's protégées.

By 1900 both Anthony and Stanton were incapacitated by age. Stanton, "lame and with failing sight," confessed fears about leaving her home. Immediately after retiring from the presidency of NAWSA, Anthony had a minor stroke. Their final letters to each other are mostly elaborate birthday greetings, as if each had made a sort of holiday out of the life of the other. Anthony's birthday was February 15, which usually coincided with NAWSA's annual meeting, at which Stanton's greetings were read. Anthony's last letter to Stanton was written

just before she died, on October 26, seventeen days
before her eighty-seventh birthday. "In age as in all else
I follow you closely," she wrote. She died four years
later at the age of eighty-six.

To Susan B. Anthony on Her Eightieth Birthday,
February 15, 1900[15]

I

My honored friend, I'll ne'er forget,
That day in June, when first we met;
Oh! would I had the skill to paint,
My vision, of that "Quaker Saint";
Robed in pale blue and silver gray,
No silly fashions did she essay.
Her brow was smooth and fair,
'Neath coils of soft-brown hair;
Her voice was like the lark, so clear,
So rich and pleasant to the ear;
The 'Prentice hand' on man oft-tried,
Now made in her the Nation's pride!

II

We met and loved, ne'er more to part
Hand clasped in hand, heart bound to heart.
We've travelled West, years together,
Day and night, in stormy weather;
Climbing the rugged Suffrage hill,
Bravely facing every ill;
While resting, speaking, everywhere,
Quite often in the open air;
From sleighs, ox-carts, and mayhap coaches,
Besieged with beetles, bugs and roaches[16]
All this for the emancipation
Of the brave women of our Nation.

III

Now, we've had enough of travel,
And, in turn, laid down the gavel,—
In triumph, having reached four score,
We'll give our thoughts to art, and lore.
In the time-honored retreat,
Side by side we will take a seat.
To younger hands resign the reins,
With all the honors, and the gains.
United, down life's hill we'll glide,
Whate'er the coming years betide;
Parted only when first in time,
Eternal joys are thine, or mine.

[Elizabeth Cady Stanton]

This birthday message was delivered to Anthony by
Harriot Stanton Blatch on her mother's behalf.

February 15 1900[17]

I bring to you, Susan B. Anthony, the greetings of your friend
and co-worker, Elizabeth Cady Stanton, greetings full of gracious
memories. When the cause for which you have worked shall be
victorious, then, as is the way of the world, will it be forgotten
that it ever meant effort or struggle for pioneers; but the friendship of you two women will remain a precious memory in the
world's history, unforgotten and unforgetable. Your lives have
proved not only that women can work strenuously together
without jealousy; but that they can be friends in times of sunshine, and peace, and stress, and storm. No mere fair-weather
friends have you been to each other.

Does not Emerson say that friendship is the slowest fruit in the
garden of God? The fruit of friendship between you has grown
through half a hundred years, each year making it more beautiful,

more mellow, more sweet. But you have not been weak echoes of each other; nay, often for the good of each you were thorns in the side. Yet disagreement only quickened loyalty. Supplementing each other, companionship drew out the best in each. You have both been urged to untiring efforts through the sympathy, the help of each other. You have attained the highest achievement in demonstrating a lofty, an ideal friendship. This friendship of you two women is the benediction for our century.

Rochester, N.Y.
Nov. 11, 1900

Dear Mrs. Stanton[18]

A happy birth-day to you—there is something magic about *eighty-five*!! Glad you have reached it. Hope you'll stay yet many a year blessed with all your children. Wish I could be with you tomorrow but I am going to try and be equal to celebrating the birthday [in] a month—yes or three weeks after the fact. If all is well and I go on improving the next three weeks at the rate I have been making, I shall go and I think there is no doubt but I shall.

I shall start the 30th or the 1st at the latest. You must be in good trim to do all the talking and we'll sit up in our big chairs & behave just the prettiest?! Good bye. With love to Harriot & Nora, Maggie & Bob, Kitt & wife, & Gatt & wife. You won't have Theodore and his wife & children! but you'll enjoy those you have & all you have. As ever yours.

Susan B. Anthony

By the end of her life, Stanton's lifelong commitment to expanding the electorate had turned into a belief in the necessity of limiting the vote to those who could read and write English. Ever since the New York suffrage campaign of 1894, at which charges were raised that woman suffrage would benefit the "vicious" more than the "virtuous," she had taken this position. The same sense of outraged entitlement that had always powered her demand for the ballot here combined with her dismay at changes in American society and politics, especially the arrival of enormous numbers of Catholic and Jewish European immigrants, who disturbed and frightened her. Stanton's position is less difficult to understand if we recognize that, at the turn of the century, immigrant men who were not yet citizens voted freely in state and municipal elections. Still, even Stanton's daughter, Harriot Blatch, caught and criticized the anti-democratic spirit of her mother's position. "As our ability to feel our own needs is not bounded by our linguistic accomplishments, neither should our power to remedy them through government be so bounded," she wrote to her mother. "Because you overlook the fact that the conditions of the poor are so much harder than yours or mine, you are led to argue that 'the ignorant classes do not need the suffrage more than the enlightened, but just the reverse.' "[19]

[Elizabeth Stanton to Susan B. Anthony, February 15, 1902, for annual convention[20]]

Miss Susan B. Anthony, Dear Friend:

It is pleasant to see that a few of our pioneers are still able to attend our Conventions in Washington.

I did hope to summon up sufficient courage this year to meet you all, and address our Judiciary Committee once more, but at the last moment my courage failed me.

Lame and with failing sight, in imagination I conjured up too many pitfalls to make the venture.

There is one point I hope you will set aside one session to thoroughly discuss, and that is "Educated Suffrage."

Whilst we all agree that every child born under our flag has a right to representation, yet as we require that every man who goes to the polls must have reached 21 years of age, so we should require that every one who votes should read and write the English language intelligently.

This is the one point I press in my speech to the Convention, on which I hope you will take a vote after its reading.

One of the greatest objections to woman suffrage today is "that it would double the ignorant vote." We should have a constitutional amendment requiring an educational qualification.

We need to throw some new dignity and sacredness around the ballot box; it seems very unwise to give all classes of humanity, the vicious as well as the virtuous, the ignorant as well as the learned, every foreigner landing on our shores, a voice in the government, of which they have no knowledge, and for which they feel no responsibility.

With the higher development of woman, we look for new safeguards in every department of government.

If all honest, honorable, educated men took a deeper interest in public affairs we should have better laws and a wiser administration of government. Unfortunately too many care more for the accumulation of wealth and family aggrandizement than for the public weal.

This is due, in a large measure, to the women of the nation.

Having no interest themselves in the government, their influence on their sires and sons is to centre their thoughts and ambitions in family life. When women feel that they have public duties as citizens of a republic, they will inspire men with a deeper devotion in national life.

Matthew Arnold says, "The first desire of every cultured mind is to take part in the great work of government.["]

When woman awakes to the beauty of science, philosophy and government, then will the first note of harmony be touched; then will the great organ of humanity be played on all its keys, with every stop rightly adjusted, and with louder, loftier strains, the march of civilization will be immeasurably quickened.

Elizabeth Cady Stanton

New York [City]
Sept. 15th, 1902[21]

Dear Susan,

Hattie and Nora arrived this morning at nine o'clock, both in good health and spirits.

I want you to take it on yourself to see that Hattie has an

official invitation to attend the State Convention in Buffalo, and to all other important convocations in this State.

For some reason, Mrs. Chapman Catt does not seem disposed to push her to the front, why, I do not know; unless she is jealous of her as a speaker.

Now we must make the most of her eloquence in our woman suffrage movement. I hope she will be able to build up a successful association in this city.

Do you intend to publish my appeal at the end of Vol. IV? A forecast of our battle for the next half-century, should it take so long.

We have just returned to the city, and are now all together at 250 West 94th St., happy, I assure you, in the reunion.

Yours as ever,
Elizabeth Cady Stanton
Per Sec

[sometime before October 26 1902[22]]

My dear Mrs. Stanton

I shall indeed be happy to spend with you November 12, the day on which you round out your four-score and seven, over four years ahead of me, but in age as in all else I follow you closely. It is fifty-one years since first we met and we have been busy through every one of them, stirring up the world to recognize the rights of women. The older we grow, the more keenly we feel the humiliation of disfranchisement and the more vividly we realize its disadvantages in every department of life and most of all in the labor market.

We little dreamed when we began this contest, optimistic with the hope and buoyancy of youth, that half a century later we would be compelled to leave the finish of the battle to another generation of women. But our hearts are filled with joy to know that they enter upon this task equipped with a college education, with business experience, with the fully admitted right to speak in public—all of which were denied to women fifty years ago. They have practically but one point to gain—the suffrage; we had all. These strong, courageous, capable young women will take our place and complete our work. There is an army of them where we were but a handful. Ancient prejudice has become so softened, public sentiment so liberalized and women have so thoroughly demonstrated their ability as to leave not a shadow of doubt that they will carry our cause to victory.

And we, dear old friend, shall move on the next sphere of existence—higher and larger, we cannot fail to believe, and one where women will not be placed in an inferior position but will be welcomed on a plane of perfect intellectual and spiritual equality.

Ever lovingly yours,
Susan B. Anthony

NOTES

1. Elizabeth Cady Stanton, diary entry, June 8, 1901, in *Elizabeth Cady Stanton as Revealed in Her Letters, Diary and Reminiscences*, ed. Theodore Stanton and Harriot Stanton Blatch (New York: Harper & Brothers, 1922), p. 358.

2. These are currently in the Susan B. Anthony Papers, Manuscript Division, Library of Congress.

3. Elizabeth Stanton, diary entry, October 1, 1896, Stanton and Blatch, *Elizabeth Cady Stanton*, p. 321.

4. Anthony Family Papers, Huntington Library, San Marino, Calif. Reproduced by permission.

5. Ibid.

6. Ibid.

7. Elizabeth Stanton, diary entry, February 20, 1902, Stanton and Blatch, *Elizabeth Cady Stanton*, p. 363.

8. Anthony to Stanton, January 27, 1884, Anthony Papers, Manuscript Division, Library of Congress.

9. Aileen Kraditor discusses this incident in *Ideas of the Woman Suffrage Movement, 1890–1920* (New York: Columbia University Press, 1965), pp. 170–72.

10. Smith Family Papers, Rare Book and Manuscript Division, New York Public Library, Astor, Lenox and Tilden Foundations. Reproduced by permission.

11. Transcript of original prepared by T. Stanton and H. S. Blatch, Elizabeth Cady Stanton Papers, Manuscript Division, Library of Congress.

12. *Woman's Journal*, Vol. 24, no. 20 (May 15, 1898), p. 153.

13. Anthony Family Papers, Huntington Library.

14. Stanton and Blatch, *Elizabeth Cady Stanton*, pp. 345–46.

15. *To Susan B. Anthony On Her Eightieth Birthday* (National American Woman Suffrage Association, 1900), pamphlet in the Clara B. Colby Papers, Wisconsin State Historical Society, Madison.

16. In the original manuscript version of this poem, the line here was "Regardless of reproaches," but Stanton must have decided not to remind her friend of their political isolation in the past, so she replaced it with a more innocuous rhyme (Stanton to Anthony, February 7, 1900, Clara B. Colby Papers, Wisconsin State Historical Society, Madison).

17. Elizabeth Cady Stanton Papers, Manuscript Division, Library of Congress.

18. Ibid.

19. Harriot Stanton Blatch, "Educated Suffrage," *Woman's Journal*, October 9, 1894, p. 325.

20. *Woman's Tribune*, Vol. 14, no. 6 (February 15, 1902), p. 21.

21. Elizabeth Cady Stanton Papers, Manuscript Division, Library of Congress.

22. *History of Woman Suffrage*, Vol. V, ed. Ida Husted Harper (New York: National American Woman Suffrage Association, 1922), pp. 740–41.

INDEX